Phoenix from the Flame

Phoenix from the Flame

Pagan Spirituality in the Western World

VIVIANNE CROWLEY

Aquarian/Thorsons
An Imprint of HarperCollins*Publishers*

The Aquarian Press
An Imprint of HarperCollins*Publishers*
77–85 Fulham Palace Road,
Hammersmith, London W6 8JB
1160 Battery Street
San Francisco, California 94111–1213

Published by The Aquarian Press 1994
10 9 8 7 6 5 4 3 2 1
1 3 5 7 9 10 8 6 4 2

© Vivianne Crowley 1994

Vivianne Crowley asserts the moral right to
be identified as the author of this work

A catalogue record for this book
is available from the British Library
ISBN 1 85538 161 3

Printed in Great Britain by
Mackays of Chatham, Kent
Phototypeset by Harper Phototypesetters Limited,
Northampton, England

To Chris who walks with me;

To Gabriel, Janet O, Majorie and Ian,
the teachers who inspired me to walk my own way;

To the three Merlins – Hans, Paul and Stein –
who bore the flame to East and North;
and to Kati-ma, who bears it in her heart;

To the Aurora Aurea too numerous to name;

To Liz who took me to Sharpham;

And to the wind which took me home to Ireland
and thence across another sea.

At the Abbey of Our Lady of Armorica,
June 1993:

Ave Ana and Blessed Be!

Contents

Introduction

As we approach the year 2000 – the turn of the millennium and our point of entry into the Aquarian Age – we stand on the brink of a transformation of consciousness. In the West, we have discovered that 'man does not live by bread alone': materialism will not satisfy our deepest needs and most heartfelt longings. In the midst of plenty, we experience inner deprivation; in our crowded cities, we experience loneliness; in our countryside, exploited to the point of ruin supposedly for our benefit, we see the harmony of Nature overthrown and our planet tottering on the brink of disaster.

In response to our inner desolation, there has reawakened in the Western psyche a spiritual current which has lain dormant for over a thousand years. The Pagan beliefs of our ancestors have risen from the flames of persecution and suppression. We have seen a return of the Old Gods and, perhaps more importantly, the return of the Goddess, without whom our society and world-view have become imbalanced and dangerous.

The second half of the twentieth century has seen an upsurge of books about Pagan religion – books on Wicca or witchcraft, books on Celtic and Norse myths, teachings of Native American Shamans and their Western interpreters, and the works of the Western Mystery and magical traditions. Many of these have focused on specific paths. This book does not aim to explain all the richness of these different paths, but to draw together the philosophy which underlies them and to answer the questions of what do Pagans believe? What does it mean to live as a Pagan? How can the beliefs of the past make sense in the twentieth and twenty-first centuries?

To write about Paganism is difficult because it is not a single entity. There are a number of Pagan religions currently being practised in the Western world and they are as different from each other as Christianity is from Buddhism. The Pagan traditions do, however, share some underlying similarities and it is these which are the focus of this book, rather than the differences between the branches of Western Paganism. To explain the similarities, it is necessary to simplify the complex philosophies and practices of these different Paganisms. This is inevitable in a book of this length and it is not designed to provide a definitive exposition of each of the paths and the major groups within them.

This book concentrates on the European Pagan Tradition, the traditional religions of Europe, but these traditions no longer belong solely to Europe. They have been taken by emigration and settlement west to the New World, south to Australasia and to many other parts of the world. The Pagan revival is not, however, confined to the West. Everywhere, those who have rejected their traditions in favour of imported religion are beginning to question their previous assumptions about the superiority of more modern religions and cultures and to reawaken contact with their own ancient Gods. Traditional religion has grown increasingly strong in Africa, for instance, where in many ways its status is more advanced. There, traditional religion can be studied as a school matriculation paper. It will be a long time before we in the West enjoy a similar privilege.

This book is a personal view of Paganism. It does not speak for all Pagans, but is the outlook of one person who has been a practising Pagan for many years. To write at all, I must generalize, but Pagans are individualists who have a wide variety of religious opinions. To encompass this richness of belief in one volume is impossible, but I hope that the coming century will see a blossoming of Pagan writing which will help those who seek the path of European traditional religion to find their way home to their ancient Gods, and those already on that path to learn the views of others and so to come to their own conclusions.

Beginning a book is always difficult. Perhaps it is the Celt in me which must always begin with a vision; for all things come to me first in pictures, then in poetry (for what is a poem but a picture in words?), then in understanding, and finally back into the words of prose, the language of explanation; and that is always the hardest thing. So I will begin with what was for me the beginning.

When I played in the stream in the woods as a child and plunged my legs up to my thighs in its soft clay mud and baked them dry beneath the sunlight, lying on my back on the bank and watching the clouds sail by above, I merged a little with the Earth. And when I made for myself garlands of ivy and climbed a tree to the highest point that would bear my weight, and entwined myself in its swaying branches and rode with it upon the wind, listening to the mysteries whispered by the rustling leaves, then I forgot for a while which was tree and which was I.

I had much freedom as a child; much more than is possible to many now, and from the age of six I would spend hours at a time in the woods, returning only to eat and to give adults the reassurance I knew they needed that all was well. Sometimes if my friend was with me, we would be out all day and would take our lunch and eat it in the treetops; but more often than not she could not come, for she lived too far away, and our nearest neighbour was a Gypsy woman who lived in a caravan in the copse, with thirty cats and a daughter who was wilder than I. Not even I played with her.

And being alone, I did not wish to be disturbed; so when people came to walk in the wood, I would hide myself so that they did not see. I learned to walk silently and to merge with leaf and tree and sometimes to 'disappear myself', so that I would move without moving. A Shaman would understand this, and some who know me now have seen it done, but I cannot really explain it so as to teach it; save only to say, that first one is in one place and then in another a little distance away, and something has passed through the brain very quickly, like two arrows crossing in flight.

I also learned to see, and this was a different kind of seeing which came first by night. For it seemed to me that sometimes I left my body and went back to the woods, which were bathed not in their night-time darkness but with golden light; and there were beings there who had no substantial shape, but seemed to me those presences whom I sensed by day, but could not see. And after a time, the memory of this seeing stayed with me, and leaves and trees and flowers were no longer solid, but were crystals of coloured light; and when I touched the pink ragged robin which grew by the edge of the marsh, I felt that I touched the garment of the universe and my fingers tingled with the softness and the beauty of it. And so it was that I spent the early part of my childhood in a kind of waking dream.

But some things penetrated the dream and one was this. I was returning one afternoon from the woods and walking up the steep road home to the farm. The tarmac was hot so that haze shimmered on the road, and I was tired. Then, shining on one side of the road, I saw what I thought was an egg. I stopped and picked it up and it was warm in my hand and heavy. It was a stone. I turned it over and there was that stopping in time and space which occurs when we first see the one we are to love, or when there is great danger; for on the other side of the stone was the face of a goat.

I took the stone home and it seemed to me a sacred thing, a thing of power; so I made an altar for it in my bedroom and covered the altar with a cloth and brought a vase of wild flowers and sat and looked at the stone until it was evening.

When I was nine, I tried to write a poem for a competition. A stag appeared to me and in his antlers he bore the Sun, and he looked at me as though to speak, but we had no common language and could not. I wrote a poem and I called him 'Majesty'. It was the first poem I wrote which did not rhyme, but it was a failure and I lost it; for I could not capture in words what I had seen.

Then for five years I sought to worship the man who was a God; until one day I saw in a vision a tall red-haired chieftain with a golden torc about his neck and gold upon his brow. His cloak was of many colours and he rode the land on a white horse, whose bridle shone with silver. The chieftain's standard-bearer rode before him and his banner was an eagle on a green field, for he honoured the Green Lady of the Meadows; though later his banner was the black-mourning of the Morrighan, for he was an exile from his own land. Behind the chieftain rode a band of warriors clad as brightly as he. They fought many battles to free the native people from a great oppression and tore down the halls of the rulers who had abused their power. But these were not his people and he was a stranger amongst them; for they were a small dark race. He, in his majesty, seemed to them a God and they bowed down before him as though to worship him. But this was not what he sought.

'I am no God,' said he,
'I am the voice of my people,
and your voice too,
if it be your will.

In your temples,
worship the Great Spirit,
the sky and the wind,
which unite both Gods and men,
give not your worship to a mortal king.'

So they took him first for their king and then, when he died, they forgot that he was not a God and they worshipped him.

It seemed that he and the stag were the same, and for a long time I could not understand what this meant. Then it came to me that no man should be worshipped and I could not find my God in prophets. Then a woman came to me in a dream and her hair was black and straight and hung to her waist, and her eyes were the grey-green of the sea. She came out of the North, walking towards me across waves and ice floes, and glittering and terrible was the jet of her eyes. As Goddess she came to me, and I knew fear and awe.

So it was the God who came to me first and I found him in trees, then in stone, then as Cernunnos Antlered One, coming out of the warmth of the Southern Sun, and then as a man, and then as none of these. For he was to me then as the breath of the Universe, and the spaces between things, and that which binds the molecules and sets them free. My God came at last as spirit, but within the world was He. And She who came out of the coldness of the North, the Goddess of the Sea, I heard her voice upon the waves and within the silence that rings with sound. And still if I do not know the answer to a thing, I will go and sit by the edge of the sea and the answer will come to me, brought in upon the waves.

All this is simply to say that the Old Ones had awoken for me and I have sought throughout my life to know their ways. And it seems to me that, in this journey of the spirit, I and others still walk that steep uphill road where I found my goat-headed stone. We reach the summit, only to find that there in the distance a hill still higher beckons, and for all the wisdom we have sought, the understanding that we gain is always less than a child's. And all our religious edifices, which serve first as staffs to help us on our way, in the end become crutches which we must discard. For there is more wisdom in the leaf on the tree than in the leaves of books that contain the thoughts of woman or of man. And the doctrines we espouse and which we hold dear are only smooth shining stones which we pick up on the road and place in our baggage. With each new dogma and doctrine, the baggage grows heavier, until we discard these pebbles, one by one, leaving them on the roadside for others to find and to carry a little further. And in the end, we have need of neither doctrine nor creed, nor to name that which we worship – for it is beyond all images and words. And who but a fool carries stone to a mountain?

> Impossible contradiction,
> how shall we name Thee?
> Unknowing, but rejoicing still,
> we hymn Thy greatness and Thy boundless will.
> Do what Thou wilt shall all the Law be,
> and Thine the Law that we obey.
> O Lady of the Night most Timeless,
> we, Thy children, ever seeking Thee,
> searching for Thy elusive shadow,
> through the woven dream of matter,
> until at last we do become Thee,
> at-one-ment in eternity.[1]

1. From *Goddess Hymn*, Vivianne Crowley, Yule 1977

Part One
What is Paganism?

1

Paganism Today

What is Paganism?

To say that you are a Pagan produces a variety of responses. Some
people think you are joking; others that you have no religion or
that you are anti-Christian. Originally, 'pagan' was a Latin word
meaning country-dweller and it implied that you were a country
bumpkin. When Christianity first began to spread, it was a
religion of the cities. Urban Christians referred to their fellow
citizens who retained their old religious ways as Pagans. Today
Paganism is the name given to a group of religions, which include
the pre-Christian religions of Europe and also other contemporary religions which share one thing in common – they do not
worship a monotheistic male god. Thus, Hinduism can be
considered a Pagan religion, whereas Islam is not.

Paganism is not a word which our ancestors would have used
to describe their religion and in many ways it was a derogatory
term. Outside Europe, Pagans often reject the term and see it as
an example of Western colonialism denigrating their traditional
beliefs. In West Africa, for instance, the followers of the
indigenous spirituality refer to it as 'African Traditional Religion'.
In the West, the equivalent term, 'European Traditional Religion',
is also used to describe the religions and spirituality of our
ancestors and, in time, may come to supplant the term 'Pagan'
which has been foisted on the indigenous religions by others. The
terms 'Elder Faith' and 'Old Religion' are also used.

The Pagan religions are undergoing an unprecedented revival
as we enter the Aquarian Age. Aquarius is a sign of the new, but
astrologically it is a fixed sign and fixedness is a quality which

roots us to the past. For our well-being, we must seek not only the knowledge of the future, but also the wisdom of our ancestors, those treasures of the intellect and spirit which have been preserved from the past. These will light our way through the darkness of the future.

Religion under Aquarius is that which goes back to the original roots of all religion. Today, under this influence, we are seeing a reflowering of ancient spiritual traditions. Paganism is once again practised throughout Europe, North and South America, Australia and New Zealand. It is an official state religion in Iceland. People are also returning to their Pagan roots in Africa and other parts of the world. All over the world, people are rejecting foreign imported religion and returning to the wisdom of their ancestors, to African Traditional Religion in Africa, to Native American religious paths in North America, and, in the Caribbean and Latin and South America, to traditions such as Santeria and Umbanda.

Under the umbrella of Paganism, all manner of deities are reverenced. The common denominator is that Pagans follow a Nature-based spirituality and worship the Old Gods who pre-existed the Middle- and Near-Eastern monotheisms. Contemporary Western Pagans may reverence the deities of a particular ethnic group such as the Celtic, Norse, German, Finnish or Baltic deities. They may also reverence the Gods through traditions which draw on a number of sources – the Great Goddess, recognizing all the different Goddesses of the world as aspects of this one deity, or the Great Goddess in combination with her consort the Lord of Life and Death.

Many Pagans take an eclectic approach to their faith, preferring to use material from a number of sources to evolve their own spiritual practice, rather than subscribing to one pantheon and a set ritual approach. Within Paganism, there are, however, distinct paths. Some of the most widely-practised are Druidry, based on the Celtic deities; Asatru, based on the Norse Gods; and Wicca, the religion of Witchcraft or Wise-craft, which worships the Great Goddess and the Horned God. There are also Goddess-worshipping groups who worship the Goddess in a variety of ways, using ideas drawn from Wicca, Greece, Rome, the Egyptian mysteries, other Goddess traditions, and combinations of all of these. Increasingly, there are also men's groups who worship ancient male deities, often in gatherings which are fairly tribal in feel. Another important strand in Paganism is

Shamanism. Shamanism is a technique rather than a religion, but it is at the heart of many traditional Pagan religions. Those practising Shamanism may draw on European and Siberian religious practice, or, in North America particularly, they may turn to Native American spirituality. Some Western Pagans see their Paganism as more modern than any of the traditional paths and prefer to describe themselves as Neo-Pagan.

Some see Paganism as an exoteric religious path which fulfils the same functions as other religions. The exoteric or outer aspect of religion is designed to promote social order and to meet all the usual human religious needs from birth to death. Some branches of Asatru have developed a strong exoteric structure. Some branches of Druidry are also now attempting to meet this need. Other Druid groups are more akin to esoteric mystery traditions, such as the Greek Eleusinian mysteries, which were essentially for adults seeking spiritual development. Similarly, Wicca was originally a mystery tradition geared towards adult initiates. From this has evolved a more open Paganism which might be termed Wiccan or Goddess-centred Paganism whose principal function is not to practise magic or to initiate into the mysteries as such.

There are traditional names by which particular Pagan paths know their Gods and Goddesses. In Wicca, the most familiar are Aradia and Cerridwen for the Goddess. In the Northern Tradition, She is worshipped as Freya and Frigga. To those following a Celtic path, She may be Bride. To others, She is Isis, or Diana. The God may be known as Odin, Cernunnos, Herne, Lugh, or by many other names. Some Pagans prefer not to name the Gods at all, but to refer to them as the Goddess and the God or the Lady and the Lord. Sometimes She is called She-Whose-Name-May-Not-Be-Spoken, and He is The-Hidden-God-who-ever-yet-Remains. Pagans may have a devotion to a particular Goddess or God, but often they worship a multiplicity of deities. This diversity can seem bewildering to an outsider; but in reality it is not so. Pagans may call their deities by different names, but most see them as aspects of the One Divine Power – different facets or personalities of the Divine Force which permeates the universe.

Many believe that the worship of the Divine as Goddess and God accords with the spirit of the Aquarian Age. In entering Aquarius, we are entering the world of the androgyne – the male and female conjoined. Before the age of the patriarchal Gods, we lived in the age of the Mother. The Great Mother's world is the

world of the dreamtime, where we are in touch with the
Otherworld, the realm of the unconscious. In the age of the
Father, our rationality awakened itself like a serpent from
the deep. I say serpent, for the conscious mind has both great
potential to climb and great capacity for betrayal. In awakening
our rationality, we lost contact with the Great Mother of All. We
turned away from the world of dreamtime, the world of night,
and reduced ourselves to the narrow world of linear thought. We
lost touch with the great creative force which lies dormant within
us and entered the world of the father, the world of the warrior.
We learned codes of honour, codes of kingship; our disparate
tribes unified under a father God and a father King, but what had
we lost?

In striving upwards, outwards, and for over-lordship, we
obeyed the dictates of the conscious mind, but we forgot the
lessons of Nature. We strove to dominate and rise above Nature,
but we cannot. We are not angels; we are made of clay. We are
physical beings inhabiting physical bodies. We lost the embrace
of the Mother and forgot that we are the Children of Earth, not
the bright and shining Children of Sun or Star. To forget this leads
to hubris and the disastrous flight of Icarus, whose wings melted
when he came too near to the Sun's rays. To live, we must breathe,
we must eat, we must have fuel to warm us and, together, in
unwitting pursuit of the rational dream, we have all but destroyed
those things which sustain our Earthly life.

Many today see the world as suffering from an overdose of
materialism; but to look at this another way, we have for the past
2,000 years suffered from an overdose of spirituality. We have
striven for heaven, we have striven for release from the Wheel
of Rebirth, and in doing so we have forgotten our responsibility
to preserve the Great Mother, the Earth which feeds us and
which is our home. We are like foolish children striving ever more
for the unobtainable and forgetting that we already inhabit a
Garden of Eden. In the Jewish myth, when Adam and Eve were
tempted by the serpent to start consuming that which was
forbidden, they began to destroy. They were cast out of the
garden and started to have new needs. Adam and Eve's desire
for clothing is a metaphor for all those new and very human
needs which we create to burden our lives and torment ourselves
with when we do not have them.

All this sounds disastrous, yet it was a necessary stage if
humankind was to evolve, to know its full potential. Now we

must return to the Elder Gods, whose messages we have forgotten in our intellectual striving. Here we seek not only to save ourselves, but to save all creation. In order to live a life in harmony with the Earth, we must become aware once more of Goddess energy – the power of the Great Mother, of whom Carl Jung said: 'She is full of snares and traps in order that man should fall, should reach the earth, entangle himself there and stay caught so that life should be lived.'[1]

How is Paganism Organized?

Paganism differs from most religions in the looseness of its organization and its lack of central authority. There are no Popes in Paganism. There are many organizations which represent particular paths such as Druidry, Wicca, Asatru, or the Paganism of particular ethnic communities. There are also a number of umbrella organizations which serve the needs of the Pagan community. In the English-speaking world, these include the Pagan Federation, Circle Network, the Pan-Pacific Pagan Alliance, PaganLink and the Irish Pagan Movement. These organizations are not churches, but information-giving and networking bodies which provide facts about Paganism and put Pagans in touch with one another. They may also organize conferences, workshops, magazines and religious gatherings. Their focus has been on helping people who have an interest in Paganism to find out more and to meet others who are Pagan.

Would-be Pagans who come from other religious backgrounds may be surprised to find that these organizations do not actively seek to convert. People are left to find their own way into Paganism. Pagans believe that people will find and remain on the Pagan path if their inner spirit and the Gods call them. The Pagan paths are not missionary religions which seek to export their Gods elsewhere. The Pagan Gods are the Gods of Nature and, since Nature is omnipresent, they are found in all cultures. There is no need for one culture to impose its view on another or to convert those in other parts of the world. Each can honour the Divine in his or her own way. Nor are the Pagan paths seeking to re-establish themselves in a day. The ancient Gods have waited for a long time for us to 'meet and remember and know them again', and their followers are content to wait for people to remember the Elder Faith and to return to it in their own time.

Where do Pagans meet to worship? In the United States and

Canada, tax laws and a tradition of a diversity of sects have encouraged the setting up of Pagan churches, but in most countries no such institutions currently exist. Many Pagans would be opposed to their existence. Currently most Pagans meet to worship outside in woods and field, in people's homes (groups can be similar to what Christians call house churches), or in rented halls. In the United States and Canada, the Pagan church organizations offer public services which anyone may attend, but in Europe and Australia worship tends to be a private affair; although this situation is rapidly changing to cope with the increasing numbers of new Pagans.

People come to Paganism in many ways: through reading the myths of our ancestors; through experiencing a sense of the Divine in Nature – a feeling that spiritual forces inhabit the trees, forests, fields and hills; through an awareness that their inner response to the Divine is not to a male but to a female deity, the Great Goddess; or through participating, sometimes purely by chance, in a Pagan festival, ceremony, conference or workshop. This may be at some gathering formally designated as Pagan, or at some other event where Pagan celebration may arise spontaneously, such as at folk festivals. Through such meetings, we may find that we share common ground with those who describe themselves as Pagans. We may choose to join an organization or to worship with others on a regular basis, but no one needs to join with others in order to worship the Gods or to practise Paganism. Some Pagans belong to formal structured groups or organizations. Others may come together on an ad hoc basis with friends. Worshipping with others has many joys and benefits and can bring deep spiritual awareness, but such awareness may also come from silence and solitude in the privacy of a quiet room or outside in Nature.

No-one can *make* us Pagans. We are Pagans if our beliefs match those of Pagan thought and we consider ourselves to be so. Particular Pagan paths may have entry through a dedication ceremony, initiation or adoption into a family or clan; but these offer gateways into their own paths only. People can be Pagans without any of these ceremonies.

Dogma

Paganism teaches that many answers to the problems of the present lie in the forgotten wisdom of the past; but unlike most

Western religions, Paganism does not claim to possess a monopoly on religious truth. In Paganism, there is no once-and-for-all revelation of the right way to approach the Divine. Pagans see their religion as one of the many on offer to the spiritual seeker. The choice of spiritual path is one of consumer preference. Paganism is non-intellectual, even at times anti-intellectual. To the Pagan, religion is born of the heart and inspiration, a deep inner knowing rather than a parroting of intellectual doctrines. The task of religion is not to categorize and classify the universe; to make it less frightening and more understandable by creating religious beliefs to explain away everything in human life which is unwelcome. The task of religion is to enable us to experience the universe and hence to come to our own understanding of what it is and its purposes.

The openness of Pagan thinking can be disorientating and disturbing to some. Those used to religions with fixed prescriptions of thought can find the lack of boundaries bewildering. Pagans are often accused of having beliefs which are diffuse and 'all things to all men', but this prejudice arises from the mistaken notion that religion must have rigid dogma and uniformity. A need for rigid dogma is more noticeable in the West than in the East and is derived from the philosophies of the monotheisms which have dominated Western society for the past two millennia. Adherents of Hinduism, to whom it is known as the Sanatana Dharma or Eternal Law, have no difficulty in dealing with a multitude of Gods and Goddesses and a wide span of beliefs. The various versions of Ultimate Reality offered by diverse spiritual teachings are seen not as separate truths, but as aspects of reality. Just as the Gods are the myriad facets of the One Divine Spirit; so religious teachings are the many pathways by which people in different places and times have attempted to communicate with the Gods. Western Paganism is akin to Hinduism, in which many diverse cults can be recognized as forming one religious framework. Hinduism happily encompasses a wide spectrum of religious belief, including the worship of Goddesses and Gods, heroes, animals, trees, plants, sacred stones and spirits. Ultimate Reality is seen as lying beyond the limitations and dogmas of the individual cults. Western Pagans agree with this Hindu view:

> To dispute the religion (Dharana) of another is the mark of a narrow mind. O Lord! O Great Magician! With whatsoever faith or feeling we call on Thee, Thou art pleased.[2]

Paganism teaches religious tolerance. The Divine has manifested in different ways at different times to suit different peoples. A Norse priest whom Christian missionaries sought to convert explained:

> I must not depart from the faith which I have held, and my forefathers before me; on the other hand I shall make no objection to your believing in the God that pleases you best. [3]

Since there are no once-and-for-all revealed scriptures in Paganism, there is little dogma. Pagans believe that truth is revealed to each of us from deep within ourselves. It is found through meditation and inner reflection. The images by which we worship our Gods are simply that – images. To kill, maim and torture others in order to convince ourselves that our human-made image of the infinite reality is superior to that of another is patently absurd.

Pagan religion is based on a core body of myth and saga which is our inheritance from our ancestors over thousands of years. Myths may pass in and out of fashion, but those myths which have endured convey universal and eternal truths. Writing from a theosophical perspective on the Norse *Eddas*, Elsa-Brita Titchenell comments:

> It truly is a miracle that these songs and stories continue to exist at all, when you consider how few of our bestselling books survive even the year of their publication. If myths recorded merely commonplace events, real or imaginary, they would have been forgotten long ago. Their longevity must be due to a built-in permanence which rests on a substratum of reality, quite independent of climatics and regional traits which lend their coloration to the stories. [4]

The religious myths of our ancestors are of great importance, because they contain the spiritual wisdom, not of one individual, but of many people over great periods of time. A Northern Tradition publication explains that every religion is mythical in its development.

> Mythology is the knowledge that the ancients had of the divine; it is religious truth expressing in poetical terms mankind's desire for personal and visible gods. . . . Our object must be to discover, with the help of our mythology,

the gods who manifest themselves throughout Nature: in
the streets and in the trees and in the rocks; in the running
streams and in the heavy ear of grain; in the splendour of
the sun by day and in the star-strewn sky at night. But it is
not the myth that Odinists believe in but the gods whom
that myth helps us to understand. [5]

The respect which Pagans have for ancient myth is different from
the attitude of those adhering to 'religions of the book' to their
scriptures. These generally rely on revelations to a single man (for
such prophets are usually male) at a particular time, and their
interpretation by his followers. This type of belief makes for
pleasing simplicity: it is easy to know what to do, think and
believe. However, like all simplifications, it does not represent
reality, which is that our understanding of the Divine is always
limited. The messages which we receive from our Gods are
filtered through the layers of our culture and personality. In
translating abstract truths into human thought, we clothe them
in our own images, drawn from our experience. Thus, in one
century, a simple peasant girl may see a vision of the Divine
Feminine and believe that she has seen the Virgin Mary. In
another place and millennium, she would see Diana the
Huntress or Cerridwen. This does not mean that the vision was
false, that there was no spiritual encounter; but that in order to
understand what we have seen, we turn to those images and
myths which are familiar to us. How else indeed are we to
interpret them?

Pagan truths are expressed in symbolic language. The myths
speak to intuition and feeling rather than to intellect.

> The bards who chanted the mythic sagas were past masters
> at suggesting majestic avenues of thought without
> specifically stating any doctrine that could be coagulated into
> set and brittle opinions. The beauty of their tales lies in the
> flights of wondering they prod the mind to take and in the
> ever-broadening vistas that are glimpsed beyond each larger
> understanding. [6]

The teachings of the Celts, Germans and Norse were conveyed
through allegory, parable, song and poetry in the age-old ways
of all religious teaching. Similarly, an African says of his religion
today:

It is the religion which has been handed down from generation to generation by the forebears of the present generation of Africans. It is not a fossil religion (a thing of the past) but a religion that Africans today have made theirs by living it and practising it. This is a religion that has no written literature, yet it is 'written' everywhere for those who care to see and read. It is largely written in the people's myths and folktales, in their songs and dances, in their liturgies and shrines, in their proverbs and pithy sayings. It is a religion whose historical founder is neither known nor worshipped; it is a religion that has no zeal for membership drive, yet it offers persistent fascination ...

The European Pagan tradition is still an oral tradition taught by myth and image. The many deities, myths and rituals can be interpreted in a variety of ways according to our level of understanding. We must study, meditate upon and grow familiar with our myths in order to discern, behind their disguises as epic and fairy-tale, the eternal values and virtues which teach us how to live. [7]

Power and Authority

In some Pagan traditions, there is a priesthood which is separate and distinct from the main body of worshippers: all groups must have people whose greater experience is recognized and who can give the lead in religious ritual. However, in most modern Pagan traditions, the priesthood is not considered to be consecrated or set apart – religious experts whose word must be obeyed as law. Most Pagans believe that the priesthood is part of the duties of an adult in society. We must work and worship and mediate with our Gods and serve the spiritual needs of those around us. Many Pagans have a view similar to that expressed by Dion Fortune:

> Know that each man has it within himself, by virtue of his manhood, to be a priest; and each woman, by virtue of her womanhood, to be a priestess . . . [8]

In the Piscean Age, we were content to follow the voice of authority – teachers recognized by the established churches. If people believed something different from those hallowed teachers, they were wrong and evil. Under Aquarius, a sign of intellectual curiosity and challenge, we are not content to follow the thought of others. We must and do question. It is this spirit of enquiry which has given birth to the scientific age. To many Pagans, the absence of beliefs imposed by hierarchical priesthoods is one of the characteristics which attracts them to Paganism. The rejection of the notion of an exclusive priesthood is shared by many religious thinkers of our time. New Age thinker William Bloom believes that a major problem of civilization has been the repression by formal religions of our true spirituality.

> We have been subject to religion and churches which allow only one kind of belief or approach to the divine unknown . . . The New Age phenomenon [is] the visible tip of the iceberg of a mass movement in which humanity is reasserting its right to explore spirituality in total freedom. The constraints of religious and intellectual ideology are falling away. [9]

Increasingly, in the West, we are beginning to see the limitations of dogmatic ideas about the infinite and the rigid power structures which have dominated religious thought for so long. Issues of power, control and domination of human beings by others are very important to Pagans. People no longer want to be told by an elite power group what to think and believe. In part, this is due to the effect of the mass media. Our leaders – political, religious and social – have been exposed to the glare of modern publicity and have been found wanting. The average young person is more likely to respect the views of a rock star than those of the religious or political establishment. When the voice of authority is not respected, it is difficult to convince people to follow hierarchical leaders (though some of Mrs Thatcher's Young Conservative followers came perilously near to worshipping the Blessed Margaret). Instead we must find new sources of authority by developing links with the voice of our own Higher Self and recovering the wisdom which lies deep within us. This weakens the authority of organized religion and leaves people in a less certain and secure world – but this may be no bad thing. Michael Perry, Archdeacon of Durham Cathedral, comments:

> There is, in any case, something to be said for the view (not confined to Wiccans) that any religion in power is, *ipso facto*, a debased and a dangerous religion. Once any religion gets power, it is more likely to suppress than to try to refute those with whom it disagrees. [10]

The Divine within All

The Aquarian Age is one of individuality. Each person finds his or her own interpretation of the Divine and is content to argue and debate with others, but not to seek to impose his or her will and world-view. Power and authority must reside within the individual and not be imposed from outside. In Wiccan lore, there is a saying:

> If that which thou seekest, though findest not within thee, thou wilt never find it without thee; for behold: I have been with thee from the beginning, and I am that which is attained at the end of desire.[11]

This is an important statement which has many levels of meaning; one of which is that spiritual knowledge is something which unfolds from within ourselves; from accessing that deeper layer of the mind which is the collective unconscious and which contains the full repository of all human knowledge, past, present and that which has yet to be revealed. Access to this timeless zone comes from learning the techniques of meditation and finding an interior stillness within ourselves where we commune with the Divine and hear the voice of the spirit penetrating the veil between the conscious and unconscious mind. It is achieving this connection with the deeper level of the Divine Self within us which is the root of our Paganism.

Although for modern Paganism a re-rooting in the past is important, the ideas which have inspired the Pagan revival are also modern ideas about human potential and human spiritual growth and the search for the Divine within us all. A Northern Tradition group explains:

> Odinists recognise man's spiritual kinship with Nature, that within himself are in essence all that is in the greater world . . . Thus there are in man the four elements, the vegetative life of plants, an ethereal body – the god-soul – corresponding to the heavens, the senses of the animals, of spiritual things and reason and understanding. Because in this way man comprises all the parts of the world within himself he is thus a true image of the gods.[12]

These ideas were found in earlier centuries in those aspects of religion which people termed esoteric. These were the mystery cults in Pagan religion, above the doors of whose temples were carved the words 'Know Thyself'. A major aim of the ancient mystery religions was to teach us about ourselves and our true relationship with our Gods. This understanding of our place in the scheme of things enables us to function as whole human beings in society. The yearning for the Mysteries has been revived in the New Age. The individualistic and questing nature of Aquarius is turned not only outwards in an effort to understand the universe, but also inwards in an effort to understand ourselves.

> The great Sun, moving in the heavenly houses, has left the House of the Fishes for the House of the Water Bearer. In the coming age shall humanity be holy, and in the perfection of the human shall we find the humane. Take up the manhood into Godhead, and bring down the Godhead into manhood, and this shall be the day of God with us; for God is made manifest in Nature, and Nature is the self-expression of God. [13]

To find the Divine in other human beings is not easy. It requires a certain optimism about humankind that can be difficult to maintain. Looking around at our world today, one can see much that is likely to invoke despair – war, hatred, ethnic strife, poverty, economic decline. There is also a disintegration of the fabric of society, as people raised without any coherent spiritual or philosophical belief, and denied entry to adult society through unemployment and society's lack of understanding of initiatory processes, turn to crime and violence as ways of satisfying their needs. Pagans see a spiritual philosophy which can help us make sense of ourselves and our place in society and the greater universe as essential to human happiness and well-being. Once societies lived in isolation and this philosophy could be imposed by a dominant power group, who would adopt the creed which most suited their own ends. We are no longer isolated. The era of mass communications means that we are constantly exposed to other viewpoints, other visions, other races and other creeds. Now the individual must make his or her own choice as to the path he or she will follow and what is right and wrong. This is the message of the Sign of the Water Bearer.

Many creeds would argue that the disintegration of society is due to people ignoring the message of their particular brand. Pagans would argue that society's problems come from ignoring not the form of a particular creed, but the underlying message:

that we cannot live selfishly and that if we do we will destroy ourselves; that human beings are tribal animals and it is only through mutual aid that we can create and maintain the complex society in which we live. In this, all the spiritual philosophies have many more similarities than differences. Each is trying to teach a way of right order and right conduct, a way in which human beings can live together in love, peace, trust and truth.

The world as a whole is best served by a uniting of its peoples and recognition of our mutual interdependence. This can only come about when we recognize and respect one another's beliefs, faiths and individuality; but many spiritual systems emphasize division and the superiority of particular cultures, religions and political systems. Instead, we need to establish a common core of ethics and honourable living which can help us to live with one another and the world around us. Paganism teaches that religious differences are the product of humanity's attempts to interpret the great truths. We may differ in how we see the details, but below the surface of the outer forms of religion is a true spirituality which can serve us all. It is a return to this true and underlying religion which Paganism represents.

The Earth is Our Mother

Pagans worship many different Gods, but a common thread which distinguishes Paganism from most other Western religions, is where it places its deities. In many religions, the Gods are separate and removed from the Earth and humankind. They live 'out there', in some insubstantial realm of the beyond, a heavenly realm which eschews the inferior world of matter and is unpolluted by it. The religions which originated in the Middle and Near East – Christianity, Islam and Judaism – conceived of the Divine as an anthropomorphic male being who created the world at a particular moment in time. This gives rise to dualism – the created universe is separate from its Creator who has given human beings dominion over it to exploit it to their heart's content. These religions also emphasize a distinction between spirit and flesh, soul and matter.

In contrast, most Pagans believe that the Divine Force is immanent or in-dwelling in the universe and is akin to the Soul of Nature: ' . . . the beauty of the green Earth, the white Moon amongst the stars and the mystery of the waters.'[14] This can be termed pantheism. All Pagans respect the Earth and the Divine in Nature. Some pantheists believe that the Divine, while present within material creation, also transcends it into a realm beyond the material universe. The Divine is both immanent and transcendent; both within the world of Nature and existing beyond it. It is the ground of everything and therefore may be contacted at all levels, in all places, in all things and through many forms.

The notion of immanence is not always easy to understand. How can the Divine be present in matter, even though we do not see it? In the Hindu scripture of the *Chandogya Upanishad*[15] Svetaketu, a young spiritual seeker, wishes to understand the nature of reality. Svetaketu is told by his father to place a lump of salt in some water and to come back the next morning. He does so and the next morning, his father tells him to retrieve the lump of salt. Svetaketu says that he cannot because it has dissolved. His father then tells him to taste the water. Svetaketu tells him that it is salty. His father then tells him:

In the same way as salt was dissolved in the water,
an invisible and subtle essence pervades the whole universe.
That is spirit. That is reality.
That is truth, and you are it.

To Pagans, the Earth is not different in substance from spirit. It is simply another expression of the Divine energy or Life Force.

The ignorant and impure man gazeth upon the face of
   Nature,
and it is to him darkness of darkness.
But the initiated and illumined man gazeth thereon
and seeth the features of God.
Be ye far from us, O ye profane,
while we adore God made manifest in Nature.[16]

Whereas Middle- and Near-Eastern religion emphasizes dualism, Western Pagans see life as a continuum of energy in different forms. They share a world-view similar to that of many Hindus: that there is no division or split between spirit and instinct, mind and matter, or between human beings and their environment.

The non-dual, formless, undefinable, and unnameable
manifests or expresses itself out of its creative play into this
universe at different levels of mind or psyche, life and

matter. . . . one spirit manifests itself at these different
levels; it alone exists and, even in its manifest state, it is one
organic whole in spite of differentiations. [17]

In the mysticism of many spiritual traditions is found the idea
that there is a single immanent Divine and unifying force at the
heart of all matter. In recent centuries, this idea has been found
more often in the teachings of the East; though it is by no means
unknown in the West. Many modern scientists have come to
share similar views. Margaret Stutley, in her book *Hinduism: The
Eternal Law,* [18] points out that molecular biologists have
discovered the underlying unity of all forms and that the
fundamental molecules of cabbage, fly or bacterium are the same
as those of man. In India, spiritual insights from the past have
led to scientific insights in the present. The Nobel Prize-winning
scientist Sir Jayadish Chandra Bose based his scientific
investigations on the ancient teaching that whatever can be found
in man and animal will also be found in vegetal life. The
crystallographer C.V. Raman, another Nobel Prize winner, based
his work on the teaching that inanimate stones are imbued with
the mysterious force of brahman which gives life. Since all life is
subject to the processes of creation, formation and decay, he
made the hypothesis, now proven, that crystals, having assumed
a certain shape, would undergo continuous change from growth
to decay.

A Green Religion

A distinctive feature of Paganism is its concern with ecological
issues: Paganism is the Green religion. Living in harmony with
Nature rather than dominance over it is one of the three *Principles
of Paganism* which many Pagans follow. While the outer forms of
Western religion have often abused the Earth, the importance of
living in harmony with Nature has been recognized by mystics
of all faiths. Thomas Traherne, in his *Centuries of Meditations,*
praises the planet.

The Earth itself is better than gold,
because it produceth fruits and flowers . . .
You never enjoy the world aright,
till the sea itself floweth in your veins,
till you are clothed with the heavens,
and crowned with the stars . . . [19]

In the Hippy era of the late 1960s and 1970s, the Incredible String Band revived these words and they became an anthem for many of the flower-child generation who returned to the ways of worship which honoured the Earth.

To Pagans, human beings are not a superior form of life which should have limitless power over other life forms, but part of the Goddess' creation. With our superior intelligence and skills, we are capable of destroying the life of the fellow creatures which share our planet. We have already destroyed a large percentage of the ozone layer, that invaluable part of the Earth's atmosphere which protects animals, plants and ourselves from the harmful constituents of the Sun's rays. The Sun is necessary for our survival but, like all forces, in excess it will destroy us. The ozone layer has been destroyed by harmful chemicals which the West has manufactured in pursuit of material comfort and wealth and which other parts of the world have emulated and are now reluctant to relinquish. Pagan writer Marian Green makes this heartfelt cry.

> Human beings are killing trees, and causing other species to become extinct *every day of the year*. We don't know the value of every small insect, every tree, shrub, herb and vine for healing, for natural contraception, for defeating cancer, but many plants in tropical rain forests have such traditional uses. Some countries are destroying stocks of mighty whales, of dolphins and other sea mammals. These large, warm-blooded, intelligent creatures deserve better than that.[20]

The challenge is for us not to destroy, but to maintain our Mother the Earth; to take responsibility for Her and to act as Her stewards, for our own benefit, for that of other species and for those that follow. There is a chant which is often used at Pagan gatherings which reflects this attitude.

> The Earth is our Mother,
> We will take care of Her,
> The Earth is our Mother,
> She will take care of us.

The future of our planet is important to all human beings (though unfortunately far too few governments have woken up to this fact); but it is particularly important to Pagans. To Pagans, the Earth is not only that which sustains the physical life of the human race, She is also a living entity – Gaia, the Great Mother. The Divine is all around us – within us and also in the world without. It permeates, impregnates, makes sacred and holy the Earth and all living beings upon it. The Great Goddess is also the sea. She is Ocean Mother as well as Earth Mother. The sea is passive and can be abused, as humans are at present doing with their pollution and over-fishing; but if She is not respected, in the end, She will rise up and overwhelm us.

The Judaeo-Christian ethic, which in recent centuries has dominated the West and those societies which in turn the West has dominated, has its virtues; but it has had a disastrous effect on our environment. Michael Perry, Archdeacon of Durham, in his book *Gods Within: A Critical Guide to the New Age*, sees the Biblical view of humanity having dominion over the earth as having had 'the direst of results in the way in which we have felt justified in treating the material creation.'

> 'Be fruitful, and multiply, and replenish the Earth, and subdue it: and have dominion over the fish of the sea, and over the fowl of the air, and over every living thing', it went in the King James Version so familiar to our forebears. We heard the word 'subdue' and forgot the word 'replenish', and we heard the word 'dominion' and forgot that the ruler who had dominion over his subjects also had responsibilities towards them. That allowed us to take and take and never give back; to squander the fossil remains of forests which had taken a million years to build up, and burn them in a generation; to make dustbowls out of wheatfields and deserts out of fruitful ground; and to believe that, as lords of creation, we were not only allowed but divinely commanded to do so. [21]

Pagans believe not that human beings are superior, but that the Great Mother finds all her creation pleasing and that each of us – humans, animals, plants – has a place and role to play in the scheme of things. The other forms of creation are there for us to live with in harmony, not to exploit. This attitude has long been that of peoples who lived in a much closer relationship to the Earth than that of the modern West. In 1855, the Native American leader Chief Seattle delivered a speech to President Franklin Pearce who proposed buying land from the tribes.

How can you buy or sell the sky –
the warmth of the land?
The idea is strange to us.
We do not own the freshness of the air
and the sparkle of the water.
How can you buy them from us?
Every part of this Earth is sacred to my people:
every shining pine needle,
every sandy shore,
every mist in the dark woods,
every clearing and humming insect
is holy in the memory and experience of my people.
We know that the white man does not understand our
　　ways.
One portion of the land is the same to him as the next;
for he is a stranger who comes in the night
and takes from the land whatever he needs.
The Earth is not his brother, but his enemy,
and when he has conquered it, he moves on. . . .
His appetite will devour the Earth
and leave behind only a desert.

The sight of your cities pains the eyes . . .
There is no quiet place in the white man's cities.
No place to hear the waves of spring
or the rustle of insect's wings. . . .
And what is there to life
if a man cannot hear the lovely cry of the whip-poor-will,
or the argument of frogs around a pond at night?
The indian prefers the soft sound of the wind
darting over the face of the pond,
and the smell of the wind itself
cleansed by a midday rain, or scented with pinion pine.
The air is precious to the redman;
for all things share the same breath –
the beasts, the trees, the man.
The white man does not seem to notice the air he breathes.
Like a man dying for many days,
he is numb to the smell of his own stench. . . .

I have seen a thousand rotting buffaloes on the prairies,
left by the white man who shot them from a passing train.

I am a savage and do not understand
how the smoking iron horse can be more important than
   the buffalo
that we kill only to live.
What is man without the beasts?
If all the beasts were gone,
men would die from great loneliness of spirit,
for whatever happens to the beast also happens to man.
All things are connected. . . .
One thing we know that the white man may one day discover.
Our God is the same God. . . .
This Earth is precious to him
and to harm the Earth is to heap contempt on its creator. . . .

When the last redman has vanished from the Earth,
and the memory is only the shadow of a cloud
moving across the prairie,
these shores and forests
will still hold the spirits of my people,
for they love the Earth
as the newborn loves its mother's heartbeat.

Chief Seattle's speech began with the phrase, 'My words are like the stars – they do not set.' May this be so.

The Native American tradition was much more alive to the need to live in harmony with animals because many Native American tribes were hunter-gatherers who depended on wild animals for their survival. Their spiritual philosophy also encouraged them to see the animals which inhabited their world as their brothers and sisters. Native American Paganism teaches that the Great Spirit is present in all things. All that is living is sacred.

What is forever but a breath to the Great Spirit?
The design of the universe is nothing.
All of time is but the snap of an arrow
in the bow of the Great Spirit.
The song of the tribes of plants was sung.
The song of the animals was sung.
The song of the tribes of man was sung.
Every world was remembered in song
and no world was forgotten.
The Great Spirit is sleeping
in all the named and nameless things. [22]

Many leading twentieth-century thinkers believe that a change of attitude to the planet and a return to the understandings of earlier epochs is essential if we are to meet the challenges which face us in the coming century. In 1965, the astronomer Fred Hoyle wrote in *Of Men and Galaxies* that our special problem today is that we are essentially primitive creatures struggling desperately to adjust ourselves to a way of life that is alien to almost the whole past history of our species. We are in that unique moment where we have lost our animal consciousness which bound us in harmony to the Earth, but we have not yet gained the insight and wisdom to use well the intellectual and scientific knowledge which has cascaded into our lives over the past century. Life has changed at a pace that would have been unthinkable a hundred years ago and unbelievable two hundred years ago. We have created for ourselves dilemmas such as the possession of forces which can destroy our world at the press of a button, without the faintest idea how to protect our world from them. The world is out of control and, as Fred Hoyle wrote, 'We find ourselves in no real contact with the forces that are shaping the future.'[23]

Many people come to Paganism because they have no faith in current Western philosophies and spiritual systems to solve the problems with which humanity is faced today. Michael Perry comments that as we teeter towards 'a wasteland of rampaging pollution in sea, earth, and ozone layer', the present spiritual bankruptcy of Western technology is evident.

> The Earth, as much as the people on it, needs to be affirmed to reach her full potential. She will not do this by factory farming and the intensive application of chemical fertilizers. The Earth herself must be honoured, seen as holy, as a Goddess – Gaia – in her own right. New Agers believe that the old, patriarchal religions can never do this. We need to go back behind them to an even older tradition, in which the feminine within deity is affirmed and the feminine values are seen as a way of salvation for the earth and her peoples. So we go back to the religions of the Mediterranean world, or the religions of other lost civilizations of what we patronisingly call the 'primitive' world, or the Old Faith which succoured the people of this land before Christianity became the ruling system.[24]

To those who honour the Earth, her sacredness is not just an abstract and mystical ideal. Many Pagans take an active role in

environmental campaigning. Campaigns to save particular
environmentally, historically and ecologically important sites
have been led by Pagans all over the world; sometimes under a
Pagan banner, but often as part of other groups such as
Greenpeace and Friends of the Earth.

The Many and The One

The earliest Pagans were probably polytheists who saw their
many Gods not as all-powerful, but as super-powerful beings
who could control some aspects of Nature and destiny, but who
were themselves subject to destiny and often to higher gods. To
our ancestors, it made sense to worship a number of deities for
different purposes, appealing to each of them for mediation in
their particular sphere.

Some modern Pagans are polytheists and see the Gods as
individual entities – powerful beings who pre-existed humanity.
Others point to the multitude of forms in which the Gods have
been worshipped in different cultures and at different times, but
which, at the same time, often have similar characteristics to
those of other times, places and peoples. To these Pagans, the
Gods are aspects of one Divine force which is 'all-pervading, all-
powerful, changeless, eternal'[25] rather than separate beings. 'All
the Gods are one God and all the Goddesses are one Goddess,
and there is one Initiator'[26] The tendency of the Aquarian Age
is towards synthesis and syncretism – a bringing-together of
disparate ideas and deities to discern their underlying Oneness.

> The Temple of Isis is built of black marble and hung with
>   silver,
> and She Herself sitteth veiled in the innermost.
> She is all Goddesses that men's hearts have worshipped,
> for they are not many things,
> but one thing under many forms.[27]

Many Pagans see the Gods as images which reflect an underlying
reality. It is not the images which are important, but the Divinity
which they represent. A publication of the Northern Tradition
explains:

> One god or many gods, it really does not matter. Our true
> gods are actually worshipped by peoples all over the world,
> using their own mythologies and adapting their worship to
> local cultures and conditions[28]

Similarly, in her preface to the 1926 edition of S.L. McGregor Mathers' classic, *The Qabalah Unveiled*, Mona McGregor Mathers wrote:

> . . . the distinction between monotheism, polytheism and pantheism . . . hardly exists for the Initiate. Verily there is little difference between a single God and a harmony of Supreme Forces. [29]

The view is also found in other contemporary Pagan traditions such as that of African Traditional Religion. In *West African Traditional Religion* [30], J. Omosade Awolalu and P. Adelumo Dopamu explain that African religion is not polytheism. The different Gods have no absolute existence, but derive from a Divine Being – the Hidden God who is ever yet Revealed – 'He who sees both the inside and outside of man, the Discerner of Hearts.' He is transcendent, but at the same time immanent: 'present, always and everywhere, ever-acting and active'.

If the Gods are many aspects of an underlying reality, why do Pagans not adopt monotheism and worship a single God? To Pagans, to reject the Gods who have sustained humanity through the millennia is a mistake. The forms or archetypes through which we worship the universal Divine Force are ways and channels for the human mind with its limitations to perceive and communicate with the infinite. The Gods can be thought of as incarnations, avatars or personalities through which the Divine unity manifests in order to help us understand and communicate with it. These images are a mutual creation of God and worshipper. Our human minds, which think in words and images, receive the abstract message of the Divine and translate it into pictures and symbols based on our knowledge and experience of the world around us. They are manifestations of the underlying spiritual force which gives rise to them – the Great Spirit which permeates all. The archetypes of the Gods are mysteries which reveal layers of meaning and wonderment which take us many lifetimes to understand and unravel. In their mysteriousness, lies some of their power. A Hindu writes:

> The more puzzling the archetypes, the nearer are we to the Unknown, because it is telling us something important: stop knowing. [31]

The archetypes are of service to us, because true reality is beyond the comprehension of the human mind. The esoteric teacher

Dion Fortune explained that 'because we are imprisoned upon the world of form':

> . . . we can only conceive the Formless
> as far as minds habituated to form can imagine it.
> But we who are men and women
> and who want to know God as He manifests in Nature –
> we see the luminous countenance of the Eternal
> in the beautiful forms of the Gods.
> And in this way we learn more, and can do more,
> than if we strive after abstract essences that elude us. [32]

The idea that the forms of the Gods are human images of reality, rather than reality itself, can be threatening to some people of great spirituality who fear the reduction of religion to mere psychology. However, as anyone who has encountered powerful archetypal forces will know, the Gods cannot be treated as though they are not real. Once we are in the grip of these forces, once we have awakened them and they have taken an interest in us, then we are indeed at the mercy of beings mysterious and ineffable which are much stronger than ourselves.

The archetypes of the Gods originate in that repository of images which is the collective unconscious of humanity. They are immensely powerful but not all-powerful. Many of our Pagan ancestors believed that if the Gods were not worshipped, they would die. Traditional witchcraft teaches that, 'The Gods are not all-powerful. They wish men well, but to aid man, they must have his help.' [33] Like many religious statements, this has many levels of meaning. One meaning is that if we do not keep ourselves open to our Gods, if we neglect their worship and forget them, then the channels of communication between us and them may be lost. This will not mean that the Gods have died, but our route to them may be forgotten. One Pagan invocation to the Horned God has the plea:

> Shepherd of Goats, upon the wild hill's way,
> lead thy lost flock from darkness unto day.
> Forgotten are the ways of sleep and night –
> men seek for them, whose eyes have lost the light.
> Open the door, the door which hath no key,
> the door of dreams, whereby men come to thee. [34]

We are in danger of losing the maps of the cosmos, which the myths of our ancestors revealed to us, to be set adrift, floating aimlessly in the starry seas of the universe, orphaned of the Gods.

Monotheisms were a natural extension of a growing rationality in the human psyche, though they are themselves based on certain irrational premises. They created over the centuries of their existence sets of beliefs far removed from the sources of inspiration which gave birth to their original revelations. They required people to believe the irrational – that which their own experience showed them to be untrue. Myths and allegories were raised to the status of objective fact. Modern Paganism has re-evaluated these, as did earlier religious movements, to cast out the outworn edifices and to replace them with a vision from the original source. Most Pagans do not approach their spiritual path from an intellectual standpoint, but come to an intuitive spiritual understanding of and relationship to their Gods, leaving it to the theologians and philosophers to argue how many angels can stand on the head of a pin. To put it another way:

All the archetypes have their origin in the same Source. The source is important. . . . Enter into the Source, and be it.[35]

1. Carl Jung, *The Collected Works of C.G. Jung*, Volume 9, Part 1, *Archetypes of the Collective Unconscious*, pages 26-7.
2. Quoted in J.M. Spiegelman and A.U. Vasavada, *Hinduism and Jungian Psychology*, page 38.
3. The Odinist Committee, *This is Odinism: Guidelines for Survival*, page 5.
4. Elsa-Brita Titchenell, *The Masks of Odin: Wisdom of the Ancient Norse*, page 4.
5. The Odinist Committee, *This is Odinism: Guidelines for Survival*, page 5.
6. Elsa-Brita Titchenell, *The Masks of Odin: Wisdom of the Ancient Norse*, page 18.
7. J.O. Awolalu, *Sin and its Removal in African Traditional Religion*, Journal of the American Academy of Religion, page 275, 44(2), 1976.
8. Adapted from Dion Fortune, *The Sea Priestess*, page 91.
9. Willian Bloom, quoted in Michael Perry, *Gods Within: A Critical Guide to the New Age*, page 21.
10. Michael Perry, *Gods Within: A Critical Guide to the New Age*, page 68.
11. From the Wiccan *Book of Shadows*, quoted in Vivianne Crowley, *Wicca: The Old Religion in the New Age*, page 161.
12. The Odinist Committee, *This is Odinism: Guidelines for Survival*, page 5.

13. Dion Fortune, *The Sea Priestess*, page 173.
14. From the Wiccan *Book of Shadows*, quoted in Vivianne Crowley, *Wicca: The Old Religion in the New Age*, page 161.
15. Eknath Easwaran, trans., *The Upanishads, Chandogya Upanisshad*, Chapter 6, verses 13.1–13.3, page 186–7.
16. Dion Fortune, *The Sea Priestess*, page 124.
17. Arwind Vasavada in J.M. Spiegelman and A.U. Vasavada, *Hinduism and Jungian Psychology*, page 163.
18. Margaret Stutley, *Hinduism: The Eternal Law*, page 11.
19. Michael Perry, *Gods Within: A Critical Guide to the New Age*, page 79.
20. Marian Green, *The Path Through the Labyrinth: The Quest for Initiation into the Western Mystery Tradition*, page 165.
21. Michael Perry, *Gods Within: A Critical Guide to the New Age*, page 78.
22. Lynn V. Andrews, *Medicine Woman*, page 96.
23. Fred Hoyle, *Of Men and Galaxies*, page 65.
24. Michael Perry, *Gods Within: A Critical Guide to the New Age*, page 23.
25. Louis Bourne, *A Witch Amongst Us*, page 205.
26. Dion Fortune, *The Sea Priestess*, page 129.
27. Dion Fortune, *The Sea Priestess*, page 121.
28. The Odinist Committee, *This is Odinism: Guidelines for Survival*, page 5.
29. S.L. McGregor Mathers, *The Qabalah Unveiled*, page x.
30. J. Omosade Awolalu and P. Adelumo Dopamu, *West African Traditional Religion*, pages 12–33.
31. J.M. Spiegelman and A.U. Vasavada, *Hinduism and Jungian Psychology*, page 21.
32. Dion Fortune, *The Sea Priestess*, page 91.
33. From the Wiccan *Book of Shadows*.
34. From an invocation to Pan in Dion Fortune, *Moon Magic*, page 176.
35. J.M. Spiegelman and A.U. Vasavada, *Hinduism and Jungian Psychology*, page 21.

2
The Return of the Pagan

In caverns deep, the Old Gods sleep;
but the trees still know their Lord,
and it's the Pipes of Pan which call the tune,
in the twilight in the wood.
The leaves they dance to the Goat God's tune,
and they whisper his name to the winds,
and the oak tree dreams of a God with horns,
and knows no other King. [1]

Paganism is the Old Religion. It is also the oldest religion. Its roots lie in the beginning of the human race. How can we understand the thought processes of our Paleolithic ancestors? Can we know how they regarded the spiritual forces which inhabit the universe? We can never fully know, but they have left us evidence of their thought. We find this in pictures and images of beautifully drawn wild animals and figures of women, pregnant and fertile. And also pictures of human beings, sometimes figures reminiscent of modern-day Shamans – men in animal skins with horned headdresses. Our early ancestors were aware of the forces which move Nature and were eager to contact and placate them. They worshipped those Gods who most affected their lives – the Gods of the hunt and of the fields. As society grew more sophisticated, they conceived of more complex pantheons. Ruler Gods were distinguished from Gods of war, Gods of love, Gods of agriculture, and all the many aspects of human and natural life.

We know much about these more complex pantheons. The Gods of Egypt, Babylon, Greece and Rome are familiar to us from the memorials which their worshippers have left – their statues, images, temples, myths and prayers. We know that religious thought underwent a complex evolution. At first, people conceived of the different forms of the Gods as separate beings. Then, as people became aware of the pantheons of other societies, they came to see different Gods as different expressions of a diverse and complex spiritual force. The Stoics and Neoplatonists of Classical Greece and Pagan thinkers in other lands realized that the myths which had been handed down by their ancestors were not merely strange tales from long ago, but allegories which explain the nature of life and the mortal world. In Europe, it was the Paganism of Greece and Rome which was most able to survive the Christian era because there were written records of its beliefs and mythology. Other than Mediterranean Paganism, it is the beliefs of our North- and West-European ancestors which have most influenced the Pagan revival.

The Pagan faiths were lost under the rising tide of monotheism which swept out of the Near and Middle East and into Europe during the first thousand years of the Piscean Age. Monotheism reached some parts of Europe much earlier than others. The Scandinavian countries – Sweden, Denmark, Norway and Iceland – became Christian between 900 and 1100 CE; the Baltic States even later. Lithuania, for instance, only became Christian in the 1400s. In the Baltics, the Pagan traditions have lived on and are some of the most vigorous Pagan movements in Europe.

Pagans are generally accepting and tolerant of the religious creeds of others, but they believe monotheism to be a mistaken view of spiritual reality and one which has caused the human race considerable suffering. In *Leaves of Yggdrasil: A Synthesis of Magic, Feminine Mysteries, Folklore*, the Norse Volva or priestess Freya Aswynn writes a spirited critique of what she describes as the 'misery of monotheism' initiated by the Egyptian Pharaoh Akenaten. Akenaten's intentions were for the best: he wished to rid himself of a corrupt priestly hierarchy, in much the same way as Martin Luther rebelled against the excesses of Rome. Freya Aswynn considers, however, that a fundamental mistake was that the new monotheism was male. This led to the ousting of the feminine principle from Nature, 'the most disastrous error in the history of human thought'[2]. There is no doubt that Akenaten was sincere in his religious inspiration and his beautiful hymn to the Sun God became part of the Jewish Bible; but monotheism is by definition intolerant. If there is only one God, those who do not view the Divine in the same way are enemies of that God. They are evil and must be punished and dissuaded from their erroneous views. The misery of the Inquisition is a logical result of such doctrines.

The earliest Gods were tribal. When tribes and peoples clashed, it was also a war of their Gods. 'My God is bigger than your God', was the notion. This type of thinking is evident in many of the myths of our ancestors and also in more recent historical records. The missionary religions of Christianity and Islam attacked the sacred groves and statues of those they sought to convert and conquer to demonstrate to the credulous the superior power of their own religion.

'Look, we have toppled your idols and the wrath of your Gods has not descended upon us. Our God is therefore more powerful than yours. Our God is the only real God.' Another reason for the success of monotheism is that it offers a simple view of the universe which cuts across the complexities of reality as portrayed in the myths of earlier faiths. 'Believe in our God and all your problems will be solved', is the message. The Pagan world which these monotheisms encountered contained many great teachings and mystical mysteries; but it was also a world where every tree, stone and other natural phenomenon was inhabited by entities. To some, this made Nature sacred and holy; to others it made Nature fearsome and strange; for onto these entities, human beings projected their inner fears. Many spirits were seen as helpful, but others were seen as mischievous and malicious forces which must be propitiated. Christianity and Islam removed many of these fears. They did so by removing the world of spirit outside the material realm. There were no longer dark forces in rock and tree. There was no longer a multiplicity of Gods with different priorities – a minefield where pleasing one deity might offend another. In monotheism there was order, simplicity and safety.

Monotheism was successful partly because it offered people simplicity in the face of the complexities of reality, but also because it did what other religions had not – it engaged in spirited marketing of its new brand of religion. With the adoption of Christianity by the Emperor Constantine in 324 CE as the official religion of the Roman Empire, the new faith harnessed an efficient distribution system for its wares. Many new religious movements have come to relatively satisfactory accommodations with older religious forms, but monotheisms have not. For the intolerant masculine monotheisms, there could be no question of coexistence alongside older religions. They were right and all other interpretations of the Divine were wrong. The attitude was uncompromising and early Christians such as Saint Augustine of Hippo preached definite views about the Pagan religions: the worship of Pagan Gods was the worship of devils. The Christian triform God was the only true God. All other representations of the Divine, both Goddesses and Gods, were evil.

The fate of some Gods and Goddesses was kinder than that of others. Often local deities were absorbed into the new system in the form of sanctified human beings – saints. It was no longer possible to make offerings to Apollo or Bride, but people could pay honour to Saint Apollinarius or Saint Bridget. Other Gods were relegated to the status of demons. The Gods of the Old Religion were made into the devils of the new. The people were no longer to worship under sky and wind which unite both Gods and men, but under roofs made by human hands and in buildings controlled by the state-approved religion.

Over the next 1,100 years, Christianity gradually became the dominant religion of Europe, having lost its hold over its own Near-Eastern place of origin in the birth throes of the newer monotheism, Islam. In some areas, people willingly embraced the new beliefs. Elsewhere, this was not the case. The new monotheism set an example for its successor, Islam, of conversion at the point of a sword. In Scandinavia, Saint Olaf made his subjects choose between conversion or death. In Germany, Charlemagne or Charles the Great conducted forced mass baptisms of Saxons by driving them at sword-point through rivers previously hallowed further upstream by his bishops. Not unnaturally this forced allegiance can never have been anything but nominal. Others, such as King Redwald of the East Saxons, compromised and kept two altars, one for the new God and one for the Gods of his ancestors.

Much has been lost of the Celtic and Norse-German religious teachings, although late versions of the myths were recorded during the Christian era. We can learn something, however, from the practices which Christianity found it necessary to forbid and suppress in Europe. Old ways died hard and bishops produced a steady flow of books denouncing Paganism. In the seventh century, Archbishop Theodore of Canterbury condemned those who celebrated the New Year dressed as a stag or bull God, sacrificing to the Old Gods and feasting in Pagan temples. In the eighth century, it was the turn of Archbishop Ecgbert of York to condemn the making of offerings to the Old Gods, witchcraft, divination, swearing vows at wells, trees or stones, and gathering herbs with non-Christian incantations. In the tenth century, King Edgar of England continued in the same vein, forbidding well worship, man worship, spells and consorting with trees and stones! In fact, trees and stones seem to have been viewed as very Pagan and suspicious. These lists of 'don'ts' are instructive. It is evident that the Pagan traditions involved man-worshipping, i.e. revering a deity incarnated in a priest or priestess for the purposes of the rite, and the worship of the Divine immanent in Nature, especially in evocative objects such as wells, trees and standing stones. The Church was not itself immune to the lure of Paganism. In the late thirteenth century, a priest in Inverkeithing in Scotland appeared before his bishop accused of leading his flock in a fertility dance around a phallic figure of a Pagan God. The bishop's reaction seems to have been rather mild, for the priest kept his parish.

Although the Church was wary of the Pagan Gods, the memory of the Gods of the Mediterranean lived on in the classical works which became increasingly available for educated men to study. These were the same works which young men had studied under Paganism, namely Plato, Socrates, Plotinus, Pliny. Ironically, the most learned men of the Middle Ages were churchmen, and paintings of Pagan deities graced the walls of cardinals and Popes. It was in the bosom of the Church itself that much Pagan thought was cherished and nurtured so that it could not die.

Knowledge of Pagan thought was also stimulated by the Crusades. Ironically, these expeditions to preserve Christianity in the East brought much Eastern and Classical Pagan thought into the West. Many Greek texts which had been lost or destroyed by the Christian Church had been preserved in the libraries of Islamic scholars. This learning infiltrated the Western intelligentsia and inspired a Renaissance, or rebirth, of Western culture. From the fifteenth century onwards, the Renaissance stimulated developments in intellectual thinking which led people to question the dogmas of the Church. This process was hastened by the corruption into which the Church had fallen. For some of the disaffected, the solution was to adopt one of the burgeoning new brands of Christianity, and a reformation of the excesses of Catholicism swept Northern Europe. For others, who were looking for something which orthodox Christianity could not offer, there were other avenues to explore.

From the Renaissance onwards, study of magical and Pagan texts became common amongst men of learning and Pagan ideas began to awaken. Some of these ideas went too far for their thinkers' own good. Depending on one's perspective, one of the more inspired or foolhardy of the Pagan revivalists was Giordano Bruno. He developed a religious system based on ancient Egyptian religion which he believed could overthrow the corruption into which Christianity had fallen. With a naivety verging on lunacy, Bruno attempted to convince the Pope of the merit of his new ideas and to enlist him as head of the new religion. Under torture he recanted his heresies, but there was a recalcitrant streak of stubbornness in Giordano Bruno. The torture over, he recanted again, this time back to Paganism. At the turn of the seventeenth century, on February 16 1600, Giordano Bruno paid the price for his impetuosity and was burned at the stake as a Pagan martyr.

Despite the attentions of the Inquisition, the rise of the thinking classes continued. The Church was fighting a losing battle in trying to hold back those developments in human thought which led, on the one hand, to that empirical study of the world around us which is modern science, and on the other to a questioning of the dogmas of Christianity. By the eighteenth and nineteenth centuries, there had been a revival of interest in Pagan religion amongst the educated classes. Education up until the seventeenth century was largely the province of priests, monks and nuns. The aristocracy had been trained in the arts of war and could barely read and write their own names. However, their heirs were taught Latin, Greek and the history of art. The Pagan pantheons became common knowledge amongst the educated and such study led inevitably to a reappraisal of Christianity's place in the scheme of things. This was stimulated by affluence. From the eighteenth century onwards, a higher standard of living for the rich meant that young men could go on 'Grand Tours' of the Mediterranean to study the culture of the Pagan Greeks and Romans. They brought back with them statues of classical Gods and Goddesses to grace the gardens of their country houses. English country winters must have been rather a shock for the average Roman God or Goddess and even more of a shock to the Egyptian Goddess Sekhmet whose ancient statues were installed in the nineteenth century in the gardens of the English stately home Chatsworth House. The nineteenth century also saw the opening of the great museums. In the cities of the Western world, people could now see for themselves the images of the ancient deities of the Pagan world.

The eighteenth century onwards also saw a revival of interest in the Paganism of our Northern European ancestors. As well as Pagan thought, the Church had also failed to suppress Pagan landscape. Although in England ignorant Puritans arranged Sunday outings to go stone bashing, there were, littered across Europe, sacred sites of our ancestors which pointed to earlier lost beliefs. Monuments such as Carnac in Brittany, Avebury and Stonehenge in Britain, New Grange in Ireland, the Externsteine in Germany, and the landscape itself, marked by burial mounds and sacred tracks, pointed to a past in which our ancestors believed in the sacredness of stone and star, and the mysteries of the Earth. These sanctuaries beneath the open sky evoked a very different feeling to that of the churches which replaced them. Here was no exaltation of a deity in human form, but a spirituality which spoke of the sacredness of the natural world. Developments in historical scholarship and the science of archaeology were important for the revival of Paganism. Archaeological advances and developments in the historical dating process led to the inevitable conclusions of the evolutionists – that the Christian version of history was wrong.

In eighteenth-century England, studies began of one of her most famous monuments, Stonehenge. There was a new romanticism about Britain's Pagan past and drawings depicting Stonehenge in its original glory went into circulation. These celebrated stones were thought to be the work of Druids and much speculation began about Druid practices. Druidry began to excite interest not only in Wales, where it was part of a Welsh cultural revival, but also in England. These Druids did not necessarily see themselves as deserting their Christianity, but believed that they would find wisdom in the works of their Pagan ancestors, and so translations of Celtic myth and legend began. The little that had been historically verified about the Druids was unfortunately supplemented by a great deal of seventeenth- and eighteenth-century romanticism. The Druids were variously credited with building Stonehenge, founding Cambridge University and being Chaldean magicians. Although historically doubtful, these romantic visions represented a yearning for genuine Pagan spirituality. Women played an important role in this revival. Lady Charlotte Guest brought together for the first time an English translation of the Welsh Celtic myths known as the *Mabinogion*[3] In Scotland, Alexander Carmichael began compiling his collection of Scots Gaelic folklore which was published at the turn of the century as the *Carmina Gadelica*. In nineteenth-century Ireland, a similar resurgence of interest in national culture began. This was not only amongst Irish speakers. Prominent Anglo-Irish families, such as those of Yeats and Oscar Wilde, were leading lights in the movement. Lady Wilde, Oscar's flamboyant Irish Nationalist mother, compiled *Ancient Legends, Mystic Charms, and Superstitions of Ireland*[4] Folk movements in other parts of Europe such as Scandinavia, Germany, the Baltics and the Balkan countries dominated by the Austro-Hungarian and Ottoman Empires began to collect and revive ancient myths, lore and traditions which formed the remnants of Pagan religion. The educated classes who were previously content to converse in the international languages of English, French, German or Swedish began to learn their native tongues and hastened to record their myths and lore before changes in European society swept them away for ever. In the mid-nineteenth century, across the seas in the New World, not a scholar but an accountant in a Boston bank, Thomas Bullfinch, laboured after his long hours at the office to compile one of the most comprehensive overviews of mythology at that time attempted – *Bullfinch's Mythology*[5] – which introduced many thousands of Americans to the cultural heritage of their European ancestors and still makes fascinating reading today.

European society met a new cultural challenge when colonization took Europeans, and especially the British, to the East. In India, Europeans discovered the rich culture of Hinduism and the profound philosophy and understanding of the psyche which had been developed and had flourished in the Indian kingdoms through the teachings of Yoga and Tantra. The meeting of East and West exported European institutions and culture to India, but it was not just a one-way exchange. Many Europeans were influenced by Hindu and Buddhist thought and adapted Eastern ideas to Western culture through Theosophy and other esoteric systems. The latter half of the nineteenth century saw the founding by Madame Helena Petrovna Blavatsky of an influential teaching organization called The Theosophical Society. Theosophy combined Buddhist and Hindu thought with ideas from Classical Paganism, principally Neoplatonism, to create an eclectic spiritual synthesis which included the notions of reincarnation and karma.

European Paganism today has many similarities to Hinduism, the major Pagan religion of the East. This is partly due to the direct influence of Hinduism on the development of modern Western thought and also partly due to underlying similarities which exist independently in these two strands of Indo-European culture. For although Hinduism is an Eastern religion, its creators came from the same Indo-European language group as the Germans and Celts. The pantheons and myths contain many overlapping stories and themes. There are, however, major differences from Western thought. The Western mind is more extraverted than the Eastern. Faced with the extreme difficulties of many people's material existence in India, it makes perfect sense to develop an introverted mode of thought which seeks to deny matter as *Maya*, illusion, and to turn inwards to enter a spiritual reality. Western Paganism also seeks the spiritual reality, but it intends not to abandon the world of Nature but to spiritualize it; to make manifest the Divine in matter rather than to flee material existence.

The Modern Pagan Revival

In recent years, Paganism has been undergoing a revival in the Western world. This has been part of a wide spiritual movement which has sought to find religious and spiritual answers outside and beyond the established religions. One of the most important impetuses to this has been the need for a Goddess-based religion. Since the nineteenth century, many thinking and spiritual people have believed that society was declining because of an over-emphasis on the masculine at the expense of the feminine. They saw this imbalance as encouraged by monotheistic, male-based religious thinking which distorted the world-view of Western society. From the late eighteenth century onwards, rapid industrialization and the rape of Europe's natural scenery and resources caused many people to feel that the time was out of joint; that common sense was being sacrificed to material progress with potentially disastrous results. This feeling increased after the horrors of the First World War. There was a desire for a return to the reverence of Nature which was evidenced throughout the 1930s by a growing following for the naturist movement, the founding of hiking and rambling societies, and the spread of Scouting and Guiding organizations. All these groups took people out of their grimy cities and sterile suburbs and into the countryside, to commune with Nature and to learn the skills of woodcraft and outdoor living which our ancestors took for granted.

The return to Nature led to a desire amongst many spiritually-minded people for a more Nature-oriented religion. One of its flowerings was Goddess-oriented Witchcraft or Wicca, which saw in the remnants of traditional village wise-craft, with its emphasis on the female, a basis on which to graft the more sophisticated blossomings of Pagan thought derived from the study of ancient Egypt, Greece, Roman, the Celtic and Norse-German revivals, and the wisdom of the East. This resulted in Wicca, a religious system based on initiation into a mystery tradition which practised rites based on the seasonal cycle, out of doors, often skyclad or in naturist fashion, and giving principal honour to the female part of the deity – the Goddess.

Other Goddess traditions and Druidry also underwent a revival. The spirituality of Paganism was woven into literature for public consumption by writers such as Dion Fortune whose novels described the religion of the Great Goddess and Horned God. The pre-Second World War period also saw the growth of a form of Paganism which was not desirable. In the German-speaking world, the Nazis saw the opportunity to prop up their political ideas with religion. The 'back to Nature' movement was subverted into a cult of physical perfection and the interest of German scholars in German national culture and its traditional religion was used to justify an aggressive warrior cult fronted by ancient Pagan symbols. This Nazi shadow has, until recent years, blocked the development of a true understanding of the Norse-German deities and the wisdom of the *Eddas*.

Despite this setback, the post-Second World War period saw a substantial growth in Paganism. It also created a climate in which people started to question authority and unilateral political and religious systems. The West saw its future lying in plurality and tolerance between races and creeds. Immigration into Europe from other parts of the world changed the face of European society forever. Gone was the isolation of the white race. Other peoples brought their religions and Gods to Europe. European cities were no longer solely the province of Christian churches. Mosques and Hindu temples now graced the city streets. In this climate, the notion that there was only one religion and one way of viewing God inevitably changed. The Christian Churches themselves had to make adjustments. Aware of the racialist horrors which European ethnocentricity could unleash, they bent over backwards to accommodate the religious expressions of the immigrant races. Europe was now a multi-racial and multi-faceted society. Those brought up in the post-Second World War period were raised in a different religious climate from that of their parents and grandparents. Comparative religion was being taught in schools and increasingly people were aware that religious adherence was as much a matter of ethnicity and parental influence as Divine inspiration. In a climate where young people were taught to question the wisdom of their elders, many began seeking their own forms of religious expression.

Many of those who have chosen Paganism as their spiritual path have also explored Eastern religions and cults. In the 1960s and 1970s, there was a movement towards Eastern mysticism fostered by the passing fad of pop groups such as the Beatles for paying visits to gurus. Rich Western youth no longer went on Grand Tours of the Mediterranean but overland to India, to sit at the feet of the Mahariji-Ji, the Mahariji Mahesh Yogi and Bhagwan Shree Rajneesh. European cities were filled with tanned young people newly-returned from India sporting orange clothing and the guru's portrait around their necks. The fashion for guruism was short-lived. The Western mind is not truly guru-oriented Pop culture moved on and, more importantly, there was increasing disillusionment with the gurus, as people became aware that their teachers, like all human beings, had feet of clay.

The teachings of Western Paganism also became more accessible. Western Paganism had been held back because, unlike Eastern Paganism, it was not well-recorded. As more books were published and Paganism became more public, people began to turn Westwards for their spiritual inspiration. The feminist movement had a great impact on the religious beliefs of both women and men. Feminism gave Goddess worship a new impetus and many people turned to Goddess-oriented spirituality as a reaction to patriarchy and in a desire for a religion which gave greater expression to feminine ideals. Some of these women identified with the label 'witch', which they saw as a power word for women and a way of manifesting latent female energy. Others saw themselves simply as Goddess worshippers. Parallel revivals occurred throughout the 1960s, 1970s and 1980s in other Pagan paths, particularly those of the Celtic and Norse-German traditions. Writers such as Caitlín and John Matthews, Elsa-Brita Titchenell, Freya Aswynn, Marian Green and Bob Stewart made accessible Celtic and Norse-German spirituality which had previously only been available to scholars and those in specialist historical, mythological and spiritual groups. All over Europe and North America, people met to enact the rituals of revived Druidry. As the fear of the Nazi past receded, there was also a growing interest in runic lore and the teachings of the Norse-German tradition. Both large organizations and smaller, more eclectic groups were formed to explore the ways of our ancestors and to enact seasonal celebrations. Similar organizations were also founded in Soviet-dominated Europe, often meeting in secret and sometimes persecuted and imprisoned for their attempts to revive the Elder Faith. Paganism was emerging from the past.

Paganism in the New Age

Pagans worship the deities of the past, but we are not living in the past. We live in the present and our religion must meet our current needs and those of the future – a future which many term the New Age. The New Age refers to our entry into a new month of the cosmic year. Once every 2,000 years or so, the position of the signs of the zodiac appears to change in relation to the Earth. This means that the sign which appears against the Eastern horizon at dawn on the Spring Equinox is no longer that of Aries, as it was when our forebears first made their astrological calculations. The zodiac signs appear to move slowly anti-clockwise around the Earth and the sign on the dawn horizon at the Spring Equinox is now that of Aquarius.

Many Pagans are wary of the term New Age, viewing New Agers as eccentric White-Lighters in turquoise track suits, waving crystals and proclaiming the arrival of new messiahs who will solve all our problems. This is the popularized downside of the New Age, but New-Age spirituality represents a much deeper and more significant transformation than these frivolous manifestations. The Age which we are now entering, the Age of Aquarius, is an Age which the psychologist Carl Jung saw as a turning point in the development of consciousness. All changes of Age are important, but the change to the Age of Aquarius may be doubly so. Aquarius is one of the few zodiac signs symbolized by a human figure – the Water Bearer. It is the sign of humanity and also of intellectual challenge. With all changes of Age, old ideas are overthrown, but under Aquarius we shall see this happening to a much faster and greater degree. In 1956, Carl Jung wrote:

> We are living in what the Greeks call the *kairos* – the right moment – for a 'metamorphosis of the gods', of the fundamental principles and symbols. This peculiarity of our time, which is certainly not of our conscious choosing, is the expression of the unconscious man within us who is changing. Coming generations will have to take account of this momentous transformation if humanity is not to destroy itself through the might of its own technology and science. [6]

Aquarius has ushered in a new aeon and evidence of its influence is everywhere. As we began to approach Aquarius at the beginning of the nineteenth century, we saw the rise of science and the overthrowing of a world-view based on religious wishful thinking which ignored the reality around us. Judaeo-Christian thinking was replaced by that of Darwin. A change of Age also brings a change in the archetypes which dominate the collective unconscious – the universal mind of humanity. On the emerald tablet of Hermes Trismegistus were carved the words: *As above, so below, but after another fashion*. When the heavens are oriented towards Aquarius, so too are our psyches and the societies which we create. Pisces is ruled by the heart. Aquarius by the throat chakra, source of inner inspiration and the Voice Within. Aquarius is attributed to the element of Air, the element of speech; but bears within it the element of Water. Here, Water means knowledge. It is a knowledge that is to be found within humanity. The message of Aquarius is that the knowledge which we seek resides within us in the deep waters of our own unconscious minds. The dominant archetype of the New Age is that of the Crowned and Triumphant Sun Child. In the language of the unconscious, both Child and Sun are symbols of the Divine Self, unpolluted by the defects of the personality. The spiritual ideal of Aquarius will be not an exterior hero, but the hero within.

Change brings danger and turmoil, both in outer society and within us. A change of Age is a time of psychological upheaval, during which our most cherished beliefs and securities are destroyed and must be rethought and rebuilt. Society can live or die, succeed or fail utterly at such a time. For society to move successfully forward into the new era, Jung considered it essential that as many people as possible should be in touch with the change of thinking and philosophy required by the transition into Aquarius and able to make what he called the psychic connection between past and future.[7] To achieve this, we must rediscover those things which have been lost to us – our ancient Gods and our ancient ways – and must reintegrate them into our lives in a new dispensation. At this point, a change of religion would be expected to occur. Christianity, the religion of the fisherman and the fish, was the great breakthrough in thought of the Piscean Age. Paganism is the religion of the Aquarian Age.

> . . . the passing of the Sun through the starry belt of the Zodiac makes the greatest of all these tides . . . and these Zodiac tides . . . are the illuminations of faith. And today, the Sun is passing over into Aquarius . . . and the Old Gods are coming back, and man is finding Aphrodite and Ares, and Great Zeus in his own heart:
> for this is the Revelation of the Aeon.[8]

1. Vivianne Crowley, *Wicca, The Old Religion in the New Age*, page 186.
2. Freya Aswynn, *Leaves of Yggdrasil: A Synthesis of Magic, Feminine Mysteries, Folklore*, pages 167–8.
3. Gantz, Jeffrey, trans., *The Mabinogion*.
4. Lady Wilde, *Ancient Legends, Mystic Charms, and Superstitions of Ireland*, pages 100–1.
5. Thomas Bullfinch, *Bullfinch's Mythology*.
6. C.G. Jung, *Past and Future, Collected Works*, 10, para 585, 586.
7. James Hillman, 'Senex and Puer: An Aspect of the Historical and Psychological Present', in Hillman, ed., *Puer Pupers*, page 4.
8. Dion Fortune, *The Sea Priestess*, page 92.

Part Two
Pagan Paths

3

The Way of the Celts

In France, Southern Germany and Austria are archaeological traces of the people who became known as the Celts which appear to date from as early as 1200 BCE. This was termed the Urnfield culture, because of the people's distinctive practice of interring their remains in urns. During the next 600 years or so, this culture spread eastwards to Bulgaria and Turkey, south into what is now Spain and Portugal, and westwards to the British Isles. The Celts were a tribal people, ruled by a chieftain chosen from among the kinsmen of the previous chief. In the English-speaking world, the most famous of these tribes is the Iceni who, led by Queen Boudicca, mounted one of the last concerted rebellions in the British Isles against the invading Romans. The rebellion failed and Celtic England was greatly Romanized. Roman influence stopped, however, at Hadrian's Wall and did not cross into Scotland; nor did the Romans ever invade Ireland. However, in southern Britain, Roman and Celtic deities often fused and Celts adopted the Roman practice of worshipping their Gods in manmade temples. Prior to this, the sacred spaces of the Celts were sacred groves of trees whose branches lifted to the stars. It was in these natural cathedrals that they conducted their worship. The word Druid may well derive from *drus*, or oak tree.

Celtic Religion

We do not know if there were any Celtic myths of creation, although it seems likely that there would have been; for in all times and places people have sought to explain their origins. Unfortunately, no Celtic creation myths as such survive. We have only fleeting commentaries from Roman writers such as Strabo, who wrote that the Druids of Gaul taught that human souls and the universe are indestructible, although one day fire and water would prevail over the world.[1] This view is not dissimilar to that conveyed by the Norse myths which are discussed later. Caesar also mentions that the Celts believed that the soul survived the body.[2]

Although our information is limited, we know that the Celts of Ireland thought of the universe as comprising four realms. These were symbolized by the four treasures of Ireland, brought there by the High Gods, the Tuatha de Danaan. These realms were *Finias*, symbolized by the Spear of Victory, which represented the heavenly realm of light; *Gorias*, symbolized by the Sword of Light, which represented the heavenly realm of heat; *Falias*, symbolized by the sacred stone, the *Lia Fail*, which represented the realm of Earth; and *Murias*, symbolized by the Cauldron of the Dagda, the Cauldron of Plenty, which represented the watery underworld. The Earth was considered to be round but flat, a disc rather than a globe, which floated on the waters of the Great Sea. Water was important in Celtic religion and was believed to have magical and healing properties. Compared with some of the other races in Europe at the time, the Celts had remarkably advanced ideas of physical hygiene – i.e. they washed. The landscape of the Celtic world – Ireland and Brittany in particular – is littered with sacred springs which serve the same purpose today as they did in earlier times – to bring the sacred waters of life to the people.

Wells were considered sacred because not only did they bring healing, they were also entrances to the Otherworld. It is also possible to reach the Otherworld by sea.

> When all is done,
> will you sail with me in *Pridwen*, my ship?
> Will you come with me
> to the silver-circled castle
> at the back of the North Wind,
> where there is peace beneath the stars,
> and the apple orchards grow?[3]

The Celts had come across the great landmass of middle Europe to the isles and coasts of the West. To them, the sea was a moat around the land. In Ireland, the west coast is still referred to as 'the edge of the Western world', and it seems natural to think of the Otherworld as just beyond the western horizon. No-one who has been to this ethereal landscape, where grey wave fades into mist, and mist into sky, can fail to be impressed with a sense of standing at the edge of time and space. It seems a border country where it is very easy to step out of the everyday world into some other reality.

The concept of the Otherworld – in Irish, *Tir na n'Og* – was very important in Celtic myth. To the Celt, the Otherworld is a beautiful realm of warmth, of nature in abundance, a perpetual early summer, heady with the smell of flowers and blossom, filled with the sound of bird song and tinkling streams. It is a land in which nothing grows old and there is no disease. To enter the Otherworld is to enter Paradise – a brighter, more beautiful version of the mundane world. In contrast with the mythology of other peoples, the Celt has a joyful, often ecstatic approach to existence. There is no preoccupation with evil and no concept of sin and punishment. There are few monsters and demons in Celtic mythology. When the spirit passes into the Otherworld, there is no doubt that it is going to a better place. In death, there is nothing to fear.

The Otherworld seems to have been thought of as another place, but also as a state of consciousness. Many of the Celtic myths which refer to the Otherworld seem to indicate remnants of Shamanic ideas of other realms. As in societies where Shamanism is still practised, the souls of the very young and the sick were thought to be in danger of wandering into the Otherworld, never to return. It is also possible to fall in love with Otherworldly beings and be enticed away.

> O come, my love, and drink with me
> the honeysuckle wine,
> O come, my love, and dwell with me
> beneath the woodbine twine.
> I will make you King, my love,
> and I shall be your Queen,
> if you will come and dwell with me,
> beneath the leaves of green. [4]

There are many stories in Celtic folklore of those who went to dwell for a while in this Land of Fairy. The Scottish story of Tam Lin is one of the better known, having been popularized in recent decades by folk groups. Tam Lin, an Earthly knight, is captured by the Queen of Fairy and becomes her consort in the

Otherworld. He seems quite happy with his role until he comes near to the end of his seven-year term of office, at the end of which he is to be sacrificed. Tam Lin's Earthly love is Janet, whose maidenhead he demanded when she was unwise enought to venture alone to the woods. The enterprising Janet becomes pregnant. She rescues Tam Lin from his fate by pulling him down from his horse when he is out riding with the Fairy Queen and her entourage. The furious Queen turns Tam Lin into a series of fearsome beasts, but Janet refuses to let him go. She clutches him to her until the Fairy Queen admits defeat and restores him to his own form – that of a naked man. She then takes him home to do his husbandly duty.

The Gods and Goddesses of the Celts are worshipped both by modern Druids and also by Witches. Given that they are so honoured in the Pagan revival, remarkably little is known about them. Like the other peoples of North and West Europe, the Celts relied primarily on an oral tradition for their sacred legends and lore; hence much has been lost to us. Celtic deities are more difficult to classify than those of other Pagan peoples. As far as we know, the Celtic Gods do not seem to have undergone the rationalization process, familiar to us from the Greek, Roman and Norse pantheons, whereby male and female deities were paired into married couples and other deities became their children. There are some family relationships between the Gods of Celtic mythology; but no coherent story of a divine genealogy has been handed down to us. The difficulty is compounded because the Celts were not one nation, but a number of tribes spread across Europe, who shared similar languages and culture. They had many deities and there are likely to have been many local variations. Identifying the Celtic Gods is not helped by the fact that the Celts were very reluctant to reveal the true names of their patron deities. In magical thinking, to know the name of something or someone is to have power over it. Caitlín Matthews comments, in *Elements of the Celtic Tradition*, that in every recorded story of Celtic tradition, people refused to name their Gods, simply saying:

I swear by the Gods that my people swear by . . .[5]

In some written collections of the Celtic myths and legends, such as that of the Welsh *Mabinogion*, deities do not figure as such. The stories purportedly describe the deeds of heroes and nobles; for reversing the process of euhemerism the Christian scholars turned deities into human beings. Euhemerus himself was a Greek philosopher who argued that deities were originally men and women who had been deified for their achievements. It seems that the Christian scribes who first committed the myths to writing preferred (or found it safer) to describe their ancient deities as humans, in the same way as the Medieval Icelandic scholar Snorri Sturluson describes Odin as a descendant of King Priam of Troy! However, the attributes and magical powers of the figures in the legends betray their divine origins.

The Irish Gods can be divided into three groups – the Tuatha de Danaan, tribal and local Goddesses, and other perhaps older deities. Dana is the Mother of the Tuatha de Danaan, and her Tribe or Clan are some of the main deities of Ireland. The principal God is the Dagda or Good God. Like Odin, the Dagda is known as the All-Father, Eochaid Ollathair, and is considered wise and knowledgeable. His weapon is a club and he also possesses a magical cauldron which can never be emptied. There are suggestions that the chalk image of a giant phallic figure with a staff which is carved into the hillside at the village of Cerne (i.e. horn) Abbas in South-West England is an image of the Dagda or his English equivalent, but modern scholars are uncertain as to the image's antiquity. Another important deity is Lugh. He is the brilliant and many-skilled God whose weapon is the spear. Lugh claims, amongst other things, to be a harper, hero, poet, healer and magician. His name was given to one of the main Celtic festivals – Lughnasadh at the beginning of August.

Three important female deities in Ireland were the Goddesses of the battlefield – Morrigan, Badhbh and Nemain – often referred to collectively as The Morrigan. Perhaps not surprisingly, given their love of carrion, their symbol is the crow or raven. The Morrigan is said to mate with the Dagda every Samhain, 31st October. This is traditionally the Festival of the Dead when the Gates between the Worlds are open and the dead may converse with the living.

The Goddess Brigid is a less darksome Goddess. Legend says that she had her chief shrine in Kildare where her vigil fire was kept perpetually burning, tended by a group of unmarried priestesses known as Inghean an Dagha, Daughters of Fire. With the Christianization of Ireland, Brigid became Saint Brigid and her holy offices were taken over by nuns. The nuns continued to tend the sacred flame until the thirteenth century, when the Bishop of Kildare decreed that the custom should be suppressed as Pagan, which indeed it was. Brigid was a patroness of learning, poetry and prophecy and also of healing and smithcraft. In a Wiccan ritual, she explains:

> Brigid they name me,
> and three gifts of fire I bring:
> first, the flame of inspiration,
> frenzy of poet and anguish of artist,
> and passion of lover for union with the beloved;
> second, the fierce fire of smith-craft,
> through whose testing all must pass;
> and third, the most precious of all,
> which eases the second's pain,
> the undying warmth of healing,
> the last and the greatest gift
> of the ever-returning Sun.[6]

Oi-melc or *Imbolc*, at the beginning of February, was an important festival in Scotland and Ireland. Imbolc celebrated the first lactation of ewes – a much-welcomed event in the countryside which is dependent on sheep and lambing. Imbolc was also sacred to Brigid, and the Christian Church later made it Saint Brigid's day. In the Western Isles of Scotland, the festival of Saint Brigid or Bride was celebrated until recent times with the making of a bed by the fireside so that the Goddess might rest there. Bride was seen as a protectress and by saying daily prayers to her, her worshippers could be kept from harm.

> Every day and every night,
> that I say the genealogy of Bride,
> I shall not be killed, I shall not be wounded . . .
> no fire, no sun, no moon shall burn me,
> no lake, no water, nor sea shall drown me.[7]

In Welsh Celtic myth, one of the most important Goddesses is Rhiannon. She appears dressed in brilliant gold clothing riding a magical white mare. Her name can be equated with Divine Queen and she may have been the same Goddess who was worshipped in France as the horse Goddess Epona and whom the Roman soldiers who joined in her worship saluted as Regina – Queen. Arianrhod, or Silver-Wheel, is the mother of the Welsh equivalent of the God Lugh. Caer Arianrhod, the Castle of Arianrhod, is placed in the Northern heavens. It is considered particularly sacred in some Wiccan traditions as the shining beacon which guides our spiritual destiny and figures in much ritual prose and poetry.

There are indications that some of the Celtic myths are based around the cycle of Nature. One recurring theme throughout the Welsh myths is that of two God-like figures fighting for the hand of one woman. Thus Pwyll and Gwawl contend for Rhiannon, Bran and Mallolwch for Branwen, and Owein and the Knight in Black for the Countess of the Fountain. There are suggestions [8] that the two rivals represent the Gods of Summer and Winter contending for the eternal Goddess. The theme emerges again in the tale of Gawain and the Green Knight from the Christian era, but under the new dispensation, Gawain resists the reward of the Lady.

He who wins the Goddess has control over the land. The relationship between Goddesses of the land and the holder of worldly power – the king – is an important theme in Celtic mythology. The Irish texts suggest that a king might be married to the tutelary Goddess of his tribe. This would take place as a Sacred Marriage with a priestess or even with the Goddess' symbolic animal. Ronald Hutton of Bristol University, in his interesting book, *Pagan Religions of the Ancient British Isles*, [9] writes that Gerald of Wales in the later twelfth century claimed that the Kings of Donegal mated with a mare and suggests that the number of royal husbands accredited to Maeve Queen of Connaught indicates that she was a Goddess rather than a mortal queen. Once the Sacred Marriage was effected, the continued health of the king was important for the tribe. Many legends point to disaster befalling the land if the king is injured. It was also essential in Irish myth that the king be free from all physical disfigurement or disability.

Other Celtic deities include Cernunnos, the Horned Lord of the animals. Today, he is worshipped primarily in Wicca. As Herne and Cern, all derivatives of the word 'horn', his name figures in many placenames in the British Isles. Two images of the Horned God appear in Celtic Europe – one of Cernunnos as a stag God and the other of a Horned God with cattle horns. In France, the cult of the Horned God of the cattle was absorbed by the Christian missionaries and he was turned into Saint Cornelly, or Cornelius in the Latinized form. This form of the Horned God is sometimes called Karnayna in Wicca. The cult of Saint Cornelly is still widespread in Brittany, most notably in Carnac, one of the most prominent Pagan sacred sites in Europe. Horned animals decorate Saint Cornelly's churches and, until recently, were brought to the churches for annual blessing by the priest. The Celtic Christians seem to have been reluctant to part with their old Gods.

In modern Wicca, Cernunnos is often thought of as the Dark Lord, a God associated with the night; but in one of the few representations of him in Britain – on a silver coin dug up in Petersfield – he is shown as a stag God with a sun-wheel between his antlers. The image of a stag crowned with the sun appears frequently in dream, poetry and myth across many cultures as an image of positive male energy. Cernunnos is also depicted in Celtic imagery as a dispenser of wealth, an attribute often associated with fertility deities.

Sun worship seems to have been prevalent amongst the Celts. The eight-spoked wheel, which has been adopted by Druids and Wiccans in the twentieth century as a symbol of the seasonal festivals, appears often upon altars and may represent the Sun. The Christian missionary Saint Patrick condemned 'those who adored the Sun' to perish eternally and insisted that Christ was the true Sun. A number of Celtic festivals involved fire, which was thought to have been brought from the Sun by a sacred bird – a swallow, wren or swift. The red markings and forked tail of the swallow were thought to be a result of scorching by the Sun's rays. Fire was used as an element of purification. At the festival of Beltane or Bright-Fire, at the beginning of May, all the fires in Ireland were extinguished. The sacred flames were then rekindled by the Druids who performed a ceremony of driving the cattle between two fires to protect them from disease. This custom of making a new fire at Beltane continued into the nineteenth century in Gaelic Scotland, as did the custom of making the Sun dance, an image which appears often in Celtic poetry. This involved reflecting the Sun's light into a bowl of water and then shaking it so that as the water rippled, the sunlight would dance about the room. The light of the Sun could be brought into the darkness of the tomb in this way. In a Celtic Spring rite, the priestess says:

> The tides of Spring are upon us,
> when the Sun shall dance,
> when water shall merge with fire,
> when the Maiden is made Mother.
> In the name of the Two and the One,
> we shall seek the mystery of unity.[10]

To see the dancing of the Sun was thought to bestow particular blessing on those who beheld it. In traditional Witchcraft, a cauldron full of water or a mirror is similarly used for Drawing Down The Moon on the night of the Full Moon.

Other insights into the Pagan deities can be found in the Celtic *Song of Amairgin* brought to Ireland by the Sons of Mil. The Sons of Mil are understood to be tribal invaders who overcame the previous settlers whose Gods were the Tuatha de Danaan. The earlier tribes retreated to the fairy hills to become the Little People of Irish legend. When the Sons of Mil first attempted to land in Ireland, the Druids of the Tuatha de Danaan sang spells against them and raised a magic wind to carry them far out to sea; but after many trials and tribulations, the Sons of Mil succeeded in making a landing. Amairgin is described by the Christian Medieval scribes as a poet and judge of the Sons of Mil and brother of the King; but he makes a declaration of thirteen statements on landing in Ireland and asks six ritual questions indicating that he was, or spoke on behalf of, a God.

> I am a wind on the sea,
> I am a wave of the ocean,
> I am the roar of the sea,
> I am an ox of seven combats,
> I am a hawk above the cliff,
> I am a shining tear of the Sun,
> I am fair amongst flowers,
> I am a boar in boldness,
> I am a salmon in the pool,
> I am a lake on the plain,
> I am the hill of poetry,
> I am a battle-waging spear,
> I am he who sets the brain afire.
> Who but I knows the mystery of the unhewn dolmen?
> Who but I knows where the Sun shall set?
> Who but I foretells the phases of the Moon?
> Who calleth the cattle from the House of Tethra?
> Whom will the fish of the laughing ocean make welcome?
> Whose is the troop, for whom the God-who-fashioneth
> edges enchantments about a spear,
> enchantments of winds?[11]

Potentially the whole of creation is found in Amairgin and he is capable of all things. Alwyn and Brinley Rees comment in *Celtic*

Heritage: Ancient Traditions in Ireland and Wales that Amairgin's utterance is similar to that of the Hindu God Krishna in the *Bhagavad-Gita*:

> I am the radiant Sun among the light-givers . . .
> among the stars of night, I am the Moon . . .
> I am the ocean among the waters . . .
> I am the wind . . .
> I am the diceplay of the cunning,
> I am the strength of the strong . . .
> I am the silence of things secret,
> I am the knowledge of the knower.[12]

The Druids

Knowledge was one of the highly-prized possessions of Celtic society and was taught by one of the highest classes of society which consisted of the Druid priesthood, the Vates or Uates, who performed magic and divination, and the Bards. There were also female prophetesses, who were the priestesses of particular Goddesses. These were called Veledas or Ueledas amongst the Gauls and by titles such as Banfili, female seer, amongst the Irish. Veledas often occupied sacred caves or groves, similar to those of their Greek sisters at the Oracle of Delphi. To these sanctuaries would come petitioners from all classes of society seeking their wisdom. Veledas exerted considerable influence and later became advice-givers at the courts of Roman emperors.

The Druids, Vates and Bards were teachers, historians, astronomers and poets. They controlled the legal system, acted as judges and supervised executions. Intellectually, Druids were living libraries and were famous and admired for their prodigious memories. The Celts developed the use of the Ogham alphabet for writing inscriptions and Julius Caesar tells us that they used the Greek alphabet for writing letters, but the Druids scorned the use of the written word for sacred and poetic thought. Each Druid was required to learn by heart the whole of their law, teachings, poetry, story, myth, religious observance, astronomy, astrology, genealogy and tribal history. This could take up to 20 years. A boy would begin his apprenticeship in early childhood and this would continue until he was considered proficient. While this is a powerful way of transmitting an oral tradition, unfortunately it has meant that with the suppression of the

Druids, most of the Celtic teachings were lost and a great treasure of Western culture destroyed.

The Druids also practised some techniques which seem Shamanic in origin. To find the answer to a question, they might eat raw bull's flesh, drink the blood, and sleep wrapped in the hide. The answer would then come during sleep. There are indications that the Celts knew of the use of bodily posture in prayer and meditation. The God Cernunnos is depicted on the Gundestrup Cauldron sitting in a meditative position reminiscent of the Buddha. In one hand he holds a snake, often used as an image of energy rising up the spinal column from the muladhara chakra at the base of the spine. The tenth-century Irish text *The Cauldron of Poesy* describes two positions conducive to prayer and one to ritual incubation, whereby a bard would lie in darkness in order to receive poetic inspiration. This involved lying flat on the back and weighing down the stomach with stones to prevent movement. This state of darkness and stillness caused sensory deprivation during which dream and vision would come to the seeker.

The Druids also had a fearsome reputation as magicians. They were believed to have the ability to raise storms, winds and mists, and to make the Sun stand still in its course. They could divine the secret names of the Gods of their enemies and call these out in battle to make the opposing tribes tremble with fear.

Despite the intellectual demands required to become a Druid, as a career it had a lot going for it. Druids were both respected and feared. In the middle of war, they could command the opposing factions to lay down their arms. Given the fiery nature of the Celts, this was probably a frequently-called for service. Druids, Vates and Bards were themselves exempt from military service and were almost immune from attack. Murder was considered by Celtic society to be a blow not just to the slain, but also to his or her family and clan. The family of the perpetrator of the crime was responsible for the actions of its members and compensation, or honour price, was payable to the relatives of the victim, with the price for those of high social status being costly indeed. The Irish hero Fionn, after avenging his father's death by slaying his killer, says, 'He dared not remain in Ireland unless he undertook poetry, for fear of the sons of Uirghriu and the sons of Morna.'[13] As a Bard, he would be relatively safe. The honour price which the family of any Bard- or Druid-murderer had to pay was so financially crippling as to be totally prohibitive.

If Druids, Vates and Bards were not quite worth their weight in gold, they were approaching it.

Modern Druidry

Today, Druidry has undergone an extensive revival all over the Western world, but particularly in the British Isles, Brittany and North America. Not all Druid orders are Pagan. Some are more akin to freemasonry and some are Christian-oriented. The Druid Orders are most familiar to the people of the British Isles from the ceremonies at the Welsh Eistedfodd, where Bards appear in their blue robes, Vates in green and Druids in white robes and headdresses. In past years, Druids were also well known for their Midsummer appearances at Stonehenge; although this ceremony has been temporarily banned by the British authorities, afraid of the size of the audience it attracts.

Some Druid groups today scorn the use of white robes, believing these originate in eighteenth-century romanticism. From a practical point of view, white does not marry well with life in muddy villages full of thatched huts. In fact, it is known that colour in clothing was an important mark of social status amongst the Celts. The higher the social status of the individual, the more colours he or she wore. Kings could wear up to twelve colours and Druids up to ten. The everyday dress of the Druids is likely therefore to have been Celtic plaid. However, there may have been differences between everyday and ritual dress. A number of independent sources from Pliny to *The Tripartite Life of Saint Patrick*[14] comment that Druids wore white robes on ceremonial occasions. Amongst the colourful plaid of the nobles, the white dress would have been a distinctive and useful focus when conducting large ceremonies and white is often used in a religious setting to denote purity. In *The Tripartite Life of Saint Patrick*, we are also told that the Druids had a tonsure, i.e. the centre of the head was shaved from forehead to back. This is often thought to be the reason why the monks of the early Celtic Church had a different shaped tonsure from the round bald patch now familiar to us from the Roman Church. Some kind of visible sign of priesthood such as shaving the head is common amongst many cultures and may have been the style of the Druids.

The practices of modern-day Druids vary between the different orders. Some teach a wide curriculum of esoteric lore. Others encourage the development of spiritual understanding through the creative arts such as music and poetry. Druids celebrate a seasonal cycle of festivals, but some Druids celebrate only those festivals which are identifiably Celtic, while others celebrate the same eight seasonal festivals as Witches.

Spirits of Place are important in many Druid traditions. Druids usually prefer to celebrate their rites outside with their feet standing upon the Earth. Pilgrimages to sacred sites and spending time outside communing with Nature are encouraged as a way of contacting the spirit of the land and learning to live in harmony with it.

> Hill walking and camping, wilderness trekking and individual or group retreats in places of great power and beauty all provide us with a sense of deep peace and connect us to the nourishment that comes when we feel ourselves as belonging in the world, as children of the Goddess. [15]

Also important is the Spirit of Time. The celebration of the seasonal cycle allows Druids to synchronize their lives with Nature. Philip Carr-Gomm, Head of the Order of Bards, Ovates and Druids, writes that time is often seen as our enemy in modern-day society. We live frenzied lives in which we constantly race against time. He advocates befriending time and learning both to make use of it and to find time each day or week for meditation and inner tranquillity. This is not self-indulgence, but helps us attune ourselves to the needs of our world. Attunement to the Sprit of the Times is considered important because Druidry is not only concerned with service to the Earth and preservation of the natural world, but also with service to humanity. Each period of history has an agenda in relation to the evolution of consciousness. Certain individuals have become great innovators and agents for the advancement of humanity, 'because they have been aware of the needs of the time and have succeeded in articulating what was already fermenting in the collective psyche.' [16] This should also be our endeavour. The role of Druid as teacher and spiritual counsellor is strongly emphasized in some Druid traditions and in the ethos of Western Paganism generally. This encourages us to be of service and open to those seeking the wisdom of the Gods. In a Druid ceremony, the participants are enjoined:

Let Unity, Harmony and Beauty be your watchwords. May you abundantly share in the Illumination. Be you ready to hear the voice of those crying out for Wisdom. Listen at the Portals – for the world is large and many are seeking. Open the Gates for them and portal after portal shall open unto you.[17]

1. See Tadhg MacCrossan, *The Sacred Cauldron: Secrets of the Druids*, page 110.
2. See Ronald B. Hutton, *Pagan Religions of the Ancient British Isles*, page 183.
3. Susan Cooper, *The Dark is Rising Sequence*, page 763.
4. From Vivianne Crowley, *Fairy Song*, 1968.
5. Caitlín Matthews, *Elements of the Celtic Tradition*, page 14.
6. Unpublished material from traditional witchcraft sources.
7. From the *Carmina Gaedelica*, trans. Alexander Carmichael, Scottish Academic Press, Edinburgh, 1972, as quoted in Caitlín Matthews, *Elements of the Celtic Tradition*, page 14.
8. Jeffrey Gantz, trans., *The Mabinogion*, pages 15–16.
9. Ronald B. Hutton, *Pagan Religions of the Ancient British Isles*, pages 172–3.
10. Unpublished material from traditional witchcraft sources.
11. Based on the R.A.S. Macalister trans. from the *Lebor Gabala Erenn,. V*, pages 114–17.
12. From the *Bhagavad-Gita*, as quoted in Alwynn and Brinley Rees, *Celtic Heritage: Ancient Traditions in Ireland and Wales*, page 99.
13. From Daithi O-hogain, *Fionn Mac Cumhail*, Gill and Macmillan, Dublin, 1988, as quoted in Caitlín Matthews, *Elements of the Celtic Tradition*, page 14.
14. Ronald B. Hutton, *Pagan Religions of the Ancient British Isles*, page 171.
15. Philip Carr-Gomm, *The Elements of the Druid Tradition*, page 86.
16. Philip Carr-Gomm, *The Elements of the Druid Tradition*, page 90.
17. Unpublished material from Druid sources

4
The Norse
and German Traditions

The Norse-German Gods were worshipped all over Northern and Western Europe by the ancestors of the Norse, Dutch, German and English peoples. Their Gods were brought to Celtic Britain by invaders from the East – the Germanic tribes of Angles, Saxons and others – who came to make their home in Britain in the tumultuous years following the withdrawal of the Roman armies from Western Europe around about 400 CE. Over the next few hundred years, these Gods were also brought to the North of England and to Eastern Scotland by the Vikings – adventurers from Scandinavia seeking a quick route to fortune and glory. These invading peoples came first with warriors and swords and later brought their families to settle and farm the eastern side of Britain. The Norse-German peoples also reached farther West and historians now believe that Viking settlers travelled as far as North America.

The Norse-German religion is often called Asatru which means 'belief in the Gods' or 'loyalty to the Aesir'. Some prefer the term Odinism, but others use Asatru, as they do not worship Odin solely. Asatru is practised all over Northern Europe and also in North America. In Iceland, in recent years, Asatru has become a strong religious movement and, along with Christianity, is one of the two official state religions. Iceland only formally became Christian in 1000 CE and her Pagan religious history is therefore nearer to her people than in some of the other Northern-European countries.

As in all Pagan paths, there is much emphasis in Asatru on the Gods as made manifest in Nature. History tells us that the German tribes near the Rhine favoured outdoor worship; though

in winter further north, this must often have been modified. The
Roman historian Tacitus writes:

> The Germans do not think it in keeping with the Divine
> majesty to confine Gods within walls or to portray them in
> the likeness of human countenance. Their holy places are
> woods and groves, and they apply the names of deities to
> that hidden presence which is seen only by the eye of
> reverence. [1]

These attitudes are similar to those of many who follow the
Norse-German tradition today. An Odinist organization tell us,
'containing the essence of the universe within themselves, the
Gods are everywhere and in everything.'

The Divine in Nature is venerated in modern Asatru in the
seasonal celebrations. Asatru is more male-oriented that some
Pagan religions (although less so than the Christian Church) but
Asatru groups are led by both men and women and both officiate
in religious ceremonies. The seasonal cycle is based around the
major festivals of Yule, the two Equinoxes – often known as
Summer-finding and Winter-finding – and Midsummer. Other
festivals of importance to the Norse-German Tradition may also
be celebrated. Yule is considered to last for twelve days, each of
which represents a month of the year to come (hence the carol
The Twelve Days of Christmas). Midsummer is celebrated as a
festival of the Sun and of the triumph of light. In Scandinavia,
it is widely observed, by Pagans and non-Pagans alike, as a public
holiday where bonfires are lit across the land.

Our Norse-German ancestors, like the Celts, relied on an oral
tradition. Their myths and religious lore were not written down
until after the coming of Christianity, but they were written
relatively sooner afterwards than were the Celtic myths, which
are overlaid with Christian, Roman and Greek influence. In
about 1220, the Icelandic scholar Snorri Sturluson, concerned to
preserve his people's traditions, wrote down what he knew in a
collection of works known as the *Prose Edda* to distinguish it from
the *Poetic Edda*. There are other Norse-German religious writings
apart from the *Eddas*, but these are less well known in the
English-speaking world.

From the *Eddas*, we learn that the Norse-German peoples
believed that the universe consists of nine worlds which together
make up the Tree of Life, Yggdrasil. Ygg is another name for Odin
and Yggdrasil means 'Odin's Steed'. Yggdrasil is so vast that its

branches stretch out over both Heaven and Earth. Yggdrasil has three roots. The first is in Asgard, the home of the High Gods, and is watered by the spring of Urd, which is the spring of Fate. It is by the Well of Urd that the Gods hold daily council. The second root of Yggdrasil is in Jotunheim, Giant-Home. Under this root is also a well – that of the giant Mimir – in which is hidden all wisdom. The third root is in Niflheim, Cloud Home, and is watered by Hvergälmer, the origin of all life-giving waters. There are a number of important animals which live on the Tree. Ratatosk the squirrel runs up and down communicating between the eagle or sacred cock at the crown and the serpent Nidhögg, Gnawer-from-Below, at its base in Niflheim. The squirrel Ratatosk is an image of the seeker of knowledge. He climbs to the heights of consciousness and down to the depths of the unconscious in order to come to awareness.

The chief God of the Aesir or High Gods is Odin in Norse or Woden in Anglo-Saxon. It was he who gave his name to Wednesday when the Anglo-Saxons adopted the Roman system of the seven-day week. The Romans attributed this day to Mercury, God of mental agility, and there are aspects of Mercury which can be equated with Odin. Odin is a God of wisdom, knowledge and communication. Elsa-Brita Titchenell, in *The Masks of Odin*, equates Odin's name with Odr or Universal Intelligence: 'the divine root of every being in all the worlds, the essence of divinity present in all life forms, in the smallest particle as well as in the cosmos itself.' Odin possesses a magical ring which dispenses eight more like itself every ninth night. These can be likened to the cycles of creation, 'recurrent motion in both time and space: the wheels within wheels of biblical symbology', and she points out that this spiral design can be found among plants and animals throughout nature, 'from the atomic worlds to the great sweeping movements of stars and galaxies in space.' [2]

Odin's consort is Frigga, the wise Mother of the Gods. She sees the future and is described as the one who 'knows every being's fate, though she herself says naught' [3] In the Tarot, this type of female energy is represented by the High Priestess. Baldur the Beautiful is Odin's son by Frigga. He is wise and merciful and his death marks the beginning of the disintegration and destruction of the world of Asgard. Baldur's death is commemorated at Midsummer when the Sun begins to wane. Bragi, from whom the English verb 'to brag' is derived, is the God of poetry. Tyr is the God of battle. Heimdall was called the White God and is said to be the son of nine maidens. He dwells beside Bifrost, the Rainbow Bridge. Loki was Odin's foster-brother and the son of a giant. He brings the forces of chaos and disorder into Asgard.

Also important in Norse-German mythology are the battle Goddesses – the Valkyries – and the three Fates or Norns, who weave the Web of Wyrd. Although Odin is considered leader of the High Gods, ultimately he is bound by the threads of Wyrd. Urd is the chief of the Norns. She rules the past. Her name means 'origin'. This is the cause of the present and future. The second sister is Verdandi, whose name means 'becoming'. She represents the present – that which is coming into being. Together the two sisters create their third, Skuld, whose name means 'debt'. Skuld represents the future; she is akin to karma and is the result of the actions of the past and present. It is Skuld who cuts the thread of life, when the individual's time comes to an end. She is depicted as wearing a veil – the past and present are known, but the future has yet to be revealed. Together the Wyrd Sisters spin the web of destiny which affects all things – Gods and men. In the *Völuspá* or *The Sibyl's Prophecy*, the functions of the Norns are described.

> A tall ash-tree stands by name of Yggdrasil,
> watered daily by white icicles,
> that drip the dew that drops in the dells.
> It stands ever green above Urd's well.
> Thence come three Maidens who know much,
> from that bower beneath the tree:
> one is named *Origin*, the second *Becoming*;
> these two fashioned the third, named *Debt*.
> They established law that determines the fates,
> of the children of ages and the lives of men.[4]

Asgard, the home of the High Gods, forms the first of the upper worlds. The others are Vanaheim and Alfheim. Vanaheim is the home of the Vanir, Gods of peace and plenty. Many believe that the Vanir were the Gods of the Bronze Age, whose followers came into conflict with the invading Iron-Age Indo-Europeans and their warrior Aesir Gods. The myths describe how a war was fought between the Gods of the two pantheons and was resolved when the two teams exchanged hostages. Freya and Njörd were sent to make their home in Asgard and Mimir and Hoenir in Vanaheim. The wily Aesir seem to have got the better of the bargain. The Vanir found Hoenir could do nothing unless advised by Mimir. Outraged, the Vanir cut off Mimir's head and returned it to Asgard, where Odin used it to learn hidden lore.

Chief amongst the Vanir are Freya and her twin brother Frey. Freya and Frey mean Lady and Lord. They are the children of Njörd. Njörd is a God of the sea, who sends winds to seafarers and protects them on their journeys. He is also associated with the planet Saturn and can be seen as Father Time. Freya is the patron and protectress of the human race. In the Tarot, she can be equated with the Empress, the Lady of Fertility, but she is also associated with the sea. One of Freya's names is Mardoll, derived from *mar*, meaning sea. Freya Asywnn[5] considers that the Norse-German Goddesses have a valuable role to play in filling a gap left by other Pagan traditions. She sees Wicca as having two main Goddess aspects – those of the Goddess as Earth and Moon. She believes that hidden within the Craft is a third current – that of Goddess as sea and the sea mysteries. This can be represented by Freya, Lady of the Vanir.

Women played an important role in Norse-German religion as Volvas and Seidkonas. The word Volva meant 'prophetess'. Seidkonas had a similar function and practised Seidr or magic. Freya was the patroness of Seidr and taught it to Odin, but Seidr was primarily a female art. Much of the practice of the Volvas was Shamanic and involved entering trances in order to communicate with the Otherworld. They also gave forth prophecy, often seated on a platform surrounded by priestesses who would perform ritual chants to help induce and maintain the trance. The role of women as prophetesses was similar to that of Veledas in Celtic society. The seeresses travelled about the country visiting different settlements to give advice and vision. Tacitus writes that the German tribes believed 'there resides in women an element of holiness and a gift of prophecy; and so they do not scorn to ask their advice, or lightly disregard their replies.'[6]

Both the God Frey and the Danish Goddess Nerthus were said to travel about the countryside in ceremonial wagons. Nerthus may have been a Vanir deity. Tacitus records[7] that Nerthus was a fertility Goddess and there is an interesting connection between Nerthus and Njörd. In Old Norse, the name Njörd is the equivalent of Nerthus, and Nerthus and Njörd may have originally been a twin pair of deities such as Freya and Frey. Some modern scholars have suggested[8] that she may have been a wife of Njörd and mother of Frey and Freya.

The role of the travelling seeress may have been connected with that of travelling deities. Nerthus visited her people in her sacred wagon, which none but her dedicated priest might touch. The priest knew the Goddess was present in her wagon sanctuary when it became heavy and he then set out with the wagon which was drawn by oxen. The reference to the heaviness suggests that at these ceremonies, a priestess would embody the Goddess. The Goddess' arrival was welcomed with great ceremony and a cessation of any tribal hostilities so that 'every weapon is put away'. The God Frey seems also to have been embodied in the person of his priest. The *Flateyjarbok,* [9] or *Book of Flatey* from the monastery of that name in Ireland, tells us that King Eric of Sweden led Frey's wagon to a certain place and waited until it became heavy. This was the sign that the God was present. The wagon was then taken into the king's hall and King Eric greeted the God, drank a horn in his honour and put various questions to him.

Alfheim, Elf-Home, also known as Ljössalfheim, Light-Elf-Home, is the world of the light elves, who are responsible for the growth of vegetation. This world was given to Frey as a teething gift. It is the natural world of fertility, plants and animals and is strongly reminiscent of the deva kingdom in other traditions. Frey is distinguished by his erect phallus and has similarities to other Nature Gods such as Cernunnos, Pan and the Egyptian Bes. At Ragnarök, the time of the destruction of the Gods, the link with the Horned God is again apparent when Frey fights Surt the destroyer with a pair of antlers, having given up his magical sword as part of a bride price.

One of the three middle worlds of Yggdrasil is Midgard, or Middle-Earth, as it is more commonly known to readers of Tolkien's *Lord of the Rings* saga. This is the human world and is ruled by Thor, who is friend of farmers and workers. Thor, or Thunor in Anglo-Saxon, whose name was given to Thursday, is Odin's son by the giantess Jord or Jorth who represents the Earth. Thor is immensely strong and one of his greatest treasures is his hammer, Mjölnir, with which he can slay giants and shatter rocks. His worship was widespread and when Saxons were converted to Christianity, he was one of the three deities they were specifically required to renounce. Like the Celtic Good God, the Dagda, Thor has certain earthy characteristics. He travels in a chariot drawn by goats. He has a zest for life and an enormous appetite for food and drink. He can literally drink his hosts dry. In the original myths, Odin may not have been the principal deity of the Aesir. Snorri Sturluson tells us in his prologue to the *Eddas* that Thor was the first of the Gods and that one of Thor's descendants 'had a son whose name was Woden, it is him that we call Odin.'[10] By the time the myths were recorded, Odin seems to have come to supremacy, in what was perhaps a later rationalization of family relationships.

Muspellheim, or Fire-Home, is the second of the three middle realms of the Tree. This is a world of creative and destructive fire, a world of pure energy in expansion. It is ruled over by Surt, the destroyer at Ragnarök. This world is balanced by Niflheim, Cloud Home, which is the world of creative and destructive frost and ice. This is controlled by the serpent Nidhögg. This world, where water vapour freezes from mist to ice, is energy in contraction. From here, Nagelfar, the Ship of the Dead, which is built out of dead men's nails, will sail forth at Ragnarök with Loki at its helm. Niflheim can be equated with *mulaprakrti* (root-nature) in Hindu philosophy – the 'primordial, undifferentiated substance out of which the matter of all range of substantiality and materiality are derived.'[11]

Of the three lower worlds, Swartalfheim, or Black-Elf-Home, is the world of the black elves or dwarves. Dwarves are useful beings, but they are greedy, treacherous and unfriendly to humans. They rule the treasures of the inner earth. Hel is the realm of the dead, but the name does not carry the negative connotations which Christianity later placed upon it. This world is ruled by the Goddess Hel, daughter of Loki, and consists of many realms both pleasant and unpleasant. Hel was not the destiny of all who died. Warriors were received into Asgard to dwell in Valhalla, the Hall of the Slain, and to feast with the Gods. Later Valhalla came to be seen as the resting place of all those who were dedicated to Odin, not just the battle-fallen. Snorri Sturluson tells us that all those whose bodies were burned after death were received by Odin, who had himself established this rite. Both men and women entered Odin's hall. To enter the realms of Odin was anticipated with great joy. The chieftain Lord Ragnor says before his death:

It gladdens me to know that Baldur's father
makes ready the benches for banquet.
Soon we shall be drinking ale from the curved horns.
The champion who comes into Odin's dwelling
does not lament his death.

I shall not enter his hall with words of fear upon my lips.
The Aesir will welcome me.
Death comes without lamenting . . .
Eager am I to depart. . . .
The days of my life are ended.
I laugh as I die. [12]

Death was not seen as the final end, but a transition to a new life. It could also be a resting place between lives. When Odin's son Baldur is killed, he can be restored to life, but only if everything on Earth will mourn him. The evil Loki who has engineered Baldur's death disguises himself as an old woman and refuses to mourn. Thus Baldur remains in the world of the dead.

There is also evidence that the Norse-German people believed in reincarnation down the ancestral line. The *Flateyjarbok* tells us that when the Christian King Olaf the Holy was born, there was great anxiety because his mother was in such long labour. The birth came about safely when a sword and a ring were taken from the burial mound of one of his ancestors, Olaf of Geistad, and presented to the child. In adult life, Olaf was believed to be the reincarnation of Olaf of Geistad. He was questioned about this on one occasion when he rode past his ancestor's burial mound.

'Tell me, Lord, . . . were you buried here? . . . They say that
when you came to this place before, you said, "Here we
were once, and here we fare now." ' [13]

Olaf, who has taken up Christianity, strongly denies that he ever said such a thing.

Jotunheim, or Giant-Home, is a hostile realm inhabited by the giants, the forces of chaos. It is a world in constant motion, which seeks to oppose anything which resists it. It acts in opposition to the creative forces of Vanaheim. The role of the giants in Norse-German mythology is an interesting one. The Gods are often equated with the highest form of consciousness present in existence, whereas the giants are seen as its opposite, all that acts against the thrust of evolution. 'They become matter only when vitalized and set in motion by the Gods and they cease to exist when the Gods depart.' [14] Freya Aswynn believes that the giants represent some of the earliest Gods of Northern Europe. These were the Gods of the Stone Age peoples who inhabited Northern Europe before the Bronze Age Vanir. She also believes that the early inhabitants of Northern Europe had an animistic outlook. What they did not understand they either worshipped or placated, and they worshipped the frost giants, mountain giants and fire giants as the raw forces of Nature.

To our Norse-German ancestors, human beings were only one of the conscious creations in the universe. Within Yggdrasil, there are a number of different conscious entities who inhabit interlocking and interacting worlds. All the different orders of creation see the same Sun, planets and stars, and undergo experiences within the same universe or multiverse; but they perceive them from the perspective of their different worlds. Their views of reality are not quite the same. In the *Allvismál* or *Lay of Allwise*, the dwarf Allwise seeks the hand of Thor's daughter. Allwise is tested by Thor on his knowledge of all aspects of creation to see if he lives up to his name. Thor asks him,

'What is the Moon that people see in every world?'
Allwise answers:

It is 'Moon' to men, to Gods 'The Ball',
'Turning Wheel' in the house of Hel;
giants say, 'Hastener', dwarfs call him 'Shine',
elves name him 'Tally of Time'.

Thor then asks, 'What is Night, Daughter of Dark, named in each world?'
Allwise answers:

Men call her 'Night', the Gods say 'Dark',
the Aesir say 'The Disguiser';
giants say 'Unlight', elves 'Joy-of-Sleep',
dwarfs call her 'Dream-Spinner'. [15]

As in many of the poems of the *Eddas*, the purpose is to instruct the audience, who learn that there are a number of worlds with different orders of being who have different viewpoints. The song also has another salutary message – that it is unwise to force the hand of Gods. Although Allwise has answered Thor's questions correctly, Thor is wilier. Unwilling to give his daughter to a dwarf, he has kept Allwise talking to dawn and the sun turns him to stone.

Creation and Destruction

Unlike Celtic mythology, the creation myths of our Norse-German ancestors have been preserved. From the *Eddas* we learn that the universe as we know it comes about through the interaction of a number of cosmic forces which result in the creation of the nine worlds which together comprise the Tree of Life. In the beginning is darkness and silence, Ginnungagap or Yawning-Void. The *Eddas* call this the time of the Fimbulvetr, Mighty-Winter, the long cold night of Non-being. During Fimbul-Winter all is not complete nothingness, for two opposing polarities exist. In Judaic mythology, these are portrayed as Chokmah and Binah – force and form, male and female, sperm and womb. In Norse-German mythology, they are not anthropomorphized, but are conceived of as Fire and Ice – Muspellheim, Fire Home, and Niflheim, Cloud Home. Matter is created when the two polarities interact – the heat of Muspellheim melts the ice of the cold world of Niflheim, thus creating vapour in the Yawning-Void. This is vapour is Ymer, the frost giant, from whom the Gods will create our world of Middle-Earth. The world of giants is a world of chaos. They create matter, but they do not know how to order it, categorize it, separate one thing from another. They are blind and unconscious forces. Ymer commences the process of creation, but this first stage alone is not sufficient to establish the manifest universe. There is neither soil, nor sea; neither Earth nor Heaven. The potential for life has been created, but not the world of form as we know it.

> Sun turned from the south, sister of the Moon,
> her right arm rested on the rim of Heaven;
> she knew not where her hall was,
> nor Moon what might he had,
> the stars knew not their constellations. [16]

For the processes of creation to develop, the active intervention of conscious forces is necessary. At this stage, Buri, Bur and the Sons of Bur are created. These are the ancestors of the Aesir, the High Gods, who are the forces of order. They have the power to bring order into chaos and to establish Middle-Earth – the world as we know it.

> Gaping abyss alone: no growth,
> until Bur's sons raised the lands,
> and brought forth magnificent Midgard.
> From southwards the Sun shone on the stony ground;
> then grew green grass in fertile soil. [17]

It is from the further interplay between order and chaos that creation comes. Both are necessary. there cannot be one without the other. Every action has an equal and opposite reaction. This balance between opposing forces is more reminiscent of Eastern thought than recent Western thought. In can be found in Eastern tradition in the interaction of Shiva and Vishnu and also in the balance of Yin and Yang. The placement of the realm of humanity is interesting. We are placed at the centre – at Middle-Earth – the mediators between the world of the giants and the forces of destruction, and the world of the creator Gods. We are in the role of Ratatosk the squirrel, with his ability to climb to the heights or plunge to the depths as we will.

In Norse-German myth, destructive forces are not evil in the dualistic sense. In all esoteric teaching, both creative, building forces and destructive, breaking down forces – anabolism and catabolism – have their role to play. Interestingly, creation is seen as atheistic in the true sense, in that no God created the universe at a single moment. The world comes about as a result of the interaction of a number of cosmic forces. The role of the Gods is to establish order once the processes of creation have begun. Here, the Gods are more akin to the qabalistic concept of Archangels – great forces with particular tasks to perform and specific powers.

In the second stage of creation, the Gods create order and rationality, allotting to the forces of the heavens their names and place.

> The High Gods gathered in council
> in their Hall of Judgement they conversed.
> To Night and Nightfall their names they gave,
> the Morning they named and Mid-Day,
> Mid-Winter, Mid-Summer, to order the year. [18]

Pagan mythology differs from Judaeo-Christian myth. Most Pagans do not believe that the universe was created in a brief space of time by a single God, that the human race is the only conscious creation in the universe, or that we, or our own planet, are the summit of that God's creation. This view is manifestly false. We inhabit only one of many potentially inhabitable planets and many other life forms must populate the universe other than our own. Creation is not a once-and-for-all event, but ever-renewing cycles and spirals of evolution and becoming. The universe which we see today will pass and fade, beings will live and die, races will come and go. The forces of creation and destruction are ever at work. The Norse-German myths speak not only of the creation of the universe, but also of its destruction. In the same way that crystals are formed and then decay, so too does our world, Middle-Earth, reach culmination and then begin to decay from within. This is the pattern of all things – our bodies, our societies, our religions, the planet itself.

The process of ecological erosion is graphically conveyed in the myths. The serpent Nidhögg gnaws through Yggdrasil's root, four stags nibble at the leaves and two goats at the bark, all gradually undermining and destroying it. Despite this continuous process of destruction, the Norse-German world-view is essentially optimistic. Wagner's opera cycle *The Ring of the Nibelungen* has given a mistaken impression that the *Eddas* convey a pessimistic religious philosophy in which the High Gods are overcome by the forces of evil. The myths describe the end of the world, but the Wagner operas stop short at the point of destruction. What they do not depict is the aftermath of Ragnarök. In the *Vaftrudnismál*, or *Lay of Illusion*, Odin in his guise as Gagnrád, Gainful-Counsel, questions the giant Vaftrudnir about the end of the world. Interestingly, the giants of chaos are portrayed as knowing more of the future than the High Gods. Odin asks Vaftrudnir what human beings will survive the Fimbul-Winter.

> *Life* and *Survivor* are hid in the Tree,
> morning dew their food will be,
> and from them will be born,
> nations to come.

Odin then asks what will happen to the Sun, 'when Fenris-Wolf has swallowed this one?'

> One daughter alone the Elf-Wheel bears
> before Fenris-Wolf o'ertakes her;
> Radiant Mane shall ride her mother's roads
> when the powers of the Gods have perished.

Elf-Wheel, or Alfrödul, is the soul of the Sun. The visible orb itself is often called Dvalin's Toy. Fenris-Wolf is Loki's son by the giantess Angrboda. From Vaftrudnir, we learn that the Sun will reappear in the form of her daughter, Radiant Mane. Many of the High Gods will be destroyed, but some will survive to found a new dynasty.

Vidar and Vale shall have the Gods' shrines
when the flames of Surt have subsided.
Mode and Magne shall then have Mjölnir
when Vingner is o'erthrown. [19]

Surt is the destroyer of the worlds. Mode (Force) and Magne
(Might) are two sons of Vingner, another name for Thor. Mjölnir
is Thor's hammer. The remaining Gods, together with a man and
a woman, Lif and Lifthrasir, Life and Survivor, who have
survived the destruction by hiding in the branches of the Tree of
Life begin a new world. In *Odens Korpgalder*, or *The Lay of Odin's
Corpse*, [20] we are told of the cessation of the phase of destruction.
As the smoke of Ragnarök dies away, the forces of destruction will
go to their lairs, the surviving Gods will rise up. Heimdall the
White, the watcher of the Gods who keeps guard upon
the Rainbow Bridge of Bifrost, blows the horn of alarm at the
beginning of Ragnarök and is there to announce that the phase
of destruction is over. His clarion call announces the dawning of
a new day. In the Pagan myths there is no irreversible finality.
The cosmos has seasons and cycles even as does the planet itself.
The phase of destruction is followed by a period of dormancy, the
Fimbul-Winter, and then by a new manifestation.

1. Tacitus, *Germania* 9, in H. Mattingly trans. *The Agricola and The
   Germania*, page 109.
2. Elsa-Brita Titchenell, *The Masks of Odin: Wisdom of the Ancient
   Norse*, page 36.
3. The *Eddas, Lokasenna* or *Loki's Flyting*, see Elsa-Brita Titchenell,
   The Masks of Odin: Wisdom of the Ancient Norse, page 217.
4. The *Eddas, Völuspá* or *Sibyl's Prophecy*, v. 19–21, see Elsa-Brita
   Titchenell, *The Masks of Odin: Wisdom of the Ancient Norse*, pages
   93–4, and W.H. Auden and Paul B. Taylor, *Norse Poems*, page 248.
5. Freya Aswynn, *Leaves of Yggdrasil: A Synthesis of Magic, Feminine
   Mysteries, Folklore*, page 2.
6. Tacitus, *Germania* 8, in H. Mattingly trans. *The Agricola and the
   Germania*, page 108.
7. Quoted in Hilda R. Ellis Davidson, *Gods and Myths of Northern
   Europe*, page 95.
8. Hilda R. Ellis Davidson, *Gods and Myths of Northern Europe*, page
   106.
9. Quoted in Hilda R. Ellis Davidson, *Gods and Myths of Northern
   Europe*, page 94.
10. Snorri Sturloson, *Edda*, Anthony Faulkes (trans.).

11. Elsa-Brita Titchenell, *The Masks of Odin: Wisdom of the Ancient Norse*, page 30.
12. From the *Lodbrok*, the *Death Song of Ragnar*, quoted in Hilda R. Ellis Davidson, *Gods and Myths of Northern Europe*, page 150.
13. Quoted in Hilda R. Ellis Davidson, *Gods and Myths of Northern Europe*, page 155.
14. Elsa-Brita Titchenell, *The Masks of Odin: Wisdom of the Ancient Norse*, page 33.
15. The *Eddas*, *Alvismál* or *The Lay of Allwise*, v.14–15, 30–31, see Elsa-Brita Titchenell, *The Masks of Odin: Wisdom of the Ancient Norse*, pages 225–30, and W.H. Auden and Paul B. Taylor, *Norse Poems*, page 248.
16. The *Eddas*, *Völuspá* or *Sibyl's Prophecy*, see Elsa-Brita Titchenell, *The Masks of Odin: Wisdom of the Ancient Norse*, page 46, and W.H. Auden and Paul B. Taylor, *Norse Poems*, page 246.
17. Ibid.
18. Ibid.
19. The *Eddas*, *Vaftrudismál* or the the *Lay of Illusion*, v.43–6, 49–50, see Olive Bray (trans.), *The Elder or Poetic Edda*, pages 55–6; Elsa-Brita Titchenell, *The Masks of Odin: Wisdom of the Ancient Norse*, pages 134–42; W.H. Auden and Paul B. Taylor, *Norse Poems*, page 232; Lee Hollander (trans.), *The Poetic Edda*, pages 42–52. Odin as Gagnrád (Gainful Counsel) questions the giant Vaftrudnir in a dialogue which is designed to educate the listener.
20. *Odens Korpgalder* or *The Lay of Odin's Corpse*, see Elsa-Brita Titchenell, *The Masks of Odin: Wisdom of the Ancient Norse*, pages 261–8.

5

Pagan Traditions
of North-East Europe

The Ways of the Finns

Finnish Paganism has roots in Shamanism and many concepts are similar to those of the Siberian and Arctic peoples. Finland stretches north beyond the Arctic Circle, and the free movement of the nomadic Sami or Lapp peoples from Siberia across into Lapland in the north of Finland has ensured a free interchange of ancient religious ideas. The way of life of many of the nomadic peoples has remained largely unchanged until recent decades and their rich cultural, religious and spiritual life has still to be fully understood by the West.

Little is recorded about the inhabitants of what is now Finland in early times, but people called *Fenni*,[1] who appear to have been Lapps, are described by Tacitus as living a simple hunter-gather existence using flint arrows for weapons and having little in the way of material possessions. These people were pushed north and partly assimilated by the Finns, who were not Indo-Europeans, from about the first century CE onwards. The Finns themselves had come westward out of Asia from an area between the River Volga and the Ural mountains over a period of two to three thousand years. Their descendants are the Finns, Hungarians, Estonians and some inhabitants of adjoining areas of the former Soviet Union.

Finnish mythology has been recorded in two works, the *Kalevala* and the *Kanteletar*, compiled in the early nineteenth century. Although this is much later than the *Eddas* or the *Mabinogion*, the lateness is relative. Finland was Christianized late and had been Christian for about the same length of time as had

Wales when its Celtic legends were first committed to paper. The *Kalevala*[2] was compiled by Elias Löhnrot and has been the main source of Finnish mythology in the English-speaking world. *Kalevala* means 'abode of Kaleva', who was an obscure giant ancestor of humankind. The poems of the *Kanteletar* are available in English, but are less well known. The *Kalevala* is oral poetry and is designed to be orated or sung by two poets. The orators would work in pairs, often sitting opposite each other and holding hands, and would rock to and fro as they sang to create a hypnotic effect on the audience. This type of singing is largely unfamiliar in the West, although there is a form of Breton song for two female voices without instrumentation which is reminiscent of it. This is sometimes sung by mother and daughter. The structure and rhythm of the *Kalevala* itself is very distinctive and designed to help the orators remember the lines. There are a number of repeated or echo lines which enable the singers to make smooth transitions from one to another and to jog one another's memories. The rhythm will be familiar to some because the nineteenth-century poet Longfellow used it for his Native American poem *Hiawatha*. This rhythm is difficult to convey in translation but is the same as that found in these lines from another poem.

> I am Fire and I am Water,
> I am that fair Witch-Queen's daughter.

Finland had been a province of Sweden since the twelfth century and was annexed by Russia at the beginning of the nineteenth century. The *Kalevala* appeared at a time when the Finnish people were beginning to want to assert their independence and it proved a great stimulus to Finnish nationalism and the revival of the Finnish language, which its upper classes used infrequently. One of Elias Löhnrot's aims in compiling the *Kalevala* was to revive the Finnish sense of identity which had been suppressed by domination from its neighbouring states. That he was successful is apparent from the fact that Kalevala Day on 28 February is now a Finnish national holiday.

In Finnish myth, the universe is created by the Goddess Ilmater, Air Daughter. At first there is no earth, only air and water. For many aeons, Ilmater floats Virgin above the waters, but she becomes lonely in the empty wastes. She decides to descend onto the surface of the waters beneath her; whereupon the wind whips up foaming waves which make her pregnant. Air

Daughter is no longer the Virgin Goddess. She is now Water Mother. Ilmater floats pregnant in the waters for 700 years, or nine ages of man, each age being about 77 years (Finns seemed to live longer than the Biblical four score and ten!); but her child does not come forth. She thrashes about in all directions in her labour pains, until she prays to Ukko, God of the Sky, for help. Ukko sends to Ilmater Water Mother a primeval duck, the scaup, or possibly a teal. This lands on her knee, which it mistakes for a green hilltop, builds a nest and lays seven eggs. One egg is of iron; the other six are of gold. Although iron is a relatively new discovery, the myth of creation bursting forth from the primeval egg is very old and is found in Egypt and in the Mysteries of Orpheus and Mithras. Dion Fortune writes of the Creatrix:

> . . . the Great Goddess is older even
> than the Gods that made the Gods,
> for men knew the function of the Mother
> long before they understood the part played by the Father;
> and they adored the Bird of Space that laid the Primordial
>   Egg
> long before they worshipped the Sun as the Fecundator. [3]

After a time, three of the eggs in Ilmater's nest hatch. Then the nest begins to irritate Ilmater and she jerks her knee. The remaining eggs fall into the water and the shell of the iron egg breaks. Ilmater uses this to create our world. The upper shell forms the heavens and the lower shell the Earth. The yolk becomes the Sun and the white the Moon. Other parts of the egg become the stars and clouds. After another nine years, Ilmater begins to create. She raises her hand and arranges the headlands. She makes hills, islands, underwater caves, rocks and reefs. After another thirty summers, Ilmater's child begins to fight his way out of the womb. Earth has been created and the conditions necessary for his survival exist. The child who emerges is Väinämöinen, the First Shaman and Immortal Bard. Väinämöinen is already old before his birth and has much wisdom. He completes his mother's work of creation and instructs the young God Sampsa Pellervoinen, 'Strong-Field', to sow the world.

The Finno-Ugric peoples had some religious ideas which were similar to those of the Norse and there may have been some common origins. In Finnish cosmology, there are three realms – the Upperworld, the Lowerworld or Underworld, and the world of everyday consciousness, the equivalent of Middle Earth. The Underworld and home of the dead is Tuonola or Manala. Tuoni is Lord of the Dead and his home of Tuonola lies on the far side of the Tuoni river, on which swims the Swan of Tuonola. The concept of a World Tree, similar to the Norse-German Yggdrasil, is also found in Finno-Ugric religion. Some Finno-Ugric peoples believed that the souls of the unborn congregate in the boughs of the World Tree and that our destinies are written on its leaves. When a leaf falls, a person dies. Their image of heaven is that of a nomadic tent-dwelling people. The sky is supported by four pillars. In the centre is the Pole Star. This is the nail from which the canopy of the heavens is hung.

Finland is divided into a number of provinces. The eastern part which borders Russia has different deities from those found in the west, but they are similar in that they are the deities of a people of the northern climes, reliant partly on agriculture, but mainly on hunting. The first list of Finnish deities was compiled very late – the mid-sixteenth century – a few hundred years after the introduction of Christianity. They were recorded on the pages of a Psalter by a Christian bishop Mikael Agricola. Other Gods and Goddesses are known to us from the *Kalevala*. One of the better-known Finnish Gods from these two sources is Ukko, the God of Sky and Thunder. Hunters would call on him to send a little snow when they were hunting bears, so that tracks might be found. Ukko is also called on to help with healing. Ukko's wife is Rauni, the Goddess of Lightning and of Winds, but also Goddess of the Earth. The Sami, the Lapp people, called her Raudna, which meant barren, for she could have no offspring. The rowan tree is sacred to her and is said to ward off lightning.

Deities of the forest were very important. Two of the best-loved deities in modern Finnish Paganism are the Goddess Mielikki and the God Tapio. Mielikki is very beautiful. She wears a blue cloak and is called Golden and The Foster-Mother of the Bear. She creates the bear from a ball of wool. The word Mielikki comes from the word *mieli*, mind, and she is equated with the intelligence or spirit of the forest. Kati-ma Koppana, in *The Finnish Gods*,[4] describes Mielikki as 'the golden summer, the forest redolent of resin, a sweet incense-like scent, the forest full of blueberries, wild mushrooms, raspberries growing on the edges and strawberries in the clearings.' She is the essence which stirs the senses, intoxicates and delights. Mielikki keeps the keys of the forest store room and lets the animals out when hunters invoke her and bring the correct offerings. Stones with hollowed-out centres for offerings of milk or honey are still found in Finland.

Tapio is called the Old Man of the Forest, Lord of the Mound, Old Man Hill, Giver of Gifts and the Strong God. Tapio also has power over the hunt. He wears animals around his belt and if hunters invoke him correctly, he will release the animals to them. Tapio wears a cloak of moss and a hat of fir twigs or pine needles. He has golden ornaments on his breast. He will make sure that the hunter's aim is true and gives advice on where to find game. The images of Mielikki and Tapio are very similar to those of Tom Bombadil and Goldberry in J.R.R. Tolkien's *Lord of the Rings*. As a reader of the *Kalevala*, Mielikki and Tapio would have been known to Tolkien and may have influenced the characters in *Lord of the Rings*. Tapio is also suggestive of Tolkien's Ents. As well as having power over the animals, he is responsible for the growth of the forest and has many attributes similar to Devas or Dryads. Tapio is said strongly to resemble an old tree. Dusty Miller, a well-known Pagan woodsman, describes Dryads.

> Each tree doesn't have a Dryad, any more than we have a
> soul, or higher self. It's the other way round; in exactly the
> same ways as our higher self has a physical body, so a
> Dryad has a group of one, or more trees, forming its
> physical body. Being a group entity, it is quite normal for a
> Dryad to have a grove, (or even a wood) or trees as the
> multiple parts of its physical body. [5]

Dusty Miller goes on to mention that each tree tribe or species has its own Dryad. In Finland, there are a number of female assistants to Mielikki called Sinipiikat, or Blue Maidens, who fulfil this function. Pihlajatar, for instance, is the Sinipiika of the rowan.

Studies of tribes of the Finno-Ugric people who practised their Pagan religion into this century indicate that religious celebrations were performed by Shamans, who could be women or men, or by the people themselves. The major feast of the Finnish seasonal cycle is Ukon Vakat, or Ukko's Day, which is held on 4 April. Ukko's Day celebrates the end of spring ploughing, an event which takes place much later in Finland than in Western Europe. This was a festive occasion, a time to relax after the hard work of early spring and before beginning the sowing. The celebrations involved much beer drinking and sexual romping.

Some similar rites to those of Mediterranean Paganism are
found in connection with the agricultural deities. There are traces
in the *Kalevala* of a vegetation God like the Egyptian Osiris. In
Finnish myth, Lemminkäinen is cut to pieces by Märkähattu and
his body thrown into a river. He is resurrected when his mother
finds his remains and pieces them together. She then calls on the
bee to bring honey and restore him. The Sacred Marriage was
performed in Finnish religion to promote the growth of the crops.
Sampsa Pellervoinen is the God who first brought agriculture to
the Finns on the instructions of Väinämöinen, the First Shaman.
Sampsa's story was sung on Ukko's Day to ensure good crops.
At Spring, he lies with his mother the Earth to promote fertility.
Some sources describe Sampsa as arriving for the ceremony in
a cart of grain.[6] Interestingly, however, he is also described as
arriving in a boat of grain,[7] which suggests that knowledge of
agriculture and its presiding deity may have been brought to
Finland by sea by settlers from countries further south.

There are other Finnish festivals. At the time of the Christian
festival of Palm Sunday, there is in West Finland a festival similar
to Hallowe'en in North America and Celtic Europe. Children
dress as witches and visit the local houses in the morning. They
carry a basket decorated with brightly-coloured feathers and
containing willow twigs. These are waved about in front of the
house and a spell cast over them before being given to the house
as a blessing. In return, the children are given sweets.

Modern Pagans in Finland have developed their own seasonal
cycle which includes Ukko's Day. Rites are simple and are
frequently conducted outdoors, even in snowy weather. In recent
years, Wicca has merged with the Finnish tradition to produce
a Finnish synthesis of the religion of the Goddess and God, in
which Mielikki and Tapio are the principle deities.

The Gods of the Balts

The Baltic countries of Lithuania, Latvia and Estonia lie to the
north-east of Europe in what was formerly the Soviet Union.
Their peoples have inhabited the area for about 4,000 years. There
are many similarities between Lithuanian and Latvian deities
which are all of Indo-European origin. The Indo-European
origins of the people are evident, particularly in Lithuania where
the language contains many Sanskrit words in almost pure form.
Estonian deities are different. Estonia lies directly across the

Baltic sea from Finland and shares common language roots. Its Gods are more similar to those of Finland and their myths are recorded in the *Kalevipoeg*, which is similar to the Finnish *Kalevala*.

Baltic Paganism is one of the most active and living traditions of European Paganism. Christianity came late to the Baltics. Its people are proud of their Pagan heritage, and boast of being the last Christianized region in Europe. Today, Pagan gatherings attract many thousands of people who believe that participating in the rites of their ancestors is an important part of their cultural heritage. In Lithuania, there is a strong Pagan church and an organization called Romuva which promotes Lithuanian Paganism and is also active amongst the Lithuanian community in the United States. There is a similar organization in Latvia.

The Baltic peoples were agricultural farming peoples and their deities reflect this. Baltic Gods and their mythology and celebrations show an earthy zest for life and love of the life force. The deities are often thought of as inhabiting farms on sacred hills or celestial mountains. The Gods are industrious and work their farms, cultivating gardens and fields.

The Baltic religion has some very strong Goddess figures. As in most Indo-European religions, the Sun is feminine. In Lithuania, she is called Saule, which means Sun. She is depicted as a beautiful woman with golden hair, silken clothing, a golden woollen shawl, a golden crown and gold rings. She is a beneficent and protective Goddess who is invoked to help human beings who are in need, and to heal the sick. She is also a fertility Goddess, a patroness of women, and is called upon to bless weddings. During the day, she drives a magnificent chariot across the sky – her course across the sky determines the length of the day. At night she sinks into the sea.

Saule lives with her brother the Moon God Meness. He has two horses, the Morning and Evening Stars. Lithuanian and Latvian mythology also has a Sky God who is called Dievs in Latvian and Dievas in Lithuanian. The word is similar in origin to Zeus. Dievas wears a silver-coloured coat and a grey hat which are reminiscent of Odin. Like Odin, he visits his people who may encounter him on his travels. He also helps with planting crops.

In Lithuanian mythology, the Earth Goddess Zemyna or Zemynele is the creatrix of the world. In Latvian she is called Zemes Mate, Earth Mother. She is the giver and the sustainer of life and brings health and prosperity. She is also the receiver of the dead who transforms death into new life.

Worship of the Goddess continued into the seventeenth century. Offerings of beer and suckling pigs were made and the harvest feast was presided over by a priestess. In Spring, she was honoured as the pregnant mother and many rituals to Zemyna accompanied the Spring planting. In Baltic Paganism, all of Nature is considered sacred and the Earth is the universal mother. Zemyna the Earth Goddess is considered holy and must not be joked with or spat upon. The earth was often kissed before starting work or going to bed. She was also invoked by those swearing oaths or seeking justice. Gifts are given to her daily as well as at festivals.

Water and fire are considered sacred elements, as they are in Celtic and other Indo-European traditions. Both figure largely in seasonal celebrations.

The fates in Lithuanian and Latvian mythology are seen as a triple Goddess, Laima-Dalia-Giltiné. Laima is depicted either as a woman or as a bird. As a woman she is seen as beautiful and fair. She is clothed in fine clothes and silver brooches and wears flowers in her hair. She determines the life path of the newborn child at birth. Offerings are made to her of woven braids and woollen threads. At weddings, she grants the newly-weds a good life. She also determines the hour of death. People made offerings to Laima on rocks which bore the impression of feet. These are called the Chairs of Laima. Dalia determines health and prosperity and the individual's fate. Giltiné is Goddess of Death. She is described as an old woman with a blue face and grey-white hair. As with the Norse-German Goddess Hel, blue is here the colour of death. Giltiné travels the world unnoticed by anyone except the dying and dogs, which are psychically sensitive enough to notice her presence.

The Vèlès are the Shades of the Ancestors. They are honoured at the household shrine which, in country areas, would have been in the same family for hundreds of years. The Vèlès may also inhabit trees.

The Baltics have a seasonal cycle of eight festivals. The solstices and equinoxes are celebrated, together with four other festivals important in the agricultural year, but these are not exactly the same as those of Western Europe. Preparations for the Winter Solstice start on the day when bears are first observed to hibernate. This, rather than the Solstice, is considered to be the first day of Winter. Winter Solstice is the time when the tides of death and life turn. On the first day of Winter, a cherry twig is placed in water, so that the twig will sprout roots in time for the Solstice to symbolize the hope of new life to come.

Winter Solstice is marked by two one-day festivals – Kucios and Kaledos. Kucios is a festival for the Vèlès or Ancestors, who spend Spring and Summer in the fields where they protect and bless the crops. They come home after the Autumn harvest. At Kucios, a grove of wooden and straw birds with a straw sun is made to decorate the house. Candles are lit and a table prepared for the Vèlès with bread, salt and Kucia bread, which traditionally consisted of thirteen different foods representing the lunar months. These include grain, peas, bean seeds, nuts and honey. With the change to the solar calendar, the foods were reduced to twelve. The living sit at another table which is covered with hay and a tablecloth. The celebrations begin when the Evening Star appears in the sky. To prepare for the ceremony, everyone bathes and quarrels are made up. The eldest person present then says an invocation to the Earth Mother and breaks the Kucia bread.

> Zemepatis, we thank thee
> for the good bread which thou hast given us.
> Help us to work the fields while blessing thee,
> that Zemynele will continue to give us thy good gifts. [8]

Beer is drunk and a libation poured for the Vèlès. There is then a feast of cranberry jelly, hot beet soup, mushroom dumplings, cabbage and fish. No meat or dairy products may be eaten. At the end of the feast, grains are poured into the hearth and a log representing the old year is burned.

Kaledos, the next festival, celebrates the rebirth of Saule Motule, Mother Sun. People carry images of the Sun through the fields and towns and wish everyone prosperity. This is also the time of the Old Man of Kaleda, who is similar to Santa Claus. Traditionally, people dressed in animal skins as goats, bulls, horses and cranes to process through the villages. This practice is interesting because it is the same New Year celebration as that which was condemned much earlier in western Europe, for example, at the end of the seventh century by Theodore Archbishop of Canterbury, as 'celebrating the New Year by dressing up in the guise of a Bull or Stag God and sacrificing to the old Gods.' [9] It was still happening in Lithuania a thousand years later – thus do such things endure.

Spring morning in Lithuania is a celebration of the vigour of life. Verbas are made which are similar to the birch twigs used to beat the skin as part of sauna treatment. Verbas are made from juniper and willow twigs as well as birch and are interwoven with flowers and coloured paper to symbolize the life force. On Spring Equinox morning, everyone tries to rise as early as possible to beat the other members of the family awake! This rather startling alternative to the alarm clock is thought to give good health. The 'whipper-in' is rewarded with a brightly-painted egg called a margutis which is symbolic of new life. The egg symbolizes the cosmic egg from which the snake Gyvate came to grant life and fertility. The Earth is also whipped to awaken the life force from its winter sleep.

At Spring Equinox, there are also fire ceremonies. The winter hearth is extinguished and a new fire is kindled outdoors using a flint. Young people go from house to house playing music and giving out eggs as good luck presents.

The Earth Goddess Zemyna's brother is Zemepathis, the protector of the farm and household. He is patron of the ritual of Sambariai which was held at the end of May to mark the end of the spring sowing. Sambariai was a household rather than a community festival. The family and workers of the farm would gather in the fields with food and drink to sing sacred songs called dainos and rounds called sutartinés. The round, whereby a group of people start a verse of a simple song or chant one after the other, is frequently used in Pagan ritual to symbolize the eternal cycle of the life force. Dainos have a similar poetic rhythm to that of the *Kalevala*. Meats are eaten and a special beer is brewed for the occasion. A blessing is drunk to wish everyone a good harvest and a libation of beer is poured on the ground in honour of Zemepatis:

Star God, we pray thee,
on grain, fields, flowers, and animals
gracefully and brightly shine.

The festival is concluded with a procession around the fields where the long dainos are sung by one group and then repeated by another. The songs are to bless the fields, to stimulate growth and to protect the harvest.

Midsummer is celebrated as the feast of Rasa, the dew. The early-morning dew of the Solstice is believed to possess exceptional healing powers and to wash naked in this would increase one's beauty. At night, sheets are dragged across the fields so that the dew is absorbed and can be used for healing. A pole, the kupole, is set up for the festival to represent the World Tree. At the top is a three-pronged branch, which in some parts of Lithuania represents the three branches of the World Tree which gave rise to the Sun, Moon and stars. The pole is similar to a Maypole and many of the Midsummer customs are similar to May customs of other warmer European countries. On Midsummer morning, women make flower crowns and men wear the oak crowns familiar in Western Europe as the crown of the Green Man. In south-western parts of Lithuania, the tree is decorated with flower wreaths and ribbons. Unmarried girls stand with their backs to the pole, throw flower crowns over their heads, and try to catch them on the tree's branches. The number of tries before they succeed is taken to be the number of years until they marry. In other parts of the Baltics, the flower crowns of the women are floated on water with the oak leaf crowns of the men. Where two crowns float together, this is seen as an omen of marriage.

At Midsummer, the hearth fire is again extinguished and a new fire is lit at the aukuras, or sacrificial bonfire. Couples jump over the fire and if they do not break grip, this is thought to ensure a successful relationship. Newly-wed couples bring the ashes of the sacrificial fire into their homes to ensure harmony in their married life. Straw dolls which represent everything old are burned and burning wheels are rolled downhill to greet the sun. During the night, there is a vigil to greet the dawn. People walk through the fields to greet the growing crops and then eat a special meal of cheese, eggs and beer laid on a cloth decorated with herbs.

Both the traditions of Finland and those of the Baltic countries are most appropriate for people in the region and those of North-East European extraction, but they have much to tell other Pagans because they represent some of the most recently-practised Pagan traditions. With the opening of contact between the Baltics and the Western world, we will have the opportunity to learn more about these thriving traditions of Paganism.

1. Tacitus, *The Germania*, 46, in *The Agricola and The Germania*, page 141.
2. Elias Löhnrot, *The Kalevala*, K. Bosley (trans.).
3. Dion Fortune, *The Sea Priestess*, page 93.

4. Kati-ma Koppana, *The Finnish Gods*, page 18.
5. Dusty Miller, *Moonshine* magazine, Birmingham, page 23, Spring 1990.
6. *Starlight* magazine, Helsinki, page 24, Time of Berries, 1989.
7. Kati-ma Koppana, *Snakefat and Knotted Threads: A Short Introduction to Finnish Magic*, page 37.
8. See *Romuva USA*, No 2, Winter Solstice, 1990.
9. *Liber Penitentialis* of Theodore Archbishop of Canterbury.

6
Wicca

Wicca is the name often given to the religion of Witchcraft, also called the Wisecraft or, more simply, the Craft. Wicca has been one of the most vigorous branches of the Pagan revival and the word Witchcraft has come to mean not just a form of magic using incantations and spells, but a whole system of Pagan philosophy and religious belief.

The word 'Witch' is a difficult one full of negative connotations of sensationalist orgies and black magic. To those familiar with the image of the Witch from fairy tales or from Shakespeare's *Macbeth* – long-nosed old women stirring cauldrons on blasted heaths, stroking black cats and riding to and fro on broomsticks – the idea that Witchcraft is a religion may seem strange. However, Witchcraft today is a Pagan religion and is often called the Old Religion. Witches worship not the Christian devil, as certain Christian fundamentalists and sensationalist newspapers with nothing better to print would have it, but two of the oldest forms of deity – the Great Mother Goddess and her consort the Horned God.

Much of the twentieth-century revival of both Wicca and more eclectic Paganism has been inspired by the work of the anthropologist Margaret Murray. In 1921, she published her famous book *The Witch-Cult in Western Europe: A Study in Anthropology*.[1] In this, she analyzes the sixteenth- and seventeenth-century European Witch persecutions and argues that the inquisitors were persecuting not Satan worshippers or unpopular old women, but an underground Pagan religious movement which worshipped the Horned God. To Margaret Murray, the followers of the Old Religion were those who had secretly kept the older faith throughout centuries of Christian persecution. In remote villages, people met together in small groups – covens – and practised in secret the rites of their ancestors and also the lore of herbs and plants, which was the traditional craft of the village wise woman and cunning man.

Margaret Murray's book was one of a number published in Europe in the nineteenth and early twentieth centuries, which re-evaluated the European Witch persecutions. In English-speaking countries, we are accustomed to thinking of Margaret Murray as the first person to see in Witchcraft the last vestiges of European Paganism, but the first modern scholars to put forward these theories were in fact nineteenth-century Germans. Karl Ernst Jarcke, a professor of criminal law at the University of Berlin, deduced from his study of the records of a seventeenth-century German trial that Witchcraft was a nature religion which was a survival of pre-Christian Pagan beliefs. Another slightly more complex theory was that of historian Franz Josef Mone, Director of Archives at Baden. There was little understanding at this time of European Pagan traditions and scholars tended to assume that any half-way sophisticated belief must have originated in Greece or Rome. Mone explained the ecstatic practices he found in the accounts of the Witch trials as having derived from the Greek cults of Hecate and Dionysus through contacts made by Germanic tribes who populated the north coast of the Black Sea. The tribes had absorbed what we would now call Shamanic practice and belief into a cult which worshipped the Horned God and practised magic. This religion survived into Medieval times until its adherents were persecuted as Witches. A French perspective based on Medieval accounts of the worship of the Goddess Herodias in France is conveyed by the historian Jules Michelet in his book *La Sorcière*, published in 1862.

The religion described by Margaret Murray, Jarcke, Mone, Michelet and others struck a chord with an enormous number of people across Europe. There was an immense psychological appeal in the idea that, in remote villages, people had for centuries practised a Paganism which gave power to the people and was also secretly practised by nobles and royals. Interest in Witchcraft as the Old Religion developed in the English-speaking world from the 1950s onwards, stimulated by the publication in the late 1940s and early 1950s of the books of Gerald Brousseau Gardner. Through his contacts with the Rosicrucian Theatre in Christchurch in the 1930s, Gerald Gardner met a group of New

Forest Witches. These were not simple village Witches, but sophisticated people with a background in ritual magic, who had contact with traditional British Witch groups. Gerald Gardner was initiated into Wicca in 1939. His fellow Witches were not keen to publicize the Craft, but Gardner gave out information under the guise of fiction in a novel, *High Magic's Aid,*[2] published in 1949 under his Witch name 'Scire', which means 'To Know', and later in two non-fiction works – *Witchcraft Today*[3] and *The Meaning of Witchcraft*[4]. These were the first accounts of modern-day Wicca.

Gerald Gardner's books were followed in the 1950s and 1960s by a spate of publicity, articles and books by and about other leading figures in Wicca, such as Alex and Maxine Sanders, Pat and Arnold Crowther, and Doreen Valiente. The religion of Wicca, with its emphasis on the Goddess, seemed a movement whose time was ripe. Wicca spread quickly, first to the United States, and then to other English-speaking countries, to non-English-speaking Europe and more recently to other parts of the world. The spread of the Craft was given further impetus in the 1970s and 1980s by the writings of Janet and Stewart Farrar, Marian Green, Starhawk, Scott Cunningham and my own work.

There are a number of similarities between Wicca and Druidry. Philip Carr-Gomm, Head of the Order of Bards, Ovates and Druids, sees them as 'brothers and sisters' who are 'within the same family and therefore sharing family characteristics but also separate, with characteristics peculiar to themselves.'[5] Both paths emphasize developing close links with Nature and their rites frequently take place out of doors. Both also stress the importance of guardianship of the Earth. Witches' magical practices are frequently geared towards the protection of sacred sites. One distinction, however, is that Druidry is more purely Celtic than Wicca. Another distinction is that Druidry is more oriented towards the Sun and Wicca to the Moon. Druid rituals usually take place in the daytime or at dawn. Wiccan rituals are conducted by the light of the Moon. Druidry is more oriented towards the God and Wicca towards the Goddess.

Traditions within Wicca

Across the world, there are four main branches of the Craft. These are known as Traditional, Hereditary, Gardnerian and Alexandrian. The Traditional groups comprise a number of different and separate localized traditions which have brought in outsiders, some of whom have subsequently transplanted the tradition to other countries many thousands of miles away from its original source. These traditions, although different, share sufficiently similar deities, forms of worship, language, symbolism and philosophy, to make them recognisable as derivations of one religion. Hereditary traditions are similar, but are passed down only through the bloodline or, sometimes, by marriage. Gardnerian and Alexandrian Wicca are derived largely from one particular tradition, based in the New Forest area of the south of England; although this has been cross-fertilized by contact with other British traditions. The term 'Wicca' is more commonly used in the Gardnerian and Alexandrian traditions; other traditions and Hereditary Witches often prefer to refer to their religion simply as the Craft; but for simplicity's sake, I am using both terms interchangeably.

Wicca has no central authority structure, but consists principally of autonomous covens run by elders. While the covens have connections with the parent covens from which the elders sprang, the structure is more like a loose net than a hierarchical pyramid. There are also Witches who prefer to worship the Gods and practise their Craft alone. They may have had one-to-one teaching from another solitary Witch, or they may have developed their own personal practice by drawing from published sources and their own inspiration.

The Deities of the Witches

Wicca worships the Divine in the forms used by some of our earliest ancient ancestors – as the Triple Goddess, whose aspects of Virgin, Mother, and Wise Woman or Crone, are associated with the waxing, full and waning phases of the Moon, and as the Horned God. The principal names by which the God is worshipped are Cernunnos or Herne, both of which mean Horned One. Herne is Celtic in origin; but in Wicca, he has absorbed a number of characteristics which originate in the Odin or Woden of our Norse and German ancestors. For instance, at Samhain, the Festival of the Dead, the God is invoked as Horned Leader of the Hosts of Air. This is a reference to Odin as Leader of the Wild Hunt. This synthesis was natural in the British Isles where successive waves of invaders brought with them similar and overlapping deities. The Goddess is frequently known by

Celtic Goddess names, but the most commonly used name is
Aradia. This is the Italian version of the name of the Classical
Goddess Herodias, whom some Medieval texts claim was widely
worshipped across southern Europe into Medieval times. The
name came into English usage via *Aradia: The Gospel of the Witches*.[6]
This is a collection of the lore and legends of the Witches of Tuscany,
gathered at the end of the nineteenth century by Charles Leland,
an American folklorist. A number of other names are also in use.
In Northern Europe, some Witches prefer the Vanir Goddess and
God names of Freya and Frey. In Finland, the forest Goddess and
God, Mielikki and Tapio, are frequently the presiding deities.
Covens may have particular patron deities. Different deities may
also be invoked at particular festivals. Thus, in some covens, the
festival of Imbolc is sacred to Bride. This multiplicity of names
does not imply Witches are worshipping a multiplicity of Gods.
The various names are seen as different epithets for the Great
Mother Goddess and Father God, who are universal and present
in all cultures and at all times. They can be called by a number
of names, in the same way that a Catholic might praise the Virgin
Mary as Tower of Ivory, Star of the Sea, etc.

Fundamental to Wicca is the idea that, although the Divine is
ultimately One, within the Divine we see a duality. The Divine
is energy. Energy is movement and change. Where there is
movement and change, there is action and reaction, transmitter
and receiver, passive and active, ebb and flow. The Divine is
therefore seen as male and female, Goddess and God. Whilst the
emphasis on the Goddess and the God differs between groups,
traditions and localities, Wicca believes that for wholeness the
image of the Divine must contain both female and male. To
worship either aspect alone will produce spiritual imbalance both
for the individual and for society.

As well as the image of the Goddess as the Triple Moon, she
is also seen as the Great Earth Mother, the Dark Goddess of the
Night and the Goddess of the Sun. The God is perceived as
primarily dual – a God of summer and a God of winter; but
within his summer aspect, we find him honoured as the Green
Man, the Sun King and the Corn King. In his winter aspect, he
is honoured at the Hunter, the Shepherd and the Lord of the
Underworld. He is also honoured at Winter Solstice as the Child
of Promise, the reborn Sun.

Teaching and Lore

A difference between Wicca and other religions is that it is not only a religion, it is also a Craft. The Craft which it practises is magic. Witches believe that the human mind has the power to effect change. As well as worshipping the Gods, Witches also perform spells for healing, or to help people with general life problems. This is seen as an integral part of the work of a Witch.

Wicca is largely an oral tradition; although much has now been recorded and published. In addition to what is learned orally, since writing became more widespread from the late-eighteenth and early-nineteenth centuries on, most Witches have kept a book of spells, lore and ritual called *The Book of Shadows* or *Black Book*. Each tradition has a core of material which is handed down. This is usually hand-copied by each Witch from his or her initiator; but each Witch's book continues to evolve throughout his or her lifetime. Traditionally, *Black Books* are highly prized and jealously guarded by their owners. This was not only because of their magical content, but because all books were rare and precious. Magical knowledge was prized in much the same way as any trade protected its secrets and cooks of great households kept and jealously guarded their recipe books. Their *Black Books* were part of the Witch's stock in trade and quite often a means of earning their livelihood. In *Snakefat and Knotted Threads*, Katima Koppana prints excerpts from an interview with Juha Kellokoski, a mid-nineteenth century Finnish tietäjä, who was persuaded to part with his *Black Book* to a folklore researcher. In the interview, Kellokoski explains that he performs most of his magic by running water – at the rapids where his familiar spirit lives. A facsimile of one page is printed in *Snakefat and Knotted Threads*. This is written in red ink on black pages and consists of the spell for getting rid of nightmares.

Black Books are spell books rather than theological treatises and little has been recorded of the world-view of Traditional Witches. *Aradia: The Gospel of the Witches*,[7] however, contains the creation myth of the Italian Witches. The Goddess Diana is spoken of as the first principle of this world, 'the first created before all creation; in her were all things; out of herself, the first darkness, she divided herself, into darkness and light was she divided.' We are told that:

All things were made by Diana,
the great spirits of the stars,

men in their time and place,
the giants which were of old,
and the dwarfs who dwell in the rocks,
and once a month worship her with cakes. [8]

However, there are also other mysterious figures, beings who pre-exist the creation of the world. They are not part of creation, for Diana is 'the first created'; but beings on another plane who are both male and female. These are described as 'the Fathers of the Beginning' and 'the Mothers, the spirits who were before the first spirit'.

In the Italian tradition, the non-physical world is seen as containing two polarities, male and female. By way of contrast, in the Faery tradition of Witchcraft, into which Starhawk was initiated, that which pre-exists creation is seen as female.

Alone, awesome, complete within Herself,
the Goddess, She whose name cannot be spoken,
floated in the abyss of the outer darkness,
before the beginning of all things.
And as She looked into the curved mirror of black space,
She saw by her own light her radiant reflection,
and fell in love with it.
She drew it forth by the power that was in Her
and made love to Herself,
and called her 'Miria, the Wonderful'.
Their ecstasy burst forth
in the single song of all that is,
was, or ever shall be,
and with the song came motion,
waves that poured outward and became
all the spheres and circles of the worlds.
The Goddess became filled with love,
swollen with love,
and She gave birth to a rain of bright spirits
that filled the worlds and became all things. [9]

Another creation myth is drawn from English Witchcraft sources. This describes the creation of the Goddess and God, but the first principle is sexless and neutral.

Ere time began, the One who is All
looked inward on Itself,
and beheld Itself as though through a reflection in a pool,
and so came to self-awareness.

And in that coming to self-awareness,
the One was made Two,
subject and object,
that which looks and that which is looked upon,
and it divided from itself.
And as the One was made Two,
so the Male and the Female were made separate . . .[10]

In other Wiccan creation myths, the cosmic principle is dual. The
polarity of light and dark, male and female, are seen as
fundamental to the universe as we know it. At the beginning,
they are separate and all is stasis. Nothing can come into
manifestation until light and dark interact. This is similar to the
role played by Fire and Cloud in the Norse-German tradition. It
also echoes the Chinese Tao philosophy; but here light is
feminine and dark masculine.

The White Goddess, the pure Light
stood one day in the centre of a magic circle,
bathing in her own radiance;
when a shadow appeared.
The Dark Lord came unto her.
He stood outside the boundary of the circle
which barred his way
and begged her to let him in.
But the Goddess feared him;
for he was large and powerful,
his strength much greater than hers.
He would rape her and hurt her;
and seek to subject her to his will.
She was light and he was darkness;
his evil would overcome her good.
She feared him
and she would not permit him to enter in.
Then he entreated:
'I seem large and threatening only because you ignore me.'
He sought only to be with her,
and to love and protect her;
he was her strength;
she had need of him,
even as he had need of her love.
Then the Dark Lord who was so full of pride
knelt down before her and wept.

His weakness melted the cold heart
of the Goddess of the Heavens;
She who sails above all,
caring for the plight of no man.
She felt a stab of pain,
a bright darkness in the whiteness of her soul,
She knew pity and love and she let him in
and they were joined as One.
As the power of the Dark Lord flowed within her,
the Goddess of Light knew a bliss
such as she had not known before.
The core of her being expanded
and flowed into the four corners of the universe
and she gave birth to planets and to stars.
The White Goddess became the Mother of All Living.
And it was love that had made her so,
the love of another who suffered for her. [11]

In this creation myth, the message is that separation brings
sorrow: the Goddess alone is barren and the God alone is forlorn.
It is only when male and female are united that the Goddess is
impregnated and creation can spring forth.

The essence of Wiccan philosophy is also conveyed in the
words of the Great Mother Charge, which each new Initiate hears
at his or her initiation.

Listen to the words of the Great Mother, who was of old
   also called amongst men Artemis, Astarte, Dione,
   Melusine, Aphrodite, Cerridwen, Diana, Arianrhod,
   Bride, and by many other names.

Whenever you have need of anything,
once in the month,
and better it be when the Moon is full,
then ye shall assemble in some secret place
and adore the spirit of me
who am Queen of all Witcheries.
There shall ye assemble,
ye who are fain to learn all sorcery,
yet have not won its deepest secrets;
to these will I teach things that are yet unknown.
And ye shall be free from slavery,
and as a sign that ye be truly free,

ye shall be naked in your rites,
and ye shall dance, sing, feast,
make music, and love,
all in my praise.
For mine is the ecstasy of the spirit;
and mine also is joy upon Earth,
for my law is love unto all beings.
Keep pure your highest ideal:
strive ever towards it;
let naught stop you or turn you aside;
for mine is the secret
which opens upon the door of youth
and mine is the Cup of the Wine of Life,
which is the Cauldron of Cerridwen,
and the Holy Grail of Immortality.
I am the gracious Goddess
who gives the gift of joy unto the heart of man;
upon Earth I give the knowledge of the Spirit Eternal;
and beyond death I give peace and freedom
and reunion with those who have gone before;
nor do I demand sacrifice, for behold:
I am the Mother of all living,
and my love is poured out upon the Earth.

Hear ye the words of the Star Goddess, She in the dust of
   whose feet are the hosts of Heaven; whose body
   encircleth the universe.

I who am the beauty of the green Earth
and the white Moon amongst the stars,
and the mystery of the waters,
and the desire of the heart of woman and of man,
call unto thy soul:
arise and come unto me;
for I am the Soul of Nature
who giveth life to the universe.
From me all things proceed,
and unto me all things must return;
and before my face,
beloved of Gods and of men,
thine inmost divine self
shall be enfolded in the rapture of the infinite.

Let my worship be within the heart that rejoiceth;
for behold all acts of love and pleasure are my rituals.
Therefore let there be beauty and strength,
power and compassion,
honour and humility,
mirth and reverence, within you.
And thou who thinkest to seek for me,
know thy seeking and yearning shall avail thee not,
unless thou knowest the mystery:
that if that which thou seekest,
thou findest not within thee,
thou wilt never find it without thee.
For behold, I have been with thee from the beginning,
and I am that which is attained at the end of desire.[12]

Since the Goddess is within the world – as the beauty of Earth
and Moon and sea, Wicca has a very positive attitude to manifest
creation. The Gods are immanent in matter, therefore the whole
of material creation – the Earth itself and the life forms which
inhabit it – are sanctified and holy. This includes the human
body: the Divine is present within ourselves.

Prayer of Praise to the Goddess

Blessed Be the Great Mother,
Without beginning and without ending,
Blessed Be her temple of pure white marble,
Blessed Be the stillness of her holy place.
Blessed Be the babe who cries to her,
Blessed Be the deer who lift their heads for her,
Blessed Be the birds who fly the skies for her,
Blessed Be the trees which shake and sigh for her,
Blessed Be the leaf which falls for her and nourishes
   the soil.
Blessed Be the wave which caresses the shore for her,
Blessed Be the sand which succumbs to its embrace,
Blessed Be the shell that is cast up from her,
Blessed Be She, the Mother of Pearl.
Blessed Be the stars which shine like jewels for her,
Blessed Be the Moon in which we see her face,
Blessed Be my spirit which soars the heights for her,
Blessed Be my soul which expands in joy for her,
Blessed Be my body, the temple of her being.[13]

Far from being seen as unclean, the body (and for women this is particularly important) is sacred and holy, a gift from the Gods, the vessel of our Divine Self.

Wicca has a very positive attitude towards women and they play an important role in Wicca. Women are essential in the priesthood. Since the Divine expresses itself as female and male, Wicca believes that the Gods are best served by priestess and priest. Usually, the rites are performed by couples who are seen as representing the two aspects of the Divine Force. Interestingly, although the popular stereotype of the Witch is female, and in the United States in particular many feminist women have turned to Witchcraft as a means of religious expression, in Europe until the past fifteen years or so, the majority of Witches were male. It is only recently that the sex ratio has evened up.

Celebrations

The positive attitude of Wicca to material creation is carried over into its attitude to religious observance, which is seen as celebration. Witches follow a seasonal cycle of eight festivals. They also worship the Gods at the thirteen full moons each year. The moon rites are called esbats. The word esbat comes from a French word meaning 'to frolic' and both sabbats and esbats are joyful occasions. While reverence for the Gods is important, it is also considered that the Gods are pleased by mirth and celebration. In the Gardnerian *Book of Shadows*, Witches are taught that 'the Gods can feel men's pleasure. The Gods love man and are pleased that he is happy.' Witches believe that their Gods want human beings to dwell on the joy of life and not on humanity's sinfulness and unworthiness. Religion should be joyful, not mournful, and should teach its followers to foster the positive side of human nature, rather than luxuriating in breast-beating self-abasement.

Wiccan teaching is that after death the spirit is reborn. Wicca differs from many of the world religions in its attitude to the material plane. To Witches, Nature is a manifestation of the Divine and life on Earth is a pleasure and a gift. It is not something from which humanity should seek to flee, but something which human beings should celebrate and for which they should be thankful. Wiccan teaching regarding life and death is conveyed in the Legend of the Goddess. This has two levels of meaning. On the one hand, the Legend describes an initiatory process and as such is used as part of an initiation rite; but it also describes what happens to the spirit after death. Like many mystery religions, teaching about the fate of the spirit after death is conveyed to initiates to sustain them through the rigours of life. The message is that which is found throughout Paganism – that death leads to new life.

The Legend of the Goddess has parallels with the story of the Vanir Goddess Freya. In Wicca, female Witches wear a necklace either of amber or of alternating amber and jet beads. The use of amber is interesting. This has long been seen in the European tradition as a Goddess stone because of its organic nature. In traditional Witchcraft, amber signifies life and jet is death. The necklace is considered sacred to the Goddess and the alternating amber and jet represents her power over life and death. In Norse-German tradition, Freya wins the magical necklace Brisingamen by descending to the underworld to retrieve it from the four dwarves who made it. In the Legend of the Goddess, the Goddess descends into the underworld to learn the secret of death and to ask the God, 'Why dost thou cause all things that I love and take delight in to fade and die?' The God tells her that he has no power to prevent the processes of aging and death, for, 'Age causes all things to wither, but when men die at the end of their time I give them rest and peace and strength, so that they may return.' The Goddess learns to accept the inevitability of death for material creation and in return the God gives her the Circle of Rebirth. 'And he taught her all his mysteries and gave her the necklace which is the Circle of Rebirth and she taught him the Mystery of the Sacred Cup which is the Cauldron of Rebirth.'

In Wiccan legend, the Mother Goddess often appears as a mediator between humanity and a sterner father God. The Legend of the Goddess teaches that: 'In ancient times our Lord the Hornèd One was as he still is, the consoler, the comforter; but men knew him as the Dread Lord of the Shadows, lonely, stern and just.' However, the Goddess, it is said, 'ever inclineth to love and mirth and happiness' and 'guardeth and cherisheth her Hidden Children in life and in death'. The concept of the Goddess as protectress of the people and a teacher of hidden wisdom is also found in *The Gospel of the Witches*. Here, in what is the earliest known form of the Great Mother Charge, Aradia explains her role and also encourages her followers to worship her at the Full Moon.

When I shall have departed from this world,
whenever ye have need of anything,
once in the month, and when the Moon is full,
ye shall assemble in some deserted place,
or in a forest all together joined,
to adore the potent spirit of your Queen,
my mother, Great Diana.
She who fain would learn all sorcery,
yet has not won its deepest secrets,
then my mother will teach her,
in truth all things as yet unknown . . . [14]

The mysteries of God and Goddess are important to Witches on many levels. They are seen as teaching us about the nature of the Gods, which is also the nature of the cosmos. They also teach us to understand ourselves and those mysteries which have power over us all: birth, sexuality, marriage, parenthood, and death. Starhawk writes in *The Spiral Dance*:

Existence is sustained by the on–off pulse, the alternating current of the two forces in perfect balance. Unchecked, the life force is cancer; unbridled, the death force is war and genocide. Together, they hold each other in the harmony that sustains life, in the perfect orbit that can be seen in the changing cycle of the seasons, in the ecological balance of the natural world, and in the progression of human life from birth through fulfilment to decline and death – and then to rebirth. [15]

Wiccan-Based Paganism

Most Wiccan traditions are not open to all; they are open only to those who have been initiated into them. All initiates are considered part of the priesthood. A woman is initiated as a priestess and witch and a man as a priest and witch. Wicca as an initiatory path has been practised in small groups which operate on an intense level and require a commitment which is really only for the dedicated few. In recent years, however, Wicca has become more widely publicized. While the core tradition remains and flourishes, there has also developed a more accessible form of Wicca which has been espoused in particular by the feminist movement in the United States and by mixed sex Pagan groups in Europe. This can be called Wiccan Paganism or

Goddess-Centred Paganism. Goddess-centred Paganism tends to be more eclectic in its approach than traditional Wicca. In the United States, for instance, Native American spiritual practices have been synthesized with Wicca. This may seem an odd marriage, but there are many aspects of the two systems which are very compatible.

Both worship within a sacred circle which calls upon the powers of the four cardinal points – the Four Quarters in Wiccan terminology. Both perceive the Divine as immanent in Nature and the Earth as sacred. Living in harmony with the Earth is emphasized in both traditions. The drumming and chanting used in tribal worship translates well into Wiccan-type celebrations. Those who have come to Western Paganism from a background in Hinduism or Buddhism have similarly brought with them concepts and practices from Eastern tradition. These include puja ceremonies to offer veneration to the Gods and meditation techniques using mantras. This type of Paganism is not only more eclectic but it has also evolved into a less formal approach than Wicca. Initiation is not seen as necessary and all are free to attend the rites to worship the Gods. Many adults who practise Wicca raise their children in this more exoteric form of Goddess-centred Paganism.

1. Margaret Murray, *The Witch-Cult in Western Europe: A Study in Anthropology.*
2. Gerald B. Gardner, *High Magick's Aid.*
3. Gerald B. Gardner, *Witchcraft Today.*
4. Gerald B. Gardner, *The Meaning of Witchcraft.*
5. Philip Carr-Gomm in Prudence Jones and Caitlín Matthews, (eds.), *Voices from the Circle*, page 63.
6. Charles G. Leland, *Aradia: The Gospel of the Witches.*
7. Charles G. Leland, *Aradia: The Gospel of the Witches*, page 18.
8. Charles G. Leland, *Aradia: The Gospel of the Witches*, page 121.
9. Starhawk, *The Spiral Dance: A Rebirth of the Ancient Religion of the Great Goddess*, page 17.
10. Vivianne Crowley, *Wicca: The Old Religion in the New Age*, page 226.
11. Another version of this appears in Vivianne Crowley *Wicca: The Old Religion in the New Age*, pages 227–8.
12. A slightly different version of this appears in Vivianne Crowley *Wicca: The Old Religion in the New Age*, pages 156–7.
13. From the Wiccan *Book of Shadows*, quoted in Vivianne Crowley, *Wicca: The Old Religion in the New Age*, page 161.
14. Charles G. Leland, *Aradia: The Gospel of the Witches*, page 6.
15. Starhawk, *The Spiral Dance*, pages 27–8.

7

The Way of the Goddess and the God

Acknowledgement of the historical origin of our deities is important to Pagans, but if we are to worship the Pagan Gods meaningfully, they must be relevant to the needs of people in the modern world. We must also recognize that our ideas of deity have evolved and that the relationship we have today with our Goddess and God is not exactly the same as that of a Viking warrior, Celtic bard or Siberian Shaman. How do we view the Goddess and God today?

The Way of the Goddess

The Goddess awakens in infinite forms and a thousand disguises. She is found where She is least expected, appears out of nowhere and everywhere to illumine the open heart. [1]

Pagans worship both God and Goddess but the Goddess receives greater emphasis in Paganism than in most religions. Some Pagans worship the Goddess alone, preferring the worship of the Mother Goddess to that of more distant Father Gods. In rediscovering the Goddess, we are returning to the worship of the Great Mother, one of the earliest forms of religious expression. To the child, the Mother is all powerful and all-providing. It is she who gives birth to us and nourishes us. To our ancestors, it was natural that the Divine should be feminine and that Nature, which gives us life, should be seen as Goddess. Many Pagans today regard the ultimate principle of the universe as female: 'From the Goddess' awakening flows forth the cosmic energy through which Gods, worlds and all creatures come into being.'

She is the manifest universe arising from the primeval sea of the unmanifest.

> She is called by many names by many men;
> but to all She is the Great Goddess –
> space and earth and water.
> As space She is called Ea,
> parent of the Gods that made the Gods;
> She is more old than time,
> She is the matrix of matter,
> the root substance of all existence,
> undifferentiated, pure . . .
> Likewise She is called Ge; for
> She is the most ancient earth,
> the first-formed from the formless . . .
> She is also the Great Deep whence life arose.
> She is all ancient and forgotten things
> wherein our roots are cast.

The role of the Goddess and women is particularly noticeable in Wicca and the Craft; but most Pagan paths place a strong emphasis on the Goddess. Even in Asatru, which has a more patriarchal group of deities than some Pagan traditions, the role of the Goddess and of the priestess, the volva or seidkona, is of growing importance. There are also groups dedicated exclusively to the worship of the Goddess. The Fellowship of Isis, which is open to both women and men, is one of the largest of these and ordains both sexes as priestesses and priests of the Goddess.

Some Goddess-worshipping paths are open to women only. One of the strongest of these, particularly in the United States, is the Dianic movement, named in honour of the Goddess Diana. This has a matriarchal focus. Many Dianic groups exclude men and see their tradition as a sisterhood, as 'wimmin's religion'. Other Dianic groups work with men, but see the role of men as less important than that of women. There are also many groups of women who meet together on an informal basis and draw inspiration for their rites from a variety of sources. Some are modelled on Wicca, other groups are more Shamanic, others have blended aspects of classical Pagan, Native American and other traditions to create an eclectic worship of the Great Goddess geared to meet modern needs.

The Women's Movement has given a strong impetus to the worship of the Goddess and has inspired many women to question and reject the religious forms which have been familiar since childhood and to turn away from the image of a patriarchal God to new spiritual pathways. It is not only women who have been concerned about the lack of the Goddess in Western religion. The Canadian writer Robertson Davies has a male academic say in his novel *The Rebel Angels*:

> I like women, and the lack of a feminine presence in
> Christianity has long troubled me. Oh, I am familiar with all
> the apologies that are offered on that point: I know that
> Christ had women among his followers, that he liked to talk
> to women, and that the faithful who remained with him at
> the foot of his cross were chiefly women. But whatever
> Christ may have thought, the elaborate edifice of doctrine
> we call his church offers no woman in authority – only a
> Trinity made up, to put it profanely, of two men and a
> bird – and even the belated amends offered to Mary by the
> Church of Rome does not undo the mischief.[2]

The negative attitude to women displayed in Christianity has derived largely from negative attitudes to sex. Having espoused celibacy as the highest good and relegated sexuality as something to be used for procreation purposes only, woman was feared and reviled. If sex is sinful then that which arouses sexual desire is sinful. For man, it is woman who most arouses his sexuality; ergo, woman is sinful. It is woman who leads men astray; therefore woman is evil. Man can best be protected from woman by segregating her and keeping her apart. Unfortunately, this only exacerbates the problem. In sexually-segregated societies, any encounter between men and women who are not relatives has sexual undertones. Interaction between men and women on the basis of friendship becomes impossible. This can only lead to the spiritual impoverishment of both sexes and thus of society. Such societies are deserts of aridity.

When sexuality is repressed, woman is seen as temptress. She is Circe, the sorceress who lures men to her sacred isle and imprisons them by her wiles. She arouses their physical desires and turns them into swine. The image of woman as seductress is bound up with another image which arouses fear – the image of woman as witch – the image of the Woman of Power. Having developed a sense of inner strength from the Women's Movement, many women have turned to Goddess religion to rediscover age-old knowledge about the innate powers of womanhood. This lost knowledge is the way of Wise Craft – the powers traditionally associated with who in Western society is called a Witch, but whom other societies call Wise Woman or priestess. Witches believe that human beings have innate powers to cause change through the use of the mind and the energy fields of the body. They also believe that consciousness is not confined to the physical realm and the laws of time, but that it can travel forwards and backwards to glimpse the past and the future. This awareness comes often first in dream, but can be developed through psychic training. Women are often considered especially gifted in this respect and many women who have become more in tune with their own psyche and energy flows have discovered that they are able to develop these powers.

In earlier societies, people were aware that women's cycles were accompanied by psychic and psychological change. Menstruating women were considered dangerous. Witches are aware that menstruating women have a high level of psychokinetic energy – the energy which causes poltergeist and other magical manifestations. At others times of the menstrual cycle, the psyche is more open to the dream world. Through attuning to their inner cycles and seasons, women become aware of their psychic tides and learn to know the times when big dreams will come, dreams which give messages which cut across the limitations of normal awareness.

It has not been easy for women to exercise the powers of Wise Craft in recent Western society. The use by women of magical powers has been strongly suppressed and condemned by the male Church. Even woman's traditional role as healer and midwife has been hijacked by a male medical establishment. However, the image of Witch, which is closely aligned to that of Shaman, offers women the possibility of harnessing this power and of using it in positive ways which benefit humankind – to heal and to change that which should be changed. There is a chant which is often used in Goddess-oriented groups:

> She changes everything She touches,
> Everything She touches changes. [3]

This is sung of the Goddess, but it speaks also to many women of their own inner powers. The power of the Goddess is seen as the heritage of every woman. Starhawk gives a group exercise in her book *The Spiral Dance: A Rebirth of the Ancient Religion of the Great Goddess* which is a Womb Chant.

Begin with a Group Breath and Power Chant. As you
breathe, imagine that you breathe through the womb. See it
glow white, like the moon, as you inhale power. See it glow
red with blood, with creative fire. Feel the power of the
womb to create – not the physical womb only, but the inner
womb where ideas and visions are generated. Let your
breath become a sound that resonates in the womb.

With each breath – feel its power – feel the woman or
man next to you – feel her power – feel how we are linked –
how strong we are when we are linked – breathe the power
of vision – breathe the womb power of creation – and let
your voice carry that power . . . [5]

Women who worship the Goddess have also become aware of
power in another sense. Women drawn to Paganism from the
Women's Movement are in some ways different from their
brothers and sisters who came earlier to the Pagan path. They are
often more politically aware. Many have come from a background
of radical campaigning and brought to their Paganism a political
stance which is anti-materialist and pro-environmental. Witches
in the United States and Europe have been at the forefront of
some of the most important anti-War and environmental
campaigns of recent years.

In taking radical political action in defence of ecological issues,
many women realized, perhaps for the first time, a sense of their
own collective power, a power to stand against the male,
patriarchal establishment. Starhawk describes how she and 600
women were imprisoned after blockading a weapons laboratory.
The guards try to remove one of the women.

The woman dives into our cluster, and we instinctively
surround her, gripping her arms and legs and shielding her
with our bodies. The guards grab her legs and pull, we
resist, holding on. The guards and the women are shouting
and in a moment, I know, the nightsticks will descend on
kidneys and heads . . . And then someone begins to chant.

The chant is wordless, a low hum that swells and grows
with open vowels as if we have become the collective voice
of some ancient beast that growls and sings . . .

'Sit down,' a woman whispers. We become a tableau,
sitting and clasping the woman as if we are healing her
with our voices and our magic. The confrontation has
become a laying on of hands.

The guards stand, tall, isolated pillars. They look
bewildered. . . . They do not know what to do.
    And so, after a moment, they withdraw. The chant dies
away. It is over. For a moment, mystery has bested
authority.[6]

Many people attracted to Paganism are individualists who have
rejected the usurpation of control of the religious function by male
priestly hierarchies. These issues are especially important to
Pagan sisterhoods. Where women have felt themselves
oppressed by the structures of patriarchal society, they have been
eager not to emulate and reproduce those structures in their own
religious movements. Women's traditions are therefore often
eclectic and loosely structured. Creativity and spontaneity are
strongly encouraged; as is free emotional expression. The
emphasis in women's groups is on immanent power – power
from within.

In Witchcraft, power is another word for energy, the subtle
current of forces that shape reality. A powerful person is
one who draws energy into the group. The ability to
channel power depends on personal integrity, courage and
wholeness. It cannot be assumed, inherited, appointed, or
taken for granted, and it does not confer the right to control
another. Power-from-within develops from the ability to
control ourselves, to face our own fears and limitations, to
keep commitments, and to be honest. The sources of power
are unlimited. One person's power does not diminish
another's; instead, as each covener comes into her own
power, the power of the group grows stronger.[7]

The images of woman as priestess and Witch are important and
empowering to women. Recent societies have taught that woman
is passive, a womb to bear children, the field which awaits the
plough, that which is to be impregnated and controlled by men
and male society. The Goddess images in Western society have
also taken on these attributes. The Virgin Mary of Christian
religion is 'the handmaid of the Lord' and woman's religious role
has for centuries been that of follower and subordinate to the
male priest. In Christianity, women have been permitted to serve
God as nuns, but only recently has women's entry to the
priesthood been contemplated. In Paganism, the image of the
Goddess is of strength and power. Woman is honoured as

priestess, Wise Woman and Woman of Power. Women are urged
not to be passive vessels at the disposal of men, but women in
control of their own destiny: 'Priestesses in their own right,
strong and proud, with their own vision.'[8]

Pagans believe that religions which portray the Divine solely
as masculine are damaging to women. In her book *Jung and
Feminism: Liberating Archetypes*, Demaris Wehr points out that:

> Symbols have both psychological and political effects,
> because they create the inner conditions . . . that lead
> people to feel comfortable with or to accept social and
> political arrangements that correspond to the symbol
> system.[9]

By worshipping the Goddess, women internalize those qualities
associated with the Goddess and learn to reject social and
political philosophies and systems which oppress women. They
learn to seek social roles through which they can function as
whole human beings, realizing all and not just part of their inner
qualities. The Goddess is worshipped as manifest in Nature,
beyond Nature and also within each individual woman. Often
ritual incorporates powerful self-affirmation and affirmation by
others.

> I am Goddess and thou art Goddess.
> Within me and without me is She,
> eternal yet ever-becoming,
> and in all Womanhood we see Her face.[10]

In recent interpretations of mythology, the Goddess is often
thought of as the Earth, the passive principle in Nature who is
activated by the warm rays of the masculine Sun. However, it is
a mistake to believe that across all cultures, the Earth is
universally portrayed as feminine and the sky as masculine. In
ancient Egyptian religion, which represented one of the most
sophisticated flowerings of Paganism, the Earth is Geb, husband
and lover of the Sky Goddess Nut, the Queen of Heaven, whose
body arches protectively over him. In the Indo-European
tradition, the Goddess is active. She is Sun and fire. Freya
Aswynn writes:

> The ancient Northern people, like all primitive peoples,
> regarded the sun as a life-giving force. It should, however,
> be emphasised that they regarded the sun as feminine. Even

in modern German the grammatical gender of 'Sonne' is
feminine. . . . The idea that the sun is feminine is evidently
very old and may well stem from a more ancient matriarchal
magical tradition. This supposition is corroborated by
evidence that in Shinto, the indigenous religion of Japan,
and in the oldest Egyptian tradition, the sun is also viewed
as a Goddess.[11]

Worshipping the Goddess inclines us to view the universe in a
different way from that of philosophies based on patriarchal
monotheism. Many branches of Western Paganism share a view
similar to that of Hindu thought. All manifestation, whether
consciousness or matter, is Shakti – the Great Mother of All.
Shakti is energy and power, but energy and power must take
shape or form. This is Shiva – the Great Father of All. This view
is the opposite of that found in the Judaic mystical tradition of
the Qabalah where the Great Mother is Binah, Mother of Form,
and the Father God is Chokmah – force. In Hindu thought, the
feminine-masculine polarity of force and form are seen as
manifesting everywhere, including within ourselves. Even when
there is no universe, these ultimate potentialities still exist,
though at rest.[12]

In Western Paganism, the Goddess is not passive but an active
and energizing force. She is the Creatrix, the dynamism which
activates the universe. She is the power which calls the power of
the God to her and, in that movement, the process of creation
begins.

> Golden Aphrodite cometh not as the Virgin, the victim,
> but as the Awakener, the Desirous One.
> As outer space She calls,
> and the All-Father commences the courtship.
> She awaketh Him to desire and the worlds are created. . . .
> How powerful is She, Golden Aphrodite,
> the awakener of manhood![13]

This Pagan image of the Goddess is very far from the
desexualized image drawn from the Semitic religions of the
barren desert. The Goddess is fertility and abundance, and the
creation of the Earth itself is seen as an act of sexuality between
two dynamic forces within the universe. This energizing image
of the feminine is very important in Paganism. Women are not
acted upon – they act. Paganism offers a spiritual path in which

women can honour the feminine aspect of the Divine and play
a full role as priestesses and celebrants of the mysteries of the
Goddess. This teaches women to internalize the qualities of the
Goddess, rather than to subordinate themselves to a male
priesthood serving a male God. The power which is offered is
not power over others, but power in the sense of inner energy
and strength – power-from-within. In taking on the role of
priestess, a woman demonstrates for herself her own inner power
and, for other women, provides a much-needed role of strong
womanhood to which they can aspire. When she has experienced
this sense of strength, she can move forward. There is a song
which is often sung at Pagan gatherings:

> We are an old people,
> We are a new people,
> We are the same people,
> Stronger than before.
> I am a strong woman,
> I am a story woman,
> I am a healer,
> My soul will never die. [14]

For many who are searching for a path through which to express
their inner spirituality, the Goddess who is present in Nature,
who is all around us, and whose essence is love, has a great
attraction. This appeal is not only to women, but also to men.
Two thousand years ago, Lucius Apuleius wrote a prayer after his
initiation into the mysteries of Isis.

> Holiest of the Holy,
> Perpetual Comfort of Mankind,
> Thou, whose bountiful grace nourishes the whole world;
> whose heart turnest
> towards all those in sorrow and tribulation
> as a mother's to her children;
> Thou, who takest no rest by night,
> no rest by day,
> but art always at hand
> to succour the distressed,
> by land and sea,
> dispersing the gales that beat upon them.
> Thy hand alone
> canst disentangle the hopelessly knotted skeins of fate,

terminate every spell of bad weather,
and restrain the stars from harmful conjunction.
The Gods above adore Thee,
the Gods below do homage to Thee,
Thou settest the orb of Heaven
spinning around the poles,
Thou givest light to the Sun,
Thou governest the universe,
Thou tramplest down the powers of Hell.
At Thy voice,
the stars move,
the seasons recur,
the spirits of Earth rejoice,
the elements obey.
At Thy nod,
the winds blow,
clouds drop wholesome rain upon the earth,
seeds quicken,
buds swell.
Birds that fly through the air,
beasts that prowl on the mountain,
serpents that lurk in the dust,
all these tremble in a single awe of Thee . . .[15]

Many men have turned to the worship of the Goddess to find there the same beauty and inner truth that was found by men millennia ago.

The Way of the God

All extremes in religious, political and spiritual thought produce an equal and opposite reaction. The dominance of our religious life by a sterile maleness returned many to the worship of the Great Goddess. An imbalance in outer society towards valuing only male activity and the male sex brought forth feminism and encouraged many, both women and men, to develop the feminine within themselves. This was of great value to men, because it returned to them a part of themselves which had been suppressed and repressed by Western society. This was male caring, creativity and joyfulness. This is, however, only one side of the lost male, which Pagan religion has needed to recover. The male is also hunter and warrior. This is not random violence or killing for the sake of it, but that use of male strength which is needed by Nature; the strength which protects, nurtures and guards the weak, and which prevents the powerful from oppressing the powerless. Having come to terms with the Goddess, many men now wish to come to terms with their own male energy. They are searching for the God.

In the 1980s we had the concept of The New Man. He changed nappies, wept buckets at the movies, and was never angry. He harboured a permanent guilt complex because his organ dangled and hers did not, and he took upon himself the sins of the male world. It was men who had persecuted women, burned them at the stake, had unleashed the dogs of war. If his ancestors had done it, then he too had done it. He was guilty by birth. Many caring men emerged from this phase frustrated that by seeking to minimize their maleness, they had not found themselves. Men had found their inner feminine. They may have rejected the stereotypical male role which they had been brought up to play and chosen other careers and other patterns of life; but there was still something missing. In rejecting the Judaeo-Christian God, all masculine deity had been abolished. It was then that the Gods of the Pagans awoke to both men and women to say, 'You rejected the God because you worshipped false idols. Do not worship the Gods of the desert. Worship the Gods of field and tree, animal and plant, Sun and Moon. Worship the forces of Life and not the God of Death!'

To play their role in society, men must come to an understanding of how to use their male energy for the greater good. The aim of Pagan religion is not to produce men who think they are women, but men in touch with their maleness. For this, the worship of God as well as of Goddess is necessary. Chris Crowley writes, in *Wicca: The Old Religion in the New Age*[16] that men are often attracted to Wicca by its emphasis on the feminine and on the Goddess. Given the strong role of the priestess in many Goddess-oriented groups, men may be content at first to adopt a somewhat supportive role. This can be a necessary antidote to male-dominated Western culture. It also provides an opportunity for men to explore the feminine side of their psyche. Chris Crowley emphasizes, however, that although reverence for the feminine principle and the feminine within never lessens, it is important that this does not become over-emphasized and negate the masculine.

In our modern era, both men and women have suffered from

false images of what they should be. They have also suffered from false male Gods. Bob Stewart writes in *Choirs of the God: Revisioning Masculinity* that:

> The God without has, for about 1500 years, been somewhat severely limited to a monosexual and imbalanced image, the 'demon Jehovah', the wrathful father, the creator of pain, suffering, inequality, restriction, elitism, misery, and so forth. This terrible image has been mitigated slightly by that of Jesus, but suffering and pain are also features of this divine son in most orthodox Christian cults or religious branches. The problem of rivalry and pain between father and son, or older and younger male, seems epitomised in the formal religions, particularly those of near-Eastern origin such as Christianity. [17]

The Christian deity offers man the image of celibacy. It denies his animal nature and seeks to emasculate him. This has led many men to seek inspiration from the worship of the Pagan Gods. In the main, men have sought and found their Pagan spirituality in mixed-sex groups following the traditional Pagan paths and the newer Pagan syntheses. In more recent years, there has also been a revival of the male mystery traditions. These include initiatory traditions familiar to us from the Graeco-Roman world (though many had their origin further East), such as those of Orpheus and that of Mithras, whose worship was widespread amongst the soldiers of the Roman Empire. Others have turned to the warrior spirituality of the Norse-German Beserkers and, in North America, to the Native American tradition, whose people lived the way of hunter and warrior into recent times. As we have seen, Pagans worship their Gods in many forms. Some have given their allegiance to Odin All-Father. Yet others have turned to one of the earliest forms of male deity – that of the Horned God – whose origins lie in a more distant past, when our ancestors were hunter-gatherers living in harmony with their prey, following the seasonal migrations of the animals on which they lived, and taking from them only what they needed, because they knew that if the animals on whom they depended died, then so too would they.

The Horned God is an image of great power which has endured in the human psyche through centuries of repression. Although newer Gods have emerged, the Horned God endured and, as Pan of the Greeks and Cernunnos of the Celts, he was a dominant force until the Christian era. With the advent of Christianity, the

Horned God was largely suppressed. He was seen as threatening, sexual and animalistic. His image became associated with that of the Christian devil. Twentieth-century Paganism has seen a rebirth and rehabilitation of the Horned God. Starhawk writes:

> The image of the Horned God in Witchcraft is radically different from any other image of masculinity in our culture. He is difficult to understand, because He does not fit into any of the expected stereotypes, neither those of the 'macho' male nor the reverse-images of those who deliberately seek effeminacy. He is gentle, tender, and comforting, but He is also the Hunter. He is the Dying God – but His death is always in the service of the life force. He is the power of feeling, and the image of what men could be if they were liberated from the constraints of patriarchal culture. [18]

The Horned God is not cerebral and celibate, but the phallic hunter God of forest and hill. The Horned God is Lord of the Animals. His body is that of a man, but his feet are hooves and his antlers or horns reach up to heaven, capturing within them the power of the Sun. He is strong and powerful; but he is also the Shepherd, the caring and protecting father. The God is old, but young; he is strong and steadfast, but he is also light, energy, movement, creativity.

> I am as old as time;
> for I sprung forth from the first breath taken;
> yet have I aged not;
> for I am born anew with each gust of wind
> and every gentle breeze.
>
> The leaves dancing on the trees,
> and still water silently mirthful with sudden ripples,
> show that I pass by.
> Fleet of foot with wingèd heels am I,
> the messenger,
> with words you all must hear.
> cascading from my silver tongue.
> I am quicksilver,
> I bring healing with my magic touch,
> I am the wind,
> the very breath of life,
> I am He. [19]

Knowledge is the spiritual goal of many Pagan paths. This is not knowledge in the sense of facts and data, but an intuitive understanding which may or may not be conscious. In many Pagan traditions, this search for understanding is conveyed through the seasonal myths which tell of the God's quest for knowledge. Chris Crowley, in *Wicca: the Old Religion in the New Age*,[20] explains the journey of the God in terms of an evolution from the freedom and natural animalism of youth, through to love, humanity, kingship, parenthood, death and sacrifice. This comes about through his interaction with the feminine, the Goddess, and also through his acceptance of the passage of time and inevitably of change. The seasonal cycle contains a message which speaks to man as well as to God and it is a message which is at the heart of male initiation. It is to male and female initiation that we now turn.

Initiation into Adulthood

One of the functions of religion is to help us to mark important transitions in the human life cycle. Birth, adulthood, marriage and death, all require us to take on new roles and responsibilities. It is one of the roles of religious ritual to show us how these things may be done. Ritual helps us make sense of the major transitions in our lives: from childhood to adolescence; from adolescence to adulthood; from mid-life to the later years when our physical strength begins to fail us and we become aware of the nearness of death. These transitions are often dealt with by specific rites of passage, but they are also approached in less direct ways. Messages about how we are to fulfil our social roles are also found in the seasonal and other myths of Paganism.

Not all, if any, of these transitions are dealt with well in modern secular societies. Initiation into adulthood in particular is a theme which is beginning to concern many people in Western society, not only Pagans. Interest in this area has grown because we recognize that we lack the processes to help our young people make a smooth transition between the worlds of childhood and adulthood. Often there is uncertainty of what is required of an adult and of an adult man or woman. This problem is cumulative; for as each generation fails to pass on the appropriate teaching, so more and more of the inner mysteries of maleness and femaleness are lost to us. We are lacking guidance on the initiatory processes of adulthood at a time when the journey into adulthood is more difficult than it has ever been. In many ways, we have more freedom. We have the choice of what occupation to follow and whether to become parents. These things are no longer decided for us by our families, the village elders, or the state. There may be pressures, both psychological and material, to conform; but we have today much greater freedom than any generation before. We are also lacking in guidance. The extended family has split up, so that there are no longer generations of elders of our own sex to whom we can turn for advice and wisdom. The nuclear family has also broken down. Fathers are frequently absent or non-existent and many men and women have no positive male role models from whom to learn.

Paganism recognizes this lack and many women and men have come to the Pagan mysteries to learn from its myths and initiatory processes a positive pattern of femaleness and maleness. Sometimes they choose to do so in groups of their own sex and sometimes in Pagan paths where both the roles of Goddess and God are positive and strong. To Pagans, the myths and rites of religion are expressions of the reality of the Divine force and allegories of how it interacts with the world. They are also templates which guide our behaviour in society. The image of the Goddess teaches a woman what it means to be female and that of the God teaches a man what it means to be male. Together they teach the nature of both sexes' responsibilities to society and how to reconcile our individual desires and wants to those of our communities. They teach the way of wholeness and how that wholeness embraces all aspects of the life cycle – good and bad, youth and age, pain and pleasure, life and death.

In his book *Iron John: A Book about Men*, Robert Bly argues that a return to the initiatory processes which were an integral part of earlier tribal societies is essential to the survival of the Western world. Many of Bly's ideas of tribal society are romanticized, but they are important. Bly argues that his own culture, that of the United States, has undergone an unmistakable decline since the 1950s. He sees initiation as a third road between the perils of rampant individualism and ego inflation, encouraged by much of our materialist culture, and the road of depression and failure, the only way out for those who cannot cope with the demands of society.

We have the grandiose road, taken by junk-bond dealers, high rollers, and the owners of private jets; and we have the

depressed road, taken by some long-term alcoholics . . .
crack addicts, and fatherless men. . . . The ancient practice
of initiation then – still very much alive in our genetic
structure – offers a third way through . . .[21]

Others, such as James Hillman,[22] a Jungian psychologist, have taken
a similar view. Hillman has made an extensive study of myths
relating to the initiation of the puer, or youth, by the senex, the older
wise man. He argues that initiation is a necessary bridge between
the world of fantasy and the harsh world of reality – a bridge which
can make reality bearable. He sees initiation as softening reality,
by filling in its background with layers of mythological perspective.
He believes that this makes the hardness of reality meaningful and
tolerable, but at the same time truly indestructible.

Robert Bly argues that the process of initiation into adulthood
is easier for women than for men.

A girl changes into a woman on her own, with the bodily
developments marking the change; old women tell her
stories and chants, and do celebrations. But with the boys,
no old men, no change.[23]

While this may have been true in tribal society, it is no longer so
today. Initiation into the traditional female mysteries has been
sadly lacking in modern society and has left many women
ignorant not only of what it means in spiritual terms to be a
woman; but also of their own bodies, their hormonal cycles, and
the mysteries of fertility and reproduction. A return to the role
of woman as midwife and healer and to natural ways of
contraception and childbirth have been a natural accompaniment
to woman reclaiming the power of the feminine. Lack of initiatory
experience from older women who have dealt with the demands
of today's society also means that many women are confused
about their role. Women today are bombarded with media images
of the Superwoman, who has it all – beauty, health, husband,
children, career, material success, inner fulfilment, fortune and
glory. Against this unrealistic image, even the most successful
woman can feel herself a failure. Creating realistic expectations
of what we can do, be and achieve requires teaching of women
by women. Many women who have created women-only Pagan
religious groups perceive their Goddess religion as a sisterhood,
in which older women teach younger women the age-old secrets
of Wise Craft and of the ways of womanhood.

In tribal society, the role of men was clear – the majority were needed to become hunters and warriors. In society today, where this need has receded and, indeed, where male violence channelled into ends which do not serve society has become a major problem, how are the initiatory processes to be managed and what are we initiating our men into becoming? Robert Bly explores what he believes is happening, or rather, not happening to men in society in the United States. Bly believes that manhood doesn't happen by itself. What is necessary is the active intervention by older men to welcome younger men into the ancient, mythologized, instinctive male world[24]

> The relevant sentence is the one accepted in New Guinea by men and women of eighty or so tribes: 'A boy cannot change into a man without the active intervention of the older men.'[25]

In Pagan tribal societies, these matters were managed well and formed an integral part of the education of young men. Often, the adolescent was separated from his parents and sent out into the wilderness to fend for himself and/or to bring back some symbol or animal which would denote that he had performed an act of courage. This type of initiation is difficult to obtain today and some men who feel the lack have been drawn to the Pagan Gods as providing images of wholeness with which to identify.

Man and the Goddess

Bly's work is based on his analysis of a fairy tale – that of Iron John. The story describes a young prince's encounter with a Wildman who takes the boy from his home and then finally sends him into the world to work for his living. He finds work in the palace of a neighbouring kingdom. He later proves his courage in war and is rewarded by winning the King's daughter for his wife. From the structure of this tale, Bly argues that every man has at the bottom of his psyche an ancient male covered with hair, whom he calls the Wildman. There are several parallels between the Wildman and the Horned God. Bly argues that in order to undergo the processes of male initiation, modern man has to get in touch with the Wildman.

Robert Bly's work, although very valuable, has spawned some unfortunate offspring. In re-evaluating the male path, there is a danger that the pendulum may swing to another extreme. The

Workshop-Attending Classes have leapt onto the Wildman bandwagon and middle-class American males now rush off to men's camps to shout for their long lost daddies and find the Wildman within. As the psychologist John Rowan points out in his book *The Horned God*, [26] this is fine, providing they also get in touch with the feminine, but otherwise it is an invitation to 'unconstructed male chauvinism'. The Wildman can become a justification for male aggression.

Robert Bly argues that initiation of men is something which must be carried out by men: Only a man can make a man. This is both true and untrue. Paganism teaches that initiation is not a one-off event, but a process with many steps. In the initiatory rites of Isis, the first initiation was that of the Goddess, the second that of the God, and the third that of the Goddess again. This is also the pattern found in the mysteries of Wicca, where the parallels with the life cycle are more explicit. What Bly describes is the stage of the initiatory process which makes us a young adult and embarks us on our life's journey. We are apprenticed to life, but still have to prove ourselves as full adults in society. This initiation must indeed be given by elders of the same sex, as only they can explain to a man what it really means to walk the male path. Similarly, only women can explain to other women what it means to be a woman and bear children and, in today's society, how to balance this with other needs for fulfilment which a woman may have.

The problem with the Iron John story is that no women figure in it other than as ciphers. The young boy in the story learns to live with the Wildman and this is a valuable lesson, but the story fades out as the young man marries the princess. He has completed one stage of the initiatory process. He has made the transition from adolescence to manhood, but what we do not learn is that there is a further initiatory process – that by the woman of the man. At this stage, we must turn to wise elders of the opposite sex to teach us. This is not woman teaching man to be New Man and to learn feminine qualities, but woman teaching man to use the attributes of his maleness for the good of the community, to protect and to serve it. This harks back to the Celtic idea of a young man going to a female warrior for the final part of his training in weapons. In the Northern traditions, women are also seen as essential instructors of men. Freya Aswynn comments:

. . . it was the wise woman's function to teach magical
practices to men, as well as to advise them in ethical
matters. In this respect there is a similarity to the older
continental tradition where women arbitrated in legal
disputes and gave advice in councils of war.[27]

Paganism emphasizes harmony and balance both in our outer
lives and within the psyche. One of the fundamental dualities in
ourselves, and also in society, is that of male and female. Many
Pagans consider that our current social and spiritual systems have
brought us out of balance because they are male dominated.
Many would call this patriarchy, but Robert Bly argues that the
society in which we live, while male dominated, is not a true
patriarchy.

The genuine patriarchy brings down the sun through the
Sacred King, into every woman and every man in the
culture; and the genuine matriarchy brings down the moon,
through the Sacred Queen, to every woman and every man
in the culture. The death of the Sacred King and Queen
means that we live now in a system of industrial
domination, which is not patriarchy.[28]

Bly believes that our current social and economic systems honour
neither male nor female modes of feeling. The system of
industrial domination determines how we live and all is sacrificed
to material ends: 'there is neither king nor queen.' Society needs
both femaleness and maleness; for when the male and female
energies within us all are brought into right harmony, then
creativity follows.

. . . the Sacred or Solar King is the principle of order and
space. When the King is present, there is sacred space free
of chaos. The King does not create order; more simply,
where he is, there is order. . . . The Queen's power is also
great. Sometimes she is in the lead, sometimes he is.
Because he and the Queen are in right space together, the
fig tree blossoms, the apple trees bear fruit abundantly,
ditches run milk and honey.[29]

Creativity is an outcome of our establishing an inner dialogue
within the masculine and feminine which reside within us all.
The psychologist Carl Jung gave a name to this contrasexual other
within us. The masculine within woman is named Animus and

the feminine within man Anima. In order to fully understand and fulfil his nature, a man must not only come into right relation with his maleness, but also achieve understanding of his inner feminine, his Anima. Hindu psychologist Arwind Vasavada believes that for men the Goddess plays a role akin to that of the Anima in Jungian psychology.

> She disturbs man from his state of ease and comfort, rouses his emotions, and all the baser instinctual shadow side of his life, drags him into the open battleground of life so that he may fulfil his destiny, but from which he always fights shy. She appears both as positive and negative mother, compassionate as well as cruel, according to the developmental stage of each individual.[30]

Dion Fortune also describes the role of the Goddess as Anima in her novel *The Sea Priestess*. The role of the Goddess is not as the passive principle. She is the muse who awakens man's consciousness into creativity.

> In the inner She is all-potent.
> She is Queen of the kingdoms of sleep.
> All the invisible workings are Hers
> and She rules all things ere they come to birth.
> Even as through Osiris Her mate
> the Earth grows green,
> so the mind of man conceives through Her power.[31]

Woman and the God

What of the God and women? The role of the God is important for women; but it is not exactly parallel to that of the Goddess for men. For long in our society, the feminine has been undervalued in worldly terms. Woman has been relegated to the bedroom and kitchen, or elevated to the heights of heaven, but she has not been permitted a voice in everyday life, 'the affairs of men'. Women have been denied part of themselves, that part which is strong, decisive, thinking, constructive. Women have been taught to look for these qualities in husbands, rather than embodying them themselves. The challenge for women is to reclaim these qualities as their own and for this, they need to understand the qualities of the Goddess; for in her are these things found.

Where women need the God is in coming into relationship with men. Many women have been damaged by maleness and have no image of what a positive male force can be. The image of the antlered God is of maleness which is strong and powerful, fierce, gentle and loving, and cares for things which are beyond his own personal needs and concerns. Women need to see the potential of what maleness can be both for their own benefit and in order to teach this to their sons; for whatever our romantic notions about tribal society, boys learn much of what is appropriate male behaviour from their earliest teachers, their mothers.

Both God and Goddess are necessary to us if we are to understand the mystery of the Divine and both mysteries are necessary and valuable if we are to understand ourselves and thus play a full role in society. In honouring both female and male, Goddess and God, we bring ourselves and our visions into right harmony. We can be all of ourselves, not denying our maleness or femaleness, but becoming who and what we truly are.

1. Starhawk, *The Spiral Dance*, page 199.
2. Dion Fortune, *The Sea Priestess*, page 121.
3. Robertson Davies, *The Rebel Angels*, page 241.
4. Lauren Liebling and Starhawk.
5. Starhawk, *The Spiral Dance*, pages 133–4.
6. Starhawk, *Truth or Dare: Encounters with Power, Authority and Mystery*, pages 4–5.
7. Starhawk, *The Spiral Dance*, page 37.
8. The Pagan Federation, *The Pagan Federation Information Pack*, page 10.
9. Vivianne Crowley, unpublished women's material.
10. Demaris Wehr, *Jung and Feminism: Liberating Archetypes*, page 22.
11. Freya Aswynn, *Leaves of Yggdrasil: A Synthesis of Magic, Feminine Mysteries, Folklore*, page 61.
12. Marvin Spiegelman in J.M. Spiegelman and A.U. Vasavada, *Hinduism and Jungian Psychology*, page 30.
13. Dion Fortune, *The Sea Priestess*, page 158.
14. Will Shepardson and the women of Greenham Common Peace Camp, England.
15. Lucius Apuleius, *The Golden Ass*, chapter XIX.
16. Chris Crowley, 'The God: Wicca and the Masculine' in Vivianne Crowley, *Wicca: The Old Religion in the New Age*, page 186.
17. R.J. Stewart, 'The God in Western Magical Arts', in John

Matthews (ed.), *Choirs of the God: Revisioning Masculinity*, page 123.

18. Starhawk, *The Spiral Dance*, page 94.
19. Chris Crowley, unpublished material, 1985.
20. Chris Crowley, 'The God: Wicca and the Masculine' in Vivianne Crowley, *Wicca: The Old Religion in the New Age*, pages 191–200.
21. Robert Bly, *Iron John: A Book About Men*, pages 35–6.
22. James Hillman, 'Senex and Puer: An Aspect of the Historical and Psychological Present', in James Hillman (ed.), *Puer Papers*, page 29.
23. Robert Bly, *Iron John: A Book About Men*, pages 86–7.
24. Robert Bly, *Iron John: A Book About Men*, page 15.
25. Robert Bly, *Iron John: A Book About Men*, pages 86–7.
26. John Rowan, *The Horned God: Feminism and Men and Wounding and Healing*, page 111.
27. Freya Aswynn, *Leaves of Yggdrasil: A Synthesis of Magic, Feminine Mysteries, Folklore*, pages 194–5.
28. Robert Bly, *Iron John: A Book About Men*, page 98.
29. Robert Bly, *Iron John: A Book About Men*, page 98.
30. Arwind Vasavada in J.M. Spiegelman and A.U. Vasavada, *Hinduism and Jungian Psychology*, page 158.
31. Dion Fortune, *The Sea Priestess*, page 123.

Part Three
Living as a Pagan

8
Rites of Passage: Making Sense of the Life Cycle

Other than entry into adulthood, major phases of the life cycle which call upon us to change our social roles are those of marriage, parenting, adjusting to the latter third of life – old age – and lastly, that greatest transition of all, whereby we transcend the material world – death. A function of religion is to help smooth the way, to prepare the psyche for the adjustments we must make and to give us the necessary inner strength and understanding of self and others to deal with these challenges by offering guidance in the form of myth and symbol as to how we are to meet their demands.

Marriage and Parenting

Early adulthood leads to relationships and usually to marriage or some other form of committed relationship. In modern Paganism, marriage is often known as handfasting. In some traditions, no permanent union is recognized. Handfasting is for a year and a day, after which the couple must renew their vows to one another. Other traditions have marriage which sets out to be permanent, although divorce is permitted. Marriage is a matter of mutual promises and of honour. If people are no longer able to keep those promises, then they must be honest and take honourable steps to dissolve the contract. Some traditions have two levels of marriage vow – those which are more of a secular contract, and more permanent vows which are usually made when the couple have been in a relationship for some time and wish to make a life-long commitment. This commitment may also endure beyond a single life-time.

By life, by love,
by heart, by my troth,
I take thee unto my hand
until the last setting of the Sun
and the last rising of the stars. [1]

Attitude to marriage and the place of sexuality within it are conveyed in this handfasting blessing. The Celebrant takes the couple's rings and places their hands on them.

Above you are the stars,
below you are the stones,
as time does pass – remember:
like a star should your love be constant,
like a stone should your love be firm.
Be close, yet not too close;
possess one another, yet be understanding;
have patience each with the other;
for storms will come but quickly go;
be free in the giving of affection and warmth;
make love often and be sensual to one another.
Have no fear, and let not the ways or words
of the unenlightened give you care;
for the Goddess and the God are with you, now and
always. [2]

In most traditions, the main requirement in marriage is that children must be cared for and safe-guarded. The gift of children is seen as a sacred trust from the Gods and their welfare is paramount. The fact that children are seen as Goddess-given does not mean that Pagans take the romantic and naive view of some humanistic psychologists that children are born good! Nor do Pagans believe in the Christian concept of original sin – that children are born evil. Children are born with the same balance of positive and negative characteristics which beset us all. They have impulses to caring, sharing and altruism, and impulses to selfishness, cruelty, anger and hate. The task of parents is to guide the child as best as they can, given their own limitations, towards those actions, thoughts and feelings which are creative, positive and likely to benefit the child and others. In our complex and materialistic world, this is a daunting task.

Since Pagans do not believe in original sin, there is no need for a ceremony after birth to frighten away the devil and to claim the child for a particular sect. However, most Pagans wish to mark the birth of their children with a naming ceremony. This is an occasion on which family and friends come together to share with the parents the joy of a new member of the human race and to welcome the child to the world. The ritual is often one of protection: to place the child under the care of the family's presiding deities and to ask for their blessing. Ceremonies are simple and will often consist of naming, anointing (with a non-toxic oil) and blessing the child and then a public commitment by the parents to raise and care for him or her. This rite can be performed by the mother and father or by a priest and priestess.

The mother or the priestess anoints the child with oil:

I anoint thy feet,
which have brought thee in our ways.
I anoint thy hands,
that they may work for what is right and true.
I anoint thy heart,
that it may beat in strength and love.
I anoint thy lips,
that they may speak no evil and give forth truth.
I anoint thy brow,
that thy mind shall seek the wisdom of enlightenment.

The mother then addresses the Goddess:

O lovely and gracious Queen of Living Light,
Thou, whose promise is that we will return after death,
to be with our own people,
and that we will know, and love,
and remember them again,
bless this child who has returned once more to her/his own.

The priest or the father then takes the child and addresses the God.

O Hornèd One, Power of Sleep and Night,
grant strength and blessing to this child.
Wrap her/him in thy cloak of thy protection
and guard her/him through the journey of life.

The parents then say:

I/we take the oath
to raise, protect and train our daughter/son (name),

given to us as a trust and sacred gift
by the Mother and Father of All,
until s/he is of age
to take responsibility for her/his own life.
We will teach the ways of our Mothers and Fathers:
love, gentleness, good example,
and firmness when called for we shall give.
Blessed Be (name) and welcome to the world!

Naming ceremonies do not generally involve 'signing up' children into a particular religious path. Parents usually endeavour to teach their children the Pagan ethos and ethics and the myths and legends of the Pagan deities, but religious choice is often seen as something which can only be made in adolescence or adulthood, when we have conscious understanding of what religion is about. In some Pagan paths, there are ceremonies of religious admission, profession or commitment which take place at adolescence. These are made when the young person is mature enough to decide that the Pagan path is right for them. Admission to a particular path may also take place much later in life.

To stand back and make no religious choice on behalf of one's child is difficult. If we have a religious or spiritual path which we hold dear, then how can we fail to want our children to share that joy with us? The Pagan ethic tends towards self-choice and love. Love is a word which is much misused. Often people speak of love when they mean need or a desire to control. What is required in parenting is that loving understanding which is sometimes called conscious love – a love combined with awareness and insight.

> Conscious love is 'the wish that the object should arrive at
> its own native perfection, regardless of the consequences to
> the lover', and this kind of giving love involves will. It is
> delight that something or someone actually exists in their
> own right. [3]

True or perfect love is a caring for others, tempered by a desire to see them grow to fulfil their own true potential. It is not imposing our beliefs on them, or insisting that they follow a religious path with which they are not compatible.

Many Pagan parents, while exposing their children to the religious beliefs and principles which they hold dear, accept that their children's spiritual needs and beliefs may evolve to be very different from their own. Other Pagans believe that in the complex world in which we live, it is essential that children are given strong religious teaching with which to guide their lives. To deny children this is seen as depriving them of what is an essential part of parental responsibility – the transmission of those values, traditions and beliefs which we hold to be best and true. These Pagan parents raise their children to follow their religious lead in the same way as the members of other faiths. Whatever we choose to do we have to remember that we must not seek to impose our view of reality or our own beliefs and dogma on others. Rather, we must aid them to find their own inner truths and to open their minds to see the importance of looking for these. This requires not authoritarianism, but gentleness – a gentleness backed up by a certain ruthlessness. The role of parent is partly that of instructor. A professor in Robertson Davies' novel, *The Rebel Angels*, talks of his role.

> To instruct calls for energy, and to remain almost silent, but watchful and helpful, while students instruct themselves, calls for even greater energy. To see someone fall (which will teach him not to fall again) when a word from you would keep him on his feet but ignorant of an important danger, is one of the tasks of the teacher that calls for special energy, because holding in is more demanding than crying out. [4]

Parenting is not just the responsibility of the physical parents. To play our full adult role in society, we must take on responsibility for raising those who follow us, our successors. For some that means taking on the responsibilities of physical parenthood, but in our over-crowded world, it is a choice which many forego. This does not mean that we are exempt from helping to raise the generations which follow us, but that our role may be other than the physical parent – that of the teacher or initiator into the world of adulthood. The initiator's task is to reveal to the fledgling adult that part of him- or herself which exists beyond the confines of everyday life and the conscious mind. It is to give the initiate some intimation of the wider, deeper, older, wiser part of us which is our true self. Robert Bly comments:

> The job of the initiator, whether the initiator is a man or woman, is to prove to the boy or girl that he or she is more than mere flesh and blood. A man is not a machine only for protecting, hunting, and reproduction; a woman is not a

machine only for protecting, gathering, and reproduction,
but each carries desires far beyond what is needed for
physical survival.[5]

To enter into the adult world, we must have an understanding
of our place in the scheme of things. This requires teaching, help
and guidance from those who have already entered adult life, to
help us understand our religious and cultural traditions and
those myths which guide our particular religious path. The aim
of such teaching is to awaken in the adolescent a sense of his or
her heritage; a heritage which implies responsibility to their
Gods, their people, their creation and their land. This provides
an unbroken sense of historical continuity – a sense of time,
place and context in which to live.

The final stage of parenting is letting go. The time comes when
the adolescent wants to establish him- or herself as an adult and
no longer wants to follow the parental rule book. We must have
the courage and strength to let the child stand on his or her own
feet. The parent must now say: 'You are adult and responsible
for yourself. My help and support are here if you need them, but
my responsibility for you is ended.' At this point, teenagers need
their own space in which to find out by trial and error the ways
of the adult world. In some societies, teenagers would live apart
in separate male and female societies, where they had to learn
to get on with young people of their own sex to survive. It was
the parent's duty to release the adolescent for this, after which
their child would enter the adult world, no longer subject to the
parents, but independent and equal.

This formal separation between adolescence and adulthood
makes the transition easier for the child and also for the parent.
In the prosperous 1960s and 1970s, many young people
unconsciously followed this example. They took to the road or
headed East, using a long journey with limited means as a way
of casting themselves into the world to sink or swim – an idea
which would be delightfully welcomed by many harassed
parents today. These journeys became rites of passage and
initiatory processes which marked the transition between
adolescence and adulthood.

In Paganism today, rites of passage which mark entry into adult
life are provided by those ceremonies of initiation and profession
by which we enter a particular Pagan path and also by ceremonies
which mark entry into womanhood and manhood. The latter

have been developed to a greater extent in the United States which, of all the countries in the Western world, seems most preoccupied with this issue. Announcements by parents of sons' and daughters' rites of passage are frequent in the social columns of the US Pagan press.

Ageing

Many people cling to their children, reluctant to allow them to fly the nest, because by recognizing that their children are adult, they will be faced with the unwelcome fact of their own ageing. If their children are young adults, then they must be middle-aged. The early stages of adulthood are welcome. They bring freedom from parental control and the opportunity to explore the world. The later stages are often feared. Many of us fear death. We also fear old age. We fear to let go of our control over the world. The temptation is to hold on to what we have achieved and to refuse to move forward. We can see this in the way in which some people cling on to their children and also in the way in which people cling to material achievement and career success. Chris Crowley writes of Wiccan mythology and how this stage of life is reached in the God's journey around the Wheel of the Year:

> This kingship is gained when the God is at his prime, only half way round the circle and at the half way stage of his life. He is at his most materially successful and at his most dominant. It would appear, both in terms of the God's progress, and in most men's, that this in itself produces a dilemma. From the vantage of this material high point, there can appear to be no further upward path. Powers at their prime now can only weaken, albeit very gradually, and the view from the top is to see a continual surging, waves of challenges from younger men, all committed to achieving their destiny and taking his place.[6]

We live in a society which is rapidly changing and in which the wisdom of our elders can seem irrelevant and outdated. This lack of respect for the older members of society is encouraged by our media who portray idealized images of physical perfection, eternal youthfulness and sexual attractiveness to which few of us can realistically aspire. The focus on the cult of youth is a great loss to society. Youth is of great value. It is energetic and idealistic.

It rejects outmoded forms and false authority; but it can also be intolerant, selfish, arrogant and lacking in the worldly wisdom to know how to implement the ideals which it espouses. The ups and downs of life, and learning to take responsibility for ourselves and for others, can teach us gentler ways and give us a wisdom which is valuable to pass down the generations. This is not to say that all our elders are founts of mystic knowledge – many are not; but society is losing something when there is no honoured place of respect for those who have served us well.

In the Pagan traditions, all phases of the life cycle are honoured. Many traditions include special ceremonies for their older members who are passing from a stage of leadership of community affairs to that of advice giver and wise counsellor. The early and middle years are seen as times for establishing ourselves in the world, for developing skills which enable us to earn a living and win status and respect, and for learning to raise others to become well-adjusted adults in society. The third part of life is seen as a time for consolidating the knowledge which we have gained. It is a time to return to study and to learn those things which we need for our onward spiritual journey. Starhawk writes:

> In the Craft, old age is a natural and highly valued part of
> the cycle of life, the time of greatest wisdom and
> understanding. Disease, of course, causes misery, but it is
> not something to be inevitably suffered: The practice of the
> craft was always connected with the healing arts, with
> herbalism and midwifery. Nor is death fearful: It is simply
> the dissolution of the physical form that allows the spirit to
> prepare for a new life.[7]

There are external forces which can help us see the need for this transition. If we are parents, our children grow up and are no longer dependent on us. Free of this, we have time and space to attend once more to our own needs. There may be needs for learning and for spiritual direction which we have had to bury and suppress in order to fulfil our parental role, but these can now come to the fore. We may, as is more customary in the East, turn to the inner quest, the spiritual adventure. Many people in fact take up the Pagan path at this stage, when they are free to pursue their own spiritual development.

Pagans are beginning to recognize the need for initiatory processes beyond those which bring us into adulthood. In some

Eastern societies, individuals who have fulfilled their social obligations to society by supporting themselves and their families will withdraw to a monastery to study, learn, contemplate and to take time for themselves. As we approach late middle age, we need to re-evaluate our role and perhaps change our life direction. Some Pagan groups have special rites which may be called Becoming an Elder or Croning. These ceremonies recognize ageing as a positive transition, when we have an opportunity to lay down some of our responsibilities and to put ourselves first and say, 'I have done my bit. It is now someone else's turn and I will concentrate on developing myself and on growing nearer to my Gods.'

Death

In Paganism, the celebrations of the seasonal cycle operate on many levels. On the one hand, they are thanksgivings for the eternally-renewing cycle of Nature. There is also another level of meaning: the seasonal myths mirror the human life cycle and also the cycle of the cosmos – the cycle of conception, birth, maturation, decay and destruction. The seasonal cycle tells us that life is continuous, but ever-changing.

There are two delusions which create much human suffering: the Delusion of Separateness and the Delusion of Rightness. There is also a third – the Delusion of Stasis. Always, humans wish to stop the passage of time and to cling to that which is outworn and has lost its usefulness; but to cling to stasis is to cling to illusion – for the message of the cosmos is change. Today, many of us are separated from the world of Nature and it is no longer outside the hut door to teach us the lessons of life and death. Separated from Nature, we grow in illusion. We forget the message of change which leads to transmutation. Our own problems assume overwhelming proportions, when in terms of the millennia in which Nature operates, they are as nothing. When our problems seem too great we can go to a high place in the countryside and there, where the cries of the animals in the fields below fade into birdsong in the skies above, we can see that our individual selves are small in comparison with the greater whole, and so too are the problems and trials which inevitably beset us through our journey in manifestation.

The method chosen by our ancestors to come to terms with the realities of existence is to celebrate the mysteries of life and death as seen in Nature; for it is in part through observation of the cycle of birth, death and rebirth in Nature that we understand that this too is our own fate – to be born, to die and to live again.

> We know how on earth with every spring the flow of forces infuses their growing power into each limb and leaf, giving beauty and perfection to blossoms, which in the course of time ripen into fruit which bears the seeds of future trees; and how, when the year draws to its close, the sap returns into the root system, nourishes it and provides firmer foundation for the next year's growth. . . . The layered cosmos expands from within, branching through all grades of matter until the limit is reached for that phase of its evolution, whereupon the life forces retreat back into the spiritual realms as the divine root receives into itself the essence or aroma of experience. [8]

The seasonal celebrations echo to Pagans the cycles of creation and destruction on the microcosmic and macrocosmic scales. Through participating in these rituals, we come to terms with the processes of ageing and death and understand that they are but part of the life process which is eternal. The following was written many years ago at Lammas when the daughter of a Pagan friend had just died.

> In the circle, I had for the first time, a sense of the life and death aspect of Lammas. Death seemed truly present. We sang a chant to Hecate and for the spirit of the child, flying free in death. I saw the greatness of the human spirit: how our lives are less than that of a butterfly's in the passing of time; how we have the vision of Gods, but are trapped in the bodies of animals; and how great is our triumph and our tragedy.

> The Summer King comes to Our Lady of the Fields,
> and we sing our songs and stories,
> and we do not care that we live or die,
> but only that the Dance of Life goes on. [9]

What we experience through participating in the cycle of the seasonal rituals is transcendence – a reaching beyond the boundaries of time, space and the material world. Carl Jung wrote that that was this transcendence which was taught in the ancient Pagan mystery traditions.

. . . the initiate takes part in a sacred rite which reveals to him the perpetual continuation of life through transformation and renewal. In these mystery-dramas the transcendence of life, as distinct from its momentary concrete manifestations, is usually presented by the fateful transformations – death and rebirth – of a god or godlike hero. The initiate may either be a mere witness of the divine drama or take part in it or be moved by it, or he may see himself identified through the ritual action with the god. . . . The initiate who ritually enacts the slaying, dismemberment, and scattering of Osiris and afterwards his resurrection in the green wheat, experiences in this the permanence and continuity of life, which outlasts all change of form and phoenix-like, continually rises anew from its own ashes. [10]

The seasonal festivals help to overcome our individual fears, despairs and griefs at the difficulties of life by showing us that we are part of a greater scheme of things which transcends our individual pain.

When all the sorrow of the past
has melted away like morning dew,
in the warmth of summer sun,
then shall we see a brighter dawn,
when love and hope and beauty are reborn. [11]

We must accept the night time and dark things of life. These are part of our legacy in incarnation and it is useless to pretend otherwise; but we can embrace and accept this in the knowledge that after darkness comes light.

My dark eyes look to the night
in the hope of dawn to come.
What do you hope for,
you, who take day as your Father and Mother,
when day is done? [12]

The great darkness which we must all face is our own mortality. Pagans are not sentimental about Nature. She has many faces: the gentle warmth of a Mediterranean spring, the fierce heat of the desert sun, the mildness of an English autumn, the cold barrenness of an Arctic night. The Goddess is both beneficent and cruel: she gives but she takes away. This duality within the

Goddess represents the true nature of the universe: a continual
struggle between life and death, dark and light. To a Hindu writer
She represents 'generation and the glories of life with the ever-
present process of disintegration and death.'[13] The Goddess has
two aspects. One is compassionate, gentle and loving; the other
fierce, cruel, violent and dark with destruction.

> Yet, even in her fierce aspect, she protects those of her
> devotees who can overcome their fears of the terrors of the
> inevitable process of continuous change and decay she
> represents, to see also her transcendent beauty and the
> eternal bliss that ultimately she bestows on her
> worshippers.[14]

The Goddess in Paganism is seen as the beautiful Virgin and
bountiful Mother. In many Pagan traditions, the Goddess is also
the Queen of Night, Lady of the Underworld and the Layer-Out
at death.

> I am the Veiled Isis of the shadows of the sanctuary.
> I am She that moveth as a shadow
> behind the tides of death and birth.
> I am She that cometh forth by night,
> and no man seeth my face.
> I am older than time and forgotten of the Gods.
> No man may look upon my face and live;
> for in the hour he parteth my veil, he dieth.[15]

This third aspect of the Goddess is one of darkness. It is an aspect
which we need to accept, but which we often fear and turn from.

> **Dark Mother**
> By the Rainbow Bridge across the Abyss,
> in the shadow of Yggdrasil tree,
> at the Well of the Origin of All-things,
> I saw them come to me.
> First, the Maiden, pale as death,
> a shroud had she for hair;
> and then the Mother, babe at breast,
> but no milk of kindness there.
> And then the Veiled One, blackest Hag,
> whose eyes were cold obsidian;
> the reeling stars reflected there,
> in silent mirrors of oblivion.[16]

Pagan ritual often calls upon this darker side of the Goddess. As Morrigan or Hecate, she is the bearer of the sickle which reaps the Corn King. The Goddess represents creation, fertility and the generation of new life; but also the continuous processes of destruction, decay and death. Both anabolism and catabolism are hers. If we can accept both sides of the Goddess' nature, we need no longer fear the trials of life, which none can escape. The death of the body is not seen as the end of existence in any of the Pagan faiths. Life and death are a cyclical process, through which we experience many states of being, both material and spiritual. Death is part of the natural and unending cycle of creation and destruction. Starhawk writes:

> Death is not an end; it is a stage in the cycle that leads on to rebirth. After death, the human soul is said to rest in 'Summerland', the Land of Eternal Youth, where it is refreshed, grows young, and is made ready to be born again. Rebirth is not considered to be condemnation to an endless dreary round of suffering, as in Eastern religions. Instead, it is seen as the great gift of the Goddess, who is manifest in the physical world. [17]

Death is a staging post in the journey of our own individual evolutionary process. It is not the end of life, but a period of peace and rest. Just as the universe goes through cycles and seasons – existence, decay, destruction, lying dormant and reawakening – so too do the cycles of Nature; and so too do the cycles of woman and man. Death is a time of rejuvenation, renewal and reunion with those who have gone before. At Samhain, the Festival of the Dead, a Wiccan priestess invokes the God as the Dread Lord of Shadows.

> Dread Lord of the Shadows,
> God of life and Giver of life,
> yet is the knowledge of Thee,
> the knowledge of death,
> open wide, we pray Thee,
> the Gates through which we all must pass.
> Let our dear ones, who have gone before,
> return this night to make merry with us,
> and when our time comes, as it must,
> O Thou, the Comforter, the Consoler,
> the Giver of Peace and Rest,
> we will enter Thy realms gladly and unafraid . . . [18]

Both the Celtic and Norse-Germanic faiths taught that the soul continues to live after the death of the body and their myths describe the realms of death. In the Northern tradition, when a human being dies, the spirit embarks on a journey to the realm of Hel, Queen of the Dead. Hel is the daughter of the mischief-making God, Loki. She depicted as half blue. This means that she is half dead, but half alive. The spirit is judged by Odin, All-father, but he takes advice from the Goddess Urd, the Norn who represents the past. The spirit then goes to its appropriate abode in Hel. This would be a pleasant realm for those whose past deeds merited it and an extremely unpleasant one for those who deeds did not.

The Hindu scriptures of the *Upanishads* tell us: 'As a man leaves an old garment and puts on one that is new, the Spirit leaves his mortal body and then puts on one that is new.'[19] Many Pagans share with Eastern philosophy a belief in reincarnation. In Wicca, ties between individuals are seen as important and these bonds will draw us to meet again those we love in future lives. The initiate is taught:

> We know,
> that when rested and refreshed among our dear ones,
> we will be reborn again,
> by Thy grace and the grace of the Great Mother.
> Let it be in the same place
> and the same time as our beloved ones,
> and may we meet, and know, and remember,
> and love them again.[20]

Reincarnation is often thought of as purely an Eastern teaching, but this is not the case. The Druids taught of the transmigration of souls – that after death the soul would incarnate again. Some in the Norse-German tradition believe that we are born once only. Others believe that individuals bound together by ties of blood and love would be reborn to meet one another again.

> It is a Northern belief that we are reincarnated into the
> same tribe or even the same family. This is connected with
> the spiritual idea of the evolution of the individual within
> the framework of a collective unit of which he is a part.[21]

This emphasis on personal ties illustrates a difference between Western and Eastern attitudes to reincarnation. Eastern philosophy teaches detachment, a releasing from the bonds of personal love. Western philosophy teaches that we can learn to love the Divine through first loving one another.

> Learn now the secret of the web
> that is woven between the light and the darkness;
> whose warp is life evolving in time and space,
> and whose weft is spun of the lives of men.
> Behold we arise with the dawn of time
> from the grey and misty sea,
> and with the dusk we sink in the western ocean,
> and our lives are strung like pearls
> on the thread of our spirit;
> and never in all our journey go we alone,
> for that which is solitary is barren. [22]

Eastern religions tend to have a negative view of material existence. The First Truth of Buddhism is that All Life is Suffering. Prince Siddhartha, who was later known as the Buddha, came to the conclusion that life could only involve suffering and was best avoided when he first managed to venture out into the world after being secluded by his father in their palace. The myth tells us he had never had to face the realities of old age, illness or death. When confronted with them, he despaired of material existence and turned away from life in the body. He left his gilded palace to live a life of asceticism as a monk.

Hindu teaching is also to seek release from material existence. The inner self consists of soul (atman) and spirit (Brahman). Atman is tied to the wheel of rebirth and can only find release by identifying itself with the spiritual world of Brahman. Human beings have no choice. They must incarnate until they gain the wisdom to free themselves from the worldly desires which bind them to the Earthly plane. These Earthly attachments include both the desire to do good and wrong-doing. Release comes from the development of detachment and selfless love.

In Western Paganism, the world is not seen as a negative place from which we must escape but, potentially at least, a place of great joy and beauty, in which there is the possibility, through Nature, to learn of the mysteries of life, death and the Gods. Rebirth is promised by the Goddess and is welcome.

> It was I who gave birth to you,
> and in the depths of my Earth,

you will find rest and rebirth,
and I will spring you forth anew,
a fresh shoot to greenness. [23]

Western Paganism also teaches that we can be released from the
Wheel of Rebirth, but this is not sought because material
existence is drudgery, but because the soul has gained all the
experience it needs of Earthly incarnation and moves on to new
experiences in other realms. The point at which we leave the
Wheel of Rebirth is illustrated in the Wiccan Autumn Equinox
rite. After the God has been cut down at Lammas, he rises again;
but not to rejoin his old life, for that is over. He has attained his
Godhead and leaves the world of men to journey to another
place. His realm is now that of the Gods, in which we transcend
our separateness and enter the unitive reality. We are at one with
our Divine source, with one another and with the cosmos itself.
When we have learned all that we can on the journey of life, the
Wheel of Rebirth ceases to turn. At that final dissolution of our
being, we return to the infinite source of all things.

The Dance of the Elements
He stepped out of his mortal body,
and bowing once in its direction,
in honour of the Earthly temple of his being,
he began the Dance of the Elements.

He danced upon the waves of sea,
and leapt the clouds across the sky,
he landed on the Earth,
and danced by light of Moon and Sun,
he danced the flashing of the lightning,
and the falling of a flake of snow,
and the journey of a leaf upon the wind,
and the dancing of the rain,
and he did not come back again.
For at the end of the elements' dance,
throwing out his arms to embrace the universe,
and saving until last, the pirouette,
he spun on tiptoe faster,
faster and more fast,
until he was no longer seen.

But do not grieve,
O do not grieve,
for behind the veil of matter,
he shall be dancing still,
weaving between the molecules,
and laughing with the atoms,
and chasing the electrons,
across the cosmos to the stars.

And he shall be in ecstasy,
and he shall be,
he shall,
he all,
all he,
Ain soph aur,
Ain soph
Ain,
No, he will not come back again.[24]

1. From an unpublished Wiccan handfasting rite.
2. Adapted from Herman Slater, *A Book of Pagan Rituals*, page 45.
3. Jean Hardy, *A Psychology With a Soul: Psychosynthesis in Evolutionary Context*, page 43.
4. Robertson Davies, *The Rebel Angels*, page 92.
5. Robert Bly, *Iron John: A Book About Men*, page 55.
6. Chris Crowley in Vivianne Crowley, *Wicca: The Old Religion in the New Age*, pages 195–6.
7. Starhawk, *The Spiral Dance*, pages 27–8.
8. Elsa-Brita Titchenell, *The Masks of Odin: Wisdom of the Ancient Norse*, page 31.
9. Vivianne Crowley, Lammas 1982.
10. Carl Jung, *The Collected Works of C.G. Jung*, Vol 9, Part 1, *Archetypes of the Collective Unconscious*, page 117.
11. Vivianne Crowley, 1977.
12. Vivianne Crowley, 1976.
13. Margaret Stutley, *Hinduism: The Eternal Law*, pages 46–7.
14. Ibid.
15. Dion Fortune, *The Sea Priestess*, page 124.
16. Vivianne Crowley, Lammas 1990.
17. Starhawk, *The Spiral Dance*, pages 27–8.
18. From the Wiccan *Book of Shadows*, as quoted in Janet and Stewart Farrar, *Eight Sabbats for Witches*, page 133.
19. *The Bhagavad Gita*, as quoted in David Lorimer, *Whole in One:*

The Near-Death Experience and the Ethic of Interconnectedness, page 125.

20. From the Wiccan *Book of Shadows,* as quoted in Janet and Stewart Farrar, *Eight Sabbats for Witches,* page 133.
21. Freya Aswynn, *The Leaves of Yggdrasil: A Synthesis of Magic, Feminine Mysteries, Folklore,* page 78.
22. Adapted from Dion Fortune, *The Sea Priestess,* page 123.
23. Vivianne Crowley, Beltane 1982.
24. Vivianne Crowley for Alex Sanders, Beltane 1988.

9
An It Harm None: Living as a Pagan

Paganism and Society

Paganism may not have a complex set of commandments, but social ethics are strongly emphasized in many Pagan traditions. The teachings of the Norse *Eddas* abound in these. The songs and stories of the *Eddas* formed part of an oral tradition. These were sung and orated in the communal hall and would be familiar to people from their earliest years. These oft-repeated maxims created a fabric of morality against which people lived their daily lives. They were not taught in a solemn way but conveyed with wit and grace.

Many of the teachings of the *Eddas* were designed to smooth the wheels of communal life. A number are gathered together in the *Hávamál* or *High One's Words*,[1] Odin is the High One.

Mead is not good they say for the sons of men;
the deeper a man drinks, the dimmer his mind.

The herd know their homing time and leave their grazing;
but a fool knows not how much his belly holds.

Boast not of your cleverness, guard your tongue well;
the wise and silent arouse no anger in the hall.
Better friend has no man than good sense.

Other teachings had a deeper meaning and conveyed group interdependence and the obligations which each person has to his or her family and society. Great emphasis is placed in any tribal society on contributing to that society, but earlier Pagan societies did not cast out those whose contribution was less than that of others. Honour decreed that the weak must be protected and it was the duty of the strong to do so. All had their place and could contribute in their own way.

> A lame man can ride;
> a handless herd cattle,
> a deaf may be a fine warrior;
> better be blind than burn on the pyre;
> no one needs a corpse. [2]

The questioning attitude and individualism of the Aquarian Age have brought us benefits, but also dangers. Positively, if we can learn to trust our own judgement, we are less likely to succumb to the tyranny of others. On the negative side, we often fail to teach people that society is not there solely to provide for their needs. They are a part of that society and must in turn give of their energy and commitment to others. If we fail to teach people that life is a two-way exchange, we produce generations who have no respect for or understanding of the ethics and values which are essential to hold societies together.

In the past, a sense of obligation was fostered by an awareness that, however strong and powerful we might be, wealth, health and strength were all transient. The idea that life was dangerous and uncertain is conveyed in the *Hávamál*.

> Fields and flocks had the rich man's sons;
> they now bear the beggar's staff;
> riches vanish in the wink of an eye,
> the most fickle of friends. [3]

It was also important to help weaker members of society because to fail to provide for the needy was to fail in honour. The attitudes of hospitality and generosity which were encouraged in Pagan society were important for the well-being of the community, but they were also important for the spiritual evolution of the giver. Attachment to material possessions binds us to the world of the transient. These things are to be experienced and enjoyed, but they are not to be clung to; for in the end all passes, all changes. Paganism teaches:

> That in the darkest time,
> there is hope of another day;
> that in the time of suffering,

we shall know release;
that all beauty is transient,
and though we honour it while it flowers,
yet do we give greater honour
to that which endures and abides:
Love, Honour, Wisdom, Truth, Courage and Compassion.

In tribal society, distributions of gifts by the rich are important social acts which bind the community together. A modern Druid, Tadhg MacCrossan, writes in *The Sacred Cauldron: Secrets of the Druids*[4] that giving is a form of sacrifice which must be practised by all and that everything we do is in some way a form of sacrifice. Giving is a way of making sacrifice and taking is a way of receiving it. The giving and taking of gifts creates bond of love and friendship. It is also a way of expressing mutual respect. The purpose is to give unconditionally, 'not for selfish reasons but for reasons of making everything better for everybody and everything.' Society helps us, protects us and gives us its gifts. In return, we must protect and help society. Freya Aswynn describes the attitude of the Northern peoples.

> When a gift was made, it definitely had an obligation
> attached to it. The exchange of gifts was a serious matter.
> The best example of this attitude was the custom, according
> to which the king acted as 'giver of rings' on the
> understanding that the recipient of the ring was prepared to
> give his life in battle for the king, if required.[5]

Religious giving, the making of sacrifice, was also very important. It represented a subordination of the interests and greed of the individual to the community and to the Gods. Religious sacrifice involved the giving of swords, shields and jewellery, as well as the sacrifice of animals. Objects given in sacrifice were considered so sacred that valuable weapons and ornaments could be placed in piles in the countryside or thrown into sacred rivers and wells and left totally untouched. No one would plunder them. Such a situation is unthinkable today. To the Celts, one of the greatest penalties which could be inflicted on a wrong-doer was to be barred from making sacrifice. Social ostracization was the result. Julius Caesar wrote that a tribe or individuals placed under such a ban were treated as impious wretches to be avoided at all costs. They had no legal rights and could hold no official position. They were believed to be unlucky and contact with them would bring misfortune.

Another social sanction was the loss of reputation, which acted as a powerful disincentive against dishonourable acts. To the warriors of Celtic and Germanic Europe, their honour amongst men was essential both for themselves in their own lifetimes, but also for their families after their death.

> Cattle die, kinsmen die;
> you yourself will die;
> but honour never dies,
> for one who has earned a good name.[6]

The tongues of the bards of Celtic society and their equivalent Nordic skalds could destroy someone's reputation and were therefore greatly feared. Mean or discreditable acts would be satirized and would echo the mead halls for generations to come.

In our enormous communities, where we no longer know our neighbours, such sanctions are irrelevant and Western society in recent years has emphasized an individualism which, taken to extremes, can do much harm. The delusion that we can stand alone without the support of others and harm them with impunity is alien to Pagan thought. It leaves us with a 'me first', grabbing and grasping society, in which the strong, under a delusion of separateness, tread down the weak. We are like waves on the ocean of being, the great sea of the collective unconscious of humanity. We see ourselves as separate and individual, but it is the sea which gives rise to us and gives us form. One wave alone disappears to be absorbed by the sand and dried by wind and sun. Together we are strong, powerful and eternal.

Bonds of friendship in Celtic, German and Norse society were extremely important and implied a definite commitment to help and defend one another. As well as reputation, it was important to have good friends on whom one could depend.

> The fir tree withers in the field,
> without shelter of bark or needles;
> such is the fate of a friendless man.
> Why should he live for long?
>
> The way is long to a faithless friend,
> though his house be by the road;
> but to a good friend there are many shortcuts
> though he live far from thee.[7]

Honour implies unselfishness and the protection by the strong of the weak. It also implies integrity. We can only have integrity if we practise truthfulness. In the tribal world, mutual help is based on friendship and friendship on trust. Trust also requires truthfulness.

> Friendship is firm when each can unburden
> his mind to the other;
> nothing is worse that a fickle mind;
> no friend is he who always flatters. [8]

In Celtic society, it was considered that if the King displayed truthfulness all would be well in the land. We are told of King Cormac mac Airt:

> It was well with Ireland in the time of that King:
> it was not possible to drink the waters of her rivers,
> on account of the spawn of her fish;
> it was not possible to travel her forests easily,
> on account of the amount of their fruit;
> it was not easy to travel her plains,
> on account of the amount of her honey;
> all of which had been granted him from Heaven,
> through the truth of his princedom. [9]

To lie, cheat and steal creates mistrust and deceit which destroy the fabric of society. The serpent is often thought of as the *Wizard of Lies* in mythology. In the Norse tradition, it is the serpent Nidhögg which gnaws at the roots of the Tree of Life undermining and destroying it. Deception also undermines our inner strength – our will. The American witch Starhawk describes the will as similar to what Victorian schoolmasters called character: honesty, self-discipline, commitment, and conviction.

> Those who would practice magic must be scrupulously
> honest in their personal lives. In one sense, magic works on
> the principle that 'It is so because I say it is so.' A bag of
> herbs acquires the power to heal because I say it does. . . .
> If I habitually lie to my lovers, steal from my boss, pilfer
> from supermarkets, or simple renege on my promises, I
> cannot have that conviction. [10]

In Celtic society also, one's word was very important. In *The Elements of the Celtic Tradition*, Caitlín Matthews quotes a famous Gaulish oath:

If I break faith with you.
may the skies fall upon me,
may the seas drown me,
may the Earth rise up and swallow me. [11]

Oath-giving is a serious matter because at stake is our integrity –
that which makes us whole and what we are. In the *Colloquy of
the Ancients*, Caoilte mac Ronan is asked by St Patrick what
qualities are most valued by the Pagan Irish. St Patrick is told that
it is truth in their hearts, strength in their arms and fulfilment
in their tongues. These ideals still hold good today. It is a pity
that more of our leaders do not practise them.

Society and Sexuality

Many religions have complex sexual taboos. This is not true of
Paganism, where on a social level, sexual morality is usually very
simple. In the Pagan view, the body has urges to fulfil its physical
functions – to eat, to sleep, to relieve itself of waste, to mate.
These things are not considered either good or evil in themselves.
They are natural functions necessary to maintain our bodies and
our species. In earlier more animalistic generations, all these
urges were fulfilled unselfconsciously in the simplest and easiest
way. We ate what was available – hence human beings are
naturally omnivores – and had sex with the nearest available
member of the opposite sex. As our thinking function developed,
we became more discriminating. We learned to appreciate that
some foods are tastier than others; we learned to cook; we
developed the art of feasting. In some cases, we developed moral
codes about our food, which included feeding ourselves in ways
which cause least harm to others – hence vegetarianism. Eating
became an aesthetic experience, a social ritual, and possibly a
matter of moral choice. Sexuality also became more complex. It
developed into an aesthetic and emotional experience. We
learned to discriminate between partners and found that we
preferred some to others. We discovered that sex could lead to
love and to deep emotional bonding.

Religion and spirituality are often confused with sexual
morality. Laws about sexual conduct are not Divinely ordained,
but are the creations of society. Early societies which lived close
to nature had very little regulation of sexuality. The main
necessity was to ensure that as many women as possible became

pregnant. This could best be served by women lying with a number of men in order to optimize their chances. Religious rites often encouraged this. In isolated societies in particular, there might be laws which discouraged in-breeding, e.g. not marrying one's own kin or clan. There might also be customs which encouraged out-breeding and maximized the gene pool, e.g. the custom of women sleeping with male travellers.

As societies become more complex, laws are enacted to regulate sexuality and to limit access to sexual partners. Often these laws are designed to protect property and to ensure that inheritance is passed on to a man's own sons rather than those of someone else. In the West, sexuality has been dominated in recent centuries by the Judaeo-Christian sexual ethos. This endorses monogamy, abstinence from sex except within marriage, and difficult divorce laws which, in the past, could only be negotiated by the rich and politically favoured. Christianity also had a very negative attitude to the human body. With the absorption of the idea that matter was evil, the body too was regarded as evil and all forms of sexuality other than for procreation purposes frowned upon. The celibate life was considered the highest good. Admirable though this ethic would have been for conserving the planet by keeping down the human population, unfortunately it was coupled in many sects with strictures against contraception for the sexually active.

To modern Pagans, there are few taboos about sexuality as such. Sexuality is considered something which can be practised between consenting adults, providing it does not cause harm to the self or others. This means that it would be wrong to have sex with someone else while one had contracted – legally or not – to be in a monogamous relationship with someone else. This would be an act of dishonesty, which would be damaging to all concerned. If we are unable to keep our promises, we must say so and break the contract. To Pagans, sexuality is a positive force. It is the force of creation which brings all things into being. For unattached adults, there are no barriers to sexual activity with other unattached adults; but we are expected to have regard to the consequences of our actions and to ensure that we do not cause unwanted pregnancy, spread sexual disease, or mislead others as to our level of commitment to the relationship. Sexuality outside of a committed relationship is acceptable providing it follows the ethic of 'An it harm none'. Sexual relationships which hurt, coerce or damage others are entirely unacceptable to

Pagans. Thus, sexuality between adults and children, or forced sex between adults without both parties' consent, is anathema. In most Pagan traditions, there is no barrier to homosexuality. Specific groups within the different traditions may have different views. Some groups in the Norse-German tradition frown upon sexual relationships between people of the same sex. Paths such as Wicca, which emphasize the polarity between Goddess and God, priest and priestess, may be unattractive to some whose orientation is not heterosexual; but there are people of all sexual orientations within Wiccan groups.

An it Harm None

One of the three Principles of Paganism which many Pagans follow is 'An it harm none, do what you will'. This ethic is a simple one and many would argue that it cannot apply in all circumstances. 'What about Hitler?' people ask. 'Surely assassinating him would have harmed him, but saved many millions of others.' No formula, whether complex or simple, can cover all situations. The more we try to create codes which will cover all eventualities, the more mechanical and unrealistic our ideas of morality become. Simple precepts provide a moral guide to which we can turn and then make the best judgements we can. The emphasis in modern Paganism is not on obeying complex sets of laws, which we must then feel guilty about breaking, but on teaching ourselves to be in tune with the Divine centre of all things, and so to make moral judgements on the basis of what is eternal and abides. The sense of what is right, true and abiding is conveyed less through direct intellectual teaching, than through symbols and myths which appeal to the unconscious. These create in the personality a solid and enduring basis of character, a centre from which to discriminate between right and wrong.

Much of Pagan ethics is about harmony and balance. This is not a striving for an impossible perfection which causes only guilt and despair when we inevitably fail, but a kinder and gentler ethic: a desire to live in a way which does not harm those around us – human beings or others whose environments we impact upon – the animal, plant and mineral life of the Great Mother's kingdom. Many Pagans have developed the concept of 'An it harm none' to take account of the greater good. In each action which we perform, there will be both a positive and a negative reaction; something will benefit and something will lose. With each breath we take, our lives are enhanced, but billions of microbes die. In order to live our lives without becoming totally neurotic, we have to accept that our very existence is a threat to the planet and to endeavour to live our lives in the way which causes least damage.

The Warrior Way

To many 'An it harm none' precludes all forms of violence, but the warrior way was integral to Celtic, Norse and German societies; just as it was to Pagan Native American and African societies. The Norse-German Aesir Gods, for instance, were Gods of an adventurous people who journeyed forth to conquer and to find new territory and wealth for themselves and their people. The words 'for their people' are important because the way of a true warrior is not the way of a thug. The true warrior serves his people by giving them his strength and his sword. His is the way of honour, which in Medieval times was translated into the concept of chivalry – the way of Arthur and his knights, fighting for a just cause.

If a warrior truly serves his people, then he enters into an initiatory path which leads to the sacrifice of all personal desires in order to serve the greater good. Valhalla, Odin's feasting hall, is the home of dead warriors; but Valhalla can also symbolize an initiatory process – the death in life. In order to enter Valhalla, the warrior must pass through a number of barriers. First there is a moat, where a werewolf fishes for men. Then there is a gate which is secured by magic. A wolf guards the door surmounted by an eagle which drips blood. Elsa-Brita Titchenell explains that each barrier is symbolic of a weakness which must be overcome.

> The warrior who would cross the River of Time (Tund) and
> the River of Doubt (Ifing) must maintain unwavering
> purpose and self-direction if he is not to be swept away by
> the turbulent current of temporal existence. He must evade
> the bestial cravings of his animal nature (the lures of
> Tjodvitner) if he is to gain the other shore. . . . Next the
> candidate for Valhalla must overcome the hounds Gere
> (Greed) and Freke (Gluttony): he must avoid desire, even
> the desire for the wisdom he is seeking, if he is to obtain it.
> To find the secret of the magic gate, he must have strength

of aspiration, purity of motive, and inflexible resolve. The
wolf and the eagle must be vanquished and transfixed over
the entrance to the hall to guard against their intrusion.
This means conquering the bestial nature (the wolf), and
pride (the eagle) – self-seeking in any guise which, like
Proteus of the Greeks, arises in ever new forms to challenge
those who approach the realms of the gods. [12]

For very valid reasons, the way of the warrior became very
unpopular in the West in the last half of the twentieth century.
Millions of young men inspired by the idea of fighting for right,
kin and country, offered their courage and their lives to this
century's supposedly just causes only to find that they were
betrayed. The cause they had thought right, they found full of
wrongness. The causes they thought just were engaged in by
cynical governments to gain economic supremacy. The way of the
warrior was betrayed.

In discovering this betrayal, our young men were not discovering anything new. Throughout the aeons, the causes for
which we have fought so often have been morally dubious. The
Viking hero who braved the seas in order to win wealth and prove
his manhood was, to those on the wrong end of his sword,
nothing more than a murderer and a ravenous wolf, destroying
other societies and taking others' lives for his greed. There can
be a warrior way which is a way of rightness, but the moral
complexities of deciding when, if ever, it is right to destroy life
have led many to reject it. Rather than lift the sword wrongly,
they choose not to lift it at all. Paradoxically, to refuse to kill may
require exactly those same qualities which are required of a good
warrior: steadfastness, cleaving to a high ideal, courage and great
moral certainty. The pacifists of our two World Wars required as
much moral courage as those who fought.

In rejecting the sword, if we do, it is important, however, not
to reject the qualities which it represents. It is a biological reality
of our species, and especially that part of it which is male, that
we need to strive and to fight. The football hooliganism which
has plagued the last two or three decades is nothing more than
the desire of young men to do as they have always done – to band
together under a common flag and cause and to prove themselves
and their manhood by fighting with other young men. In
societies which needed warriors to protect them, these young
men had a valued role. In societies which are striving for peace,

not war, then they are a liability. Freya Aswynn writes:

> In modern society aggression is seen as a solely negative
> force. People are encouraged to be docile and the weak rule
> the strong by denying them the right to be strong. However,
> aggression can also be seen as a creative force, a force that
> breaks down outworn forms [Geburah] and builds new
> ones. Aggression expresses itself in the survival instinct, the
> unconscious force which urges one to struggle and to
> survive against all odds. Correct application of this force, i.e.
> when controlled by personal discipline, makes us both
> resourceful and persistent. [13]

The way of the warrior is a way of struggle and conflict. It is to
meet the world head on and grapple with it for loss or for victory.
To many of us, who avoid confrontation, who live our safe lives
in our safe jobs, such a way is unimaginable. It is the way of the
adventurer, the seafarer and voyager, who journeys out boldly to
tread where no one has trod before.

Many branches of modern Paganism encourage those virtues
which are valued in pioneering societies – courage, truth,
honour, fidelity, discipline, hospitality, industriousness, self-
reliance and perseverance. These qualities are valuable not to
make war against other tribes, but to channel them into causes
which are positive for society – to fight against injustice, the
oppression of the weak, and the destruction of our planet by
those forces portrayed as the snares on the way to Valhalla – the
hounds of Greed and Gluttony which impel Western civilization
to immerse itself in materialism and sow the seeds of its own
destruction.

Love and Kinship for Nature

The Pagan ethos encourages us to live in harmony with our
environment. One of the Three Principles of the Pagan
Federation is:

> Love and kinship with Nature: rather than the more
> customary attitude of aggression and domination over
> Nature . . . [14]

Western civilization has lost sight of the need to live in harmony
with the planet, a need which was obvious to societies
supposedly much less sophisticated than ours. Living in

harmony with Nature means finding a balance between our needs and those of the animal and plant kingdoms. Conservation of our plant environment is very important to Pagans. Many Pagans practise the old witch idea of explaining to any plant we pluck or tree we fell why we are taking its life. Holding conversation with plants and trees may seem odd to some; hence some of the ribald press coverage when Britain's Prince of Wales admitted doing so. Regardless of our beliefs about plant life, the idea of stopping to think about what we are doing to the plant and tree life we use makes much sense. A related tradition is that of offering a gift in return for what we take. If we take fruit from a tree, we should offer something in return. If we cut down a tree, we should plant one or two more. We are much less likely to destroy wantonly if we stop to consider why we need to take something and what we are going to give in return.

Many interpret 'An it harm none' to mean that meat-eating and the killing which it entails should be avoided. In becoming vegetarians, they are following in the footsteps of many of their more sophisticated Pagan ancestors. The priests and priestesses of the Goddess Isis were permitted to eat eggs and lentils but not fish or meat. The Neoplatonists, with their concept of all Gods and Goddesses being manifestations of the One transcendent Divinity, were also vegetarians. To many of today's Pagans, the Pagan ethic is not compatible with taking life unnecessarily. To kill animals for meat represents such an unnecessary taking of life. Coming from the other direction, many vegetarians see Paganism as their natural spiritual path.

Other Pagans would argue strongly against this. For many people, the return to the religion of their ancestors means a return to a more natural way of life. These Pagans would argue that human beings are hunters, natural omnivores, eating both fruit and flesh, fish and fowl. Many country-living Pagans raise their own animals for food and believe that to give an animal a good natural life and then to kill it cleanly and painlessly is entirely acceptable. They would argue further that it makes no sense to eat plants and not to eat animals. Killing a plant deprives it of life in just the same way as killing an animal. Others, while not complete vegetarians believe that we should eat down the protein chain, consuming those things which will experience least harm and suffering.

Whatever Pagans decide about meat-eating, there is a general agreement that certain aspects of meat production are not compatible with 'An it harm none'. Many meat-eating Pagans endeavour to avoid factory-farmed meat and eggs. Others believe that excessive meat consumption by Westerners encourages environmentally-damaging intensive farming methods and has a bad effect on Third World countries by forcing them to grow foodstuffs for Western livestock rather than for themselves. In this way, Western greed distorts the world economy to the detriment of the economically less powerful. Pagans believe that we should take from the Earth only what we need. In Lynn Andrews' book *Medicine Woman*, her Native American teacher Agnes explains to her the attitude of a true hunter.

> The path of the hunter is sacred. Never thoughtlessly kill anything – not even a bug. Imagine if something huge were to flatten *you* thoughtlessly. . . . I want to spend my days as a warrioress and recognize the beauty in all things. An animal is a child of the universe, like you and me. Taking the life of a wild and free animal should be done with the understanding of your own death. Otherwise leave it be. [15]

The respect for Nature which is evident in the Native American path is similar to that of European Paganism. Baltic Paganism, for instance, teaches the sacredness of nature, respect for ancestors, and promotes the search for harmony. Harmony is an important concept in Paganism. Harmony in Lithuania is Darna. The aim of existence is to seek Darna within ourselves, within the home and within the community. The essence of Darna is preserved in this old Lithuanian prayer.

> That I may love and respect my mother, my father and old
> people;
> that I may protect their graves from rending and
> destruction;
> that, for their rest,
> I may plant in cemeteries
> oaks, junipers, wormwoods and silverweed.
> Those who do not love and respect their bearers
> will find hardship in their old age,
> or will not grow old at all.
>
> That my hands may never become stained by human blood.
> That the blood of animals, fish or birds
> may not taint my hands,

by my killing them satiated and not hungry.
Those who today kill animals with delight
will tomorrow drink of human blood.
The more hunters live in Lithuania,
the further fortune and a happy life escape us.

That I may love and respect bread.
If a crumb should accidentally fall,
I will lift it, kiss it and apologise.
If we all respect bread,
there will be no starvation or hardship.

That I may never hurt anyone;
that I may always give the correct change;
that I may not mistakenly steal even the smallest coin.
The Gods always punish offences.

That I may not denigrate foreign beliefs
and may not poke fun at my own faith.

That I may not fell a single tree without holy need;
that I may not step on a blooming field;
that I may always plant trees.
The Gods look with grace
upon those who plant trees along roads,
in homesteads, at holy places,
at cross roads, and by houses.
If you wed, plant a wedding tree.
If a child is born, plant a tree.
If someone beloved dies,
plant a tree for their soul.
At all festivals,
during all important events,
visit trees.
Prayers will attain holiness through trees of thanks.
So may it be! [16]

Similar concepts are found in traditional English witch lore which
teaches:

May we be no man's enemy,
and may we be the friend of that which is eternal and
abides.

May we never devise evil against any man,
and if any devise evil against us,
may we escape unharmed
and without the need of hurting them.
May we never quarrel with those nearest to us,
and if we do, may we be reconciled quickly.
May we love, seek and attain only those things good and
   true
which are the gifts of the Ancient Ones:
love, freedom, happiness and peace.[17]

Harmony is important to all societies, but especially to agricultural peoples. Harmony is much more of a preoccupation of peoples who live in settled land conditions than in hunter-gather or nomadic herding societies. When communities engage in agriculture, the cooperation of a large number of people is essential if the community is to survive. War is counter-productive because it disrupts the cycle of ploughing, planting and harvesting, which if not done at their correct time will mean that the community will starve. The disastrous effect of war on agriculture is readily observable in many famine-ridden parts of the world today.

The Way of Balance

The way of life which causes least harm to others is often the way of balance. This ideal can be found in Celtic ethics where it is seen as the fitness of things. This sense of fitness is found in the teachings of Cormac son of Airt. Cormac was a King of Ireland in about the third century CE. He was a foster-son of King Lugaid mac Con and from an early age displayed such great wisdom that he was considered to be a receptacle of truth. In the *Tecosca an Righ* or *Instructions of King Cormac mac Airt*,[18] he describes to his grandson Cairbre how he behaved as a young prince.

I was a listener in the woods,
I was a gazer at the stars,
I was blind where secrets were concerned,
I was silent in a wilderness,
I was talkative among many,
I was mild in the mead-hall,
I was stern in battle,

I was ready to watch,
I was gentle in friendship,
I was a physician to the sick,
I was weak towards the powerless,
I was strong towards the powerful,
I was never hard, lest I be satirised,
I was not feeble, lest I have my hair stripped off,
I was not close, lest I should be burdensome,
I was not arrogant, though I was wise,
I was not given to promising, though I was strong,
I was not venturesome, though I was swift,
I did not deride the old, though I was young,
I was not boastful, though I was a good fighter,
I would not speak about anyone in his absence,
I would not reproach, but I would praise,
I would not ask, but I would give;
for it is through those habits
that the young become old and kingly warriors.[19]

Cairbre then goes on to ask Cormac what is good for him. 'Not hard to tell,' said Cormac. 'If you listen to my teaching.'

Do not deride any old person, though you are young;
nor a poor man, though you are rich;
nor a naked one, though you are well-clad;
nor a lame one, though you are swift;
nor a blind one, though you are keen-sighted;
nor an invalid, though you are strong;
nor a dull one, though you are clever;
nor a fool, though you are wise.[20]

In another passage, Cormac tells Cairbre how he can best maintain his own self-respect.

If you be too wise, they will expect too much of you;
if you be too foolish, you will be deceived;
if you be too conceited, you will be thought vexatious;
if you be too humble, you will be without honour;
if you be too talkative, you will not be heeded;
if you be too silent, you will not be regarded;
if you be too harsh, you will be broken;
if you be too feeble, you will be crushed.[21]

The aim is to be none of these things, i.e. to avoid extremes. King

Cormac's instructions represent a model of balanced behaviour and right conduct. The ideals he expresses are akin to those conveyed in the Great Mother Charge in Wicca.

> . . . let there be beauty and strength, power and compassion, honour and humility, mirth and reverence within you. [22]

This is the balance which Paganism teaches.

1. The *Eddas*, the *Hávamál*, or *High One's Words*, see Elsa-Brita Titchenell, *The Masks of Odin: Wisdom of the Ancient Norse*, pages 110–30, W.H. Auden and Paul B. Taylor, *Norse Poems*, pages 147–67, and Lee M. Hollander, *The Poetic Edda*, pages 14–41.
2. *Hávamál*, verse 71.
3. *Hávamál*, verse 78.
4. Tadhg MacCrossan, *The Sacred Cauldron: Secrets of the Druids*, page 54.
5. Freya Aswynn, *The Leaves of Yggdrasil: A Synthesis of Magic, Feminine Mysteries, Folklore*, page 31.
6. *Hávamál*, verse 76.
7. *Hávamál*, verses 50 and 36.
8. *Hávamál*, verse 123.
9. Quoted in Anne Ross, *Everyday Life of the Pagan Celts*, page 150.
10. Starhawk, *The Spiral Dance*, page 111.
11. Caitlín Matthews, *The Elements of the Celtic Tradition*, page 13.
12. Elsa-Brita Titchenell, *The Masks of Odin: Wisdom of the Ancient Norse*, pages 75–6.
13. Freya Aswynn, *The Leaves of Yggdrasil: A Synthesis of Magic, Feminine Mysteries, Folklore*, page 12.
14. The Pagan Federation, *Pagan Federation Information Pack*, page 4.
15. Lynn V. Andrews, *Medicine Woman*, pages 129–31.
16. Old Lithuanian prayer based on the translation of Jonas Trikunas in *Romuva USA* 8.
17. Unpublished material from witchcraft sources.
18. Kuno Meyer (trans.) *The Instructions of King Cormac mac Airt* page 17.
19. Kuno Meyer (trans.) *The Instructions of King Cormac mac Airt* page 17.
20. Kuno Meyer (trans.) *The Instructions of King Cormac mac Airt* page 21.
21. Kuno Meyer (trans.) *The Instructions of King Cormac mac Airt* page 45.
22. From the Wiccan *Book of Shadows* as quoted in Vivianne Crowley, *Wicca: The Old Religion in the New Age*, page 161.

10
Stepping Into the Dark

Good and Evil

Many Pagans believe in a universe in which order and chaos are in a perpetual struggle. These two forces are not the good and evil of Christian and other Middle and Near Eastern dualisms, but anabolism and catabolism, creation and destruction. Both are necessary for the existence of the universe. To Pagans, evil is human-made and is the result of ignorance and a lack of understanding of the true nature of reality. The universe is neutral and has its own purposes, which may or may not be perceived as good in human terms.

Pagans often speak of the Goddess as the transcendent power which moves the universe. Often the Gods are not seen as personal deities possessed of the human moral values, but as great natural tides, which are beyond the concept of good and evil in the sense understood by human beings. In *The Dark is Rising*, Susan Cooper describes how a young girl perceives the power of the Goddess in the making of the Greenwitch, a nature Goddess figure, by the women of a Cornish village.

When she turned back again towards the sea, the Greenwitch was finished. The women had drawn away from the great figure; they sat by the fire, eating sandwiches, and laughing, and drinking tea. As Jane looked at the huge image that they had made, out of leaves and branches, she could not understand their lightness. For she knew suddenly, out there in the cold dawn, that this silent image somehow held within it more power than she had ever sensed before in any creature or thing. Thunder and storms

and earthquakes were there, and all the force of the earth
and sea. It was outside Time, boundless, ageless, beyond
any line drawn between good and evil.[1]

Human beings take the androcentric and egocentric view that
those things which benefit us are good and that which opposes
us is evil; but on a cosmic scale good and evil are seen very
differently. The Gods represent forces which are neither light nor
dark. They are the power of the natural world, the force of life
itself, which seeks ever to renew itself and to express itself.

This where we live is a world of men, ordinary men, and
although in it there is the Old Magic of the earth, and the
Wild Magic of living things, it is men who control what the
world shall be like. . . . But beyond the world is the
universe, bound by the law of the High Magic, as every
universe must be. And beneath the High Magic are two . . .
poles . . . that we call the Dark and the Light. No other
power orders them. They merely exist.[2]

This does not mean that the Gods will allow evil to grow
unchecked. Our Gods lean towards equilibrium, to a balancing
of the forces of order and chaos. There is a struggle between the
two inherent tendencies of the life force – existence and non-
existence, creation and destruction – and it is a struggle which
may have an ultimate resolution; but this will be within a time-
frame way beyond the comprehension of human beings, who as
a race are but a blip in the on-going history of the universe. Nor
is that resolution perceived as an ultimate triumph of good over
evil, but rather a stilling and a calm, the ultimate dissolution into
non-being which is beyond both these poles of activity. The
nature of good and evil as envisaged by Pagans is conveyed in
The Dark is Rising by a Merlin figure.

. . . you have heard me talk of Logres. It was the old name
for this country, thousands of years ago; in the old days
when the struggle between good and evil was more bitter
and open than it is now. That struggle goes on all round us
all the time, like two armies fighting. And sometimes one of
them seems to be winning and sometimes the other, but
neither of them has ever triumphed altogether. Nor ever
will, . . . for there is something of each in every man.[3]

Most Pagans do not see their Gods as good guys opposed by the universe's baddies. The Divine emerges into action out of eternal tranquillity and contemplation and returns to stillness once more when each phase of creation is done. There is good and evil, but it lies within humanity, not the cosmos. This standpoint is found in many traditions. In some Judaic traditions, the fallen angel Lucifer opposes Jehovah because he believes that an animal such as man is not wise enough to be given free will and to exercise independent judgement. Man will defy the Gods and unleash evil in the world. This idea is also found in the Greek myth of Pandora's box. All the troubles of the world are kept securely in a chest and Pandora is instructed never to open it. However, her human curiosity and intelligence, which are both humanity's blessing and its curse, prompt her to open the forbidden box and evil is unleashed into the world. Evil arises when there is the possibility of choice and action. Human beings have the option of performing acts which serve the greater good or acts which promote misery and destruction. These choices, which face us daily, are subject to our conflicting emotions – love, hate, pity, cruelty, greed, selfishness and altruism – all the realities of the human heart.

Fate and Free Will

Ethical choice implies free will; for how can we choose between right and wrong unless we are free to make that choice? Pagans believe in free will, but we also believe that our lives are influenced by fate, wyrd or destiny – hence the popularity of divination as a way of seeing into the pattern of fate. How can these things be reconciled?

Different branches of Paganism have varying ideas on the amenability of fate to change. Some would take the more fatalistic Hindu approach:

> . . . that we all are guided by fate, the Unknown. It takes us
> through the tortuous journey of our life to our
> Individuation – to Wholeness. We may refuse this guidance
> at our own cost. Truly, we cannot even refuse it for long. It
> is more powerful than our will. [4]

True to their Western outlook, those following the European Pagan tradition tend to be less deterministic than their brothers and sisters in the East. Most Western Pagans believe that we are not bound by fate, though guided by it, and that we have free will and moral choice. The Norse-German tradition teaches that the Web of Wyrd creates situations and demands which we must meet – this is our destiny or wyrd – but the way in which we meet our destiny depends on us. We can choose the way of honour and right, or we can choose the way of dishonour and wrong. We can choose the way which benefits others, or that which harms and injures them. Having seen into the pattern of the Web of Wyrd, the possibilities are to succumb, to fight or to change our destiny.

Pagans have no notions which match those of the Christian original sin. To Pagans, the child is born neither good nor evil. Its destiny is a blank sheet on which the world and the child itself will write. Our circumstances and upbringing may influence us for good or ill in these choices, but in the end the responsibility for the decisions we make and the consequences of our actions are ours. In some traditions, but not all, the concept of reincarnation may mean that the child already has a legacy from its past actions, both good and bad, which will help determine its future. This Karma is the accumulated consequences of our own past actions. We will not be punished for them, but we will continue to be confronted by them until we learn more adaptive ways of behaving.

The concepts of original sin and reincarnationary karma are ways in which human beings have attempted to make sense of the fact that life is not fair: that bad things do happen to good people. Most Western Pagans do not attempt to reconcile themselves to this problem by demanding some philosophical construct which will make sense of the unfairness and illustrate that 'it's all right really': people do deserve what they get and get what they deserve. The Pagan view is that the universe is much more arbitrary than that. The Gods are not concerned about seeing that we individually are seen right. They have better things to do. Human beings are not the centre of the universe. We are but small cogs in its machinery. The universe is not run for our benefit to ensure that we make a profit on our karmic balance sheet. Bad things do happen to good people and we have to put up with them, make the best of them, learn as best we can from our experience and mistakes, and triumph over them.

Guilt and Sin

For Pagans evil exists, not in the form of some external tempter or demon, but in the form of actions of human beings. The Divine itself is neither good nor evil. In the words of Mahatma Gandhi:

> The only devils in the world are those running around in
> our hearts. That is where the battle should be fought.

Sometimes we successfully fight this battle and sometimes we do
not. When we fail, the knowledge of our own wrong-doing
creates guilt and a feeling of sinfulness. Paradoxically, we may
become most aware of our deficiencies if we decide to try to
follow a spiritual path and to live our lives in a better way. The
nearer we draw to our Gods and the source of all being, the more
aware we become of ourselves. Often in Paganism it is taught that
one of the purposes of life is to 'Know thyself' – to learn to see
ourselves as we truly are. This involves a spiritual quest and, if
we go on a spiritual quest, we cannot expect the way to be easy.
The hero in fairy tales must face monsters and dangers before he
achieves his destiny. If we set out on a path seeking spiritual
knowledge, the Gods will grant us what we seek; but the initial
results may not be entirely welcome. Enlightenment brings clear-
seeing and revelation. In the clear light of the Gods we perceive
our own deficiencies and have insight into our own failings. This
often produces feelings of guilt, inferiority and worthlessness.
From the perspective of the Northern Tradition, Freya Aswynn
writes:

> Anyone who evolves along a spiritual path, whatever that
> path may be, will develop a set of personal ethical values by
> which he or she chooses to live. However, human nature
> being what it is, we do not always live up to our self-
> imposed standards and consequently experience a sense of
> failure. This sense of failure smashes a dent in our self-
> esteem and restricts us in our creativity. All this is
> necessary, however, and is unavoidable if we are to learn
> from our mistakes. . . . Nidhögg gnaws at the roots of
> Yggdrasil in an attempt to destroy the Tree. We can interpret
> this myth psychologically. Nidhögg can be viewed as the
> shadow in the unconscious, gnawing at or undermining the
> sense of Self symbolised by Yggdrasil. [5]

Many religions deliberately capitalize on and even encourage
feelings of guilt and inferiority in their followers. Paganism
teaches that each individual is worthy and holy; that his or her
individuality is to be respected; and that each of us is needed in
the world and has a role to play. Marian Green writes:

You are unique, your life is valuable, and you can learn to shape Creation to bring health, to bring joy and to bring fulfilment, if you follow the path of your spirit, as it wanders through the tangle of life's lessons. Within you are the seeds of greatness, and only you can release them, nurture them that they may flower and fruit for the benefit of the whole universe.[6]

Guilt is an extremely negative emotion which creates anxiety and doubt, as well as feelings of inferiority. Doubt and anxiety make us believe that our wishes and hopes are without value and inhibit us from living at our full capacity and achieving the maximum we can within the range of our abilities. The paralysing effect of doubt is conveyed by the *Eddas*.

Doubt is the river that flows between
the ground of the Gods and the giants;
it shall flow free and open forever;
no ice may form on *Ifing*.[7]

In order to make our spiritual quest, we must overcome these barriers. Doubt and anxiety sap our courage and our will and are purposeless emotions. The *Hávamál* or *High One's Words* of the *Eddas* contains some very homely advice.

A fool lies awake at nights
worrying of this and that;
weary is he when morning breaks,
and all is still as before.[8]

Different religious paths have evolved different ways of dealing with guilt. Catholic Christianity has the confessional. The believer is taught that the priest has the power to forgive his sins and can lift the burden of guilt from his shoulders. Some branches of Protestantism teach that, providing one believes in the right version of God (i.e. their version), one is saved. It doesn't matter what one does or how repulsive one's conduct, one has an assured seat in heaven. These attitudes do not accord with Pagan belief which is that we are each responsible for our own actions. Buddhist belief is more similar to the Pagan. This, like Paganism, teaches that our spiritual state should be one of joy. Breast-beating when we have done something wrong and lapsing into guilt and shame will not help matters. When things go wrong we have to live with it and we also have to live with the knowledge of our own wrong-doing. We cannot be forgiven or saved by anyone else. We are responsible for our own actions. Marian Green writes:

> . . . you only need to admit your failure to yourself, and to the immortal Gods, not to receive absolution, but to be given guidance as to how to put right what you made wrong. You must examine every action you make, admit your faults at least to yourself, and deal with them. You must cope with personal guilt feelings, not by getting someone else to bless them away, but by actually striving to repair what was harmed. [9]

Pagans believe in the concept of balance. If we have committed wrong actions, we must seek out opportunities to redress the balance and to give something back in return for what we have taken. Once we have admitted our mistakes to ourselves and done whatever is possible to put them right, we must put them behind us and begin again. Ritual can be helpful here, for it is a way of marking a transition between one state and another. We can create our sacred space, perform actions of cleansing and purification and then emerge again to start life anew.

Below is an adaptation of a ceremony for dealing with guilt and regrets by Starhawk which she calls the *Indrinking Spell*. [10] Here the ceremony is addressed to the Mother Goddess but it could also be addressed to the God. We can perform the ceremony by creating sacred space in whatever way is familiar to us. The Gods can also be invoked in the customary manner. We sit facing north, the point of the Sun's nadir, and light a candle. There should be a large bowl of earth at the centre of our sacred space or on the altar, together with a cup of water and some wine, beer, mead or milk. We take the cup filled with clear water. Then we are told:

> Visualize all the negative things that you are feeling about yourself, the mistakes you have made, the things you have done wrong. Talk to yourself and admit you feel bad. Tell yourself, out loud, exactly what you have done wrong, and why. Let your emotion build energy, and project it all into the cup. Breathe on the water.

We next visualize the Goddess as a forgiving Mother and imagine her hands covering ours. She is saying:

> I am the Mother of all things,

My love is poured out upon the Earth.
I drink you in with perfect love,
Be cleansed. Be healed.
Be whole. Be changed.

We pour the water into the bowl of earth and fill the cup with
the wine, beer, mead or milk and visualize ourselves as we would
like to be – free of guilt and sorrow, changed so that we will not
repeat the same errors. We charge the cup with strength and the
power to be the person we want to be. We then visualize the
Goddess once more, her hands covering ours, and she says:

Mine the Cup and Mine the Wine of Life.
Drink deep!

We then drink the charged liquid and feel ourselves filled with
strength. We know that we have changed, that we are, from that
very moment, a new person, not bound by the patterns and
errors of the past. The ritual is then closed in accordance with
our tradition and the negatively-charged earth is scattered to the
four winds. The rite can be performed alone or in a group
situation if people wish.

Within us is our own darkness, that which Jung called the
Shadow. Within the greater mind of humanity is also a greater
darkness, the collective Shadow, the negativity of humankind.
One of the most important functions of our religious and spiritual
philosophies is to help us resolve this most formidable of
problems which has beset the human race since its rise into
consciousness. In order to come into the light we must pass
through the places of darkness; we must confront those aspects
of ourselves which lie deep and hidden and integrate them into
our lives in their true place where those very qualities which we
have sought to repress may become of value to us. We must
transmute anger into energy and complacency into true serenity
born of knowledge, not the complacency of ignorance. This is
essential not only for ourselves but also for society. If we succeed
we shall be as the Gods; if we fail we shall perish utterly, a
forgotten experiment in the laboratory of time.

We picked some flowers and they were fair,
but as we watched they withered there;
the petals fell from our trembling hands;
blood red stains on virgin sand.

We tried to fly but only fell,
down the dark to the Gates of Hell,
and the twinkling stars went twinkling on,
and did not notice we had gone. [11]

1. Susan Cooper, *The Dark is Rising Sequence*, page 383.
2. Susan Cooper, *The Dark is Rising Sequence*, page 599.
3. Susan Cooper, *The Dark is Rising Sequence*, page 59.
4. Arwind Vasavada in J.M. Spiegelman and A.U. Vasavada, *Hinduism and Jungian Psychology*, page 14.
5. Freya Aswynn, *The Leaves of Yggdrasil: A Synthesis of Magic, Feminine Mysteries, Folklore*, pages 44–5.
6. Marian Green, *The Path Through the Labyrinth*, page 4.
7. The *Vaftrudnismál*, verse 16.
8. *Hávamál*, verse 23.
9. Marian Green, *The Path Through the Labyrinth*, page 65.
10. Starhawk, *The Spiral Dance*, pages 116–7.
11. From *Illusions*, Vivianne Crowley, Autumn Equinox 1970.

Part Four
What Pagans Do

11
Worshipping the Gods

Why do we worship the Gods? Pagans do not worship because they have to. They are not bound to attend religious services because of social or family pressures. They are not afraid that if they do not give due reverence to their Gods, they will be punished and burn eternally in Hell. They worship their Gods because they love them. Pagans also worship their Gods because they enjoy it! We enjoy worshipping our Gods because in those moments we draw nearer the ineffable, the profound mystery of the universe, the life force which sustains us all. To draw nearer to this source is to come like a thirsty man to a pool of cool, clean water. We drink and every organ of our body absorbs the water and draws nourishment from it. So too does our spirit drink, when we return to the great pool of the infinite which is our source.

Pagans also worship the Gods because their views of life are very different from many of the values of Western society. Material well-being is not seen as the prime objective of life. The material world is important – we ignore it at our peril – but material things alone will not satisfy our deepest needs. For this, we must have spiritual sustenance and we must be linked with those forces who create and maintain the universe. If we lose this link we are orphans of the universe; separated forever from the Mother and Father of All.

The Role of Ritual

Many people, while believing that they are Pagans, baulk at the word ritual. They feel that ritual is an empty parade and show which is not for them. They may have been over-exposed to

empty religious rituals as children or have seen them only at a
distance on television programmes or at the occasional wedding.
Ritual is seen as something pompous, overwordy, boring and
authoritarian; a chance for a priest to talk down to a fidgeting
congregation. Pagan ritual is very different from this. It is not
something which is done to us, but something which we do.
Most Pagan ritual is highly participative.

> You become the priest, understand the Mystery and
> participate fully in the presence of the Gods and the
> communion between all levels of being.[1]

In earlier societies, ritual functioned to mark the transitions
between different life stages. Birth, sexual maturation, marriage,
giving birth, kingship, war and death were all marked by rites
which gave us patterns of behaviour with which to meet their
demands. Vestiges of such rites do remain in our largely secular
society, but for many people these rituals have become hollow
and meaningless. This is unfortunate because religious rituals are
important.

They show us the meaning of our lives and how we as
individuals fit into a greater whole. Ritual speaks through a
symbolic language which allows us to come to an understanding
of those processes of life and death which are our lot, and to
praise, honour, and thank our Gods, who nourish and care for
us. The ancient myths and rituals which are the cultural treasure
house of our ancestors contain truths about the development of
the human race. Many would say that they represent meta-
physical realities: that they are dramatic representations of the
interplay of the Gods, the Divine forces of the universe. However,
it is not necessary to believe this in order to find value in religious
ritual. The rites are not only a way of contacting the Divine
outside us, but also a way of understanding our inner psyche and
contacting the Divine within. If we neglect our myths and rituals,
we lose the sense of the endless cyclical process of the life force
which endures in the face of the changing seasons and the brief
shooting star of our individual lives.

Our ancestors believed that if the correct rites were not
performed at the correct times, then the Sun might fade and die,
that summer might not return to the land. Empirical observation
shows that this is not so; but if in espousing science we reject the
myths which have sustained the human race over the millennia,
then we miss the point entirely. Myth is not objectively true, but

that which is psychologically true. It is what Jung called 'the bridge to all that is best in humanity.'[2] Robert Bly, in his book *Iron John*, mourns the loss of humanity's myths. He believes that people in the West lost their ability to think mythologically around the year 1000.

> Perhaps because Christianity would not allow any new stories, or new gods, or perhaps because after the Renaissance the exciting pursuit of science absorbed more and more imaginative energy, the layer was never reconstituted. European men and women gradually stopped feeding the abundant gods and goddesses with their imaginative energy. The inner heaven collapsed and we see all around our feet its broken glass.[3]

Pagan Rites

Pagan rites bring to the minds of many people lurid pictures of naked orgies by bonfires. Fun though these activities might be, the reality is much more prosaic. Pagans may perform their rites in ordinary clothes, in special ritual dress, or, going back to nature, in nothing at all; but, whatever their garb, the purpose is the same – to worship the Gods of their ancestors and to revere the Divine force which gives birth to us, sustains us and will ultimately receive us when this phase of our existence on Earth is done.

Pagan celebrations may be based on ritual drawn from a particular tradition, or they may be spontaneous and eclectic rites created by the participants solely for that occasion. Whatever the differences in rituals between traditions, the emphasis in all Pagan traditions is on a cycle of activity – the wheel of the year and the wheel of death and rebirth – of which we are all a part. There are rituals to celebrate the important phases of the life cycle, the phases of the year and, in some traditions, the phases of the moon. Pagan ritual may be as simple as sitting together in silence beneath a tree and meditating for a while, or it may be as complicated as a Latin high mass. It may be similar to a tribal gathering with drums, fire and feasting; or it may be formal and ceremonial in white robes and with elaborate temple furnishings.

Celebrating at least some of the rites outside in Nature is considered important in Paganism. Some of our Pagan predecessors had beautiful temples which were the work of highly-cultured civilizations, but in many parts of the world, they had much simpler places of worship. In most of Western and North Europe, the idea of worshipping our Gods in temples built by human beings was an alien idea brought to us by the invading Romans. Their culture was essentially urban, even taking its name from a city. Modern Paganism does not reject cities, but we seek to worship, when we can, beneath trees, sky, sun, moon and stars, by the sound of rushing water, ever-flowing sea, wind and the cry of the birds. Being practical people, however, Pagans recognize that outdoor worship is not always possible. A visit to a sacred site at dawn is fine at weekends, but not in the middle of the working week. Some of us are fortunate enough to have secluded gardens, but others are not. A cliff top is a pleasant place on a summer's day, but not the most congenial of spiritual venues in a December rainstorm with two screaming toddlers. Some rites must take place indoors and those who have sufficient space will often set aside a room within their homes as a temple. Others use a living room or hired hall. Some Pagans decorate their rooms with beautiful altars, hangings and statues of the Gods. Others have plainer tastes. Outdoors, Pagans rely on the beauties of nature.

There are in effect temple Pagans and tribal Pagans. Some lean towards the beautiful edifices of the temples of Egypt, Greece and Rome; others to the simple forest and natural sites of the Celts, Germans and our early ancestors. Most appreciate both.

Since Pagans often do not have specially consecrated temples, the concept of creating sacred space is seen as important. This involves the marking off of ritual space in some way to indicate that, for the duration of the rite, this is holy ground. Pagans may emphasize that they are entering sacred space by removing shoes and watches – for the world of the sacred is outside the normal laws of time – or by wearing special robes or being skyclad – the term used by witches for ritual nudity.

Sacred space in Paganism is often thought of as a meeting point between the worlds. This is between the worlds of humans and Gods, and between the worlds of humans and other aspects of creation such as the devas. In many traditions the blessing of the devas on a rite is considered very important and where possible rites are held outside in natural surroundings which form the devas' habitat. Places where two or more elements are present in abundance are considered particularly powerful. Marian Green comments:

Anywhere where two elements meet: earth and air; water

and earth; air and water; or earth and fire – provides a
sacred interface. Most of these are obvious outdoor locations
like the edges of the sea and land, high in the hills, near
lakes or waterfalls, but the last is the domestic hearth, the
original centre of the homestead. Even today people still use
the mantelpiece as a kind of altar, placing on it favourite
ornaments, photographs of loved ones, and even candlesticks
ready for any power cut. It is important to acknowledge the
sanctity of a particular place and be able to recognise the
subtle atmosphere which differs from a similar unblessed
place, even if it is one corner of a bedsitter or the attic of a
mansion or an ancient church or Stone-Age ritual site.[4]

Wiccan and Goddess-oriented ritual frequently takes places in
circular sacred space. This is not necessarily a physical circle;
though some people have created stone circles in their gardens
for this purpose. The circle is made at the beginning of the ritual
by drawing it either in the air or on the ground with a ritual
sword, knife or staff. The circle will then be consecrated with the
four elements of the wise: Air, Fire, Water and Earth. The
Guardians of the Four Quarters are then called to protect the
circle for the duration of the rite.

The symbol of the circle guarded by the Guardians of the
Quarters is the circle-cross. This symbol appears frequently in
Celtic mythology. Some Celtic traditions create sacred space in
the shape of a circle surrounded by a square. The circle is sacred
to the Goddess and the earth forces and the square to the God
and the powers of the heavenly bodies. When the circle of the
mundane plane is surrounded by the square of heaven, then we
are entering the realm where Gods and humanity may meet. The
concept of squaring of the circle, found in many magical
traditions, is reminiscent of this Celtic cosmology.

The shape of the sacred space we create to commune with our
Gods is important. It is an indicator of the underlying cosmology
and religious beliefs which give rise to it. In Christianity, apart
from the innovations of that interesting group the Knights
Templar, who had round churches, church space is rectangular.
God sits at one end and humanity at the other, often separated
by a barrier or screen which only the chosen male – a priest –
may penetrate. In modern Goddess worship, with its circular
consecrated space, the worshipper is considered to re-enter the
womb of the Goddess. Asatru and more patriarchal Paganism

may favour the square or rectangle, but the concept of a central altar is retained.

Once sacred space has been created, Pagans will call on their Gods. Different conventions apply when invoking the Gods in different Pagan paths. In some traditions, the Gods are invoked into an individual who enters into a state of union with the Divine force and then speaks as the God or as the Goddess for the duration of the rite. In other traditions, the Gods are called upon through poetry, prayers and praise. They may then be considered to be present in the sacred space and/or within all the ritual participants. In some Pagan traditions, the names given to the Goddess and the God are not considered very important. In the Wiccan tradition, the priest invokes the Goddess as 'Astarte, Dione, Melusine, Aphrodite, Bride . . .'. These Goddesses from diverse Pagan pantheons are seen as aspects of the one Great Goddess. Invoking the force behind the different manifestations of the Divine masculine or feminine is acceptable; but invoking two or more deities from different pantheons may not be a very good idea. A friend who invoked Isis and Odin in the same ritual decided, as more and more things started to go wrong, that there was a problem: 'They just didn't get on!'.

At seasonal celebrations, the invocation of the Gods will be followed by an enactment or reading of the seasonal myth. This may be solemn or mirthful. The seasonal mystery will often be followed by the singing and chanting of songs to the Gods. In Wiccan groups, this may be preceded by spell-working, in which case dances and chants to raise energy and power may be used. A ceremonial partaking of cakes and wine, or cakes and mead or ale, is then usual. Libations may also be poured for the Gods. This is the only type of sacrifice which is usual in modern-day Paganism, although our ancestors would have sacrificed animals at their rites.

Ritual feasting, which was always a feature of tribal society, is important in Paganism. In Celtic and Germanic society, feasts were a means of showing hospitality, itself a sacred act, and feasts would be presided over by Druids and chieftains. Pagans believe that religion should be joyful and celebratory, not miserable and totally solemn; though solemnity has its proper place. Modern Pagan celebrations often end with a feast, the playing of music, drinking of beer, wine or mead. This is not in most cases considered an aftermath to the ritual, but an integral part of it. To feast with the Gods is a sacred act and after such feasts a portion of food and drink will be left out for the Gods. This is usually done by pouring a libation to the Earth and by leaving food for the birds and wild animals. The rite will end with a bidding farewell to any Guardians who have been summoned and a thanking of the Gods.

Seasonal Rites

Different Pagan traditions have special days on which they celebrate, but all the Pagan traditions celebrate a cycle of seasonal festivals. These celebrations come easily to us because their remnants are found everywhere in the folk traditions of Western culture. To recreate our rites, we draw on our own experiences and also on the wealth of mythology, folklore, fairy tale and village custom, which lingers in our heritage.

The seasonal cycle followed by most Western-European Pagans is derived principally from the festivals of Celtic and Norse-German mythology. The four Celtic festivals are Imbolc or Oi-melc, held on February 1, when the first flowers appear to herald the coming spring; Beltane or May Eve on 30 April, which marks the beginning of summer; Lughnasadh, which is also known by its Saxon name of Lammas or Loaf Mass on 1 August; and Samhain, Summer's End, or Hallowe'en, on 31 October. It should be emphasized, however, that these dates apply only to the northern hemisphere. In the southern hemisphere with its reversed patterns of seasons, these festivals are usually held at different times. Samhain takes place at the beginning of May, Imbolc at the beginning of August, Beltane at the beginning of November, and Lammas at the beginning of February.

The Celtic festivals marked important points in the agricultural calendar of Western Europe, such as ploughing, harvesting and the winter slaughter of animals. Originally, they would not have been held on fixed dates, but when the people had finished their seasonal tasks. As we moved into the world of calendars and the recording of time, the dates of these festivals gradually became fixed.

The other four major festivals in the Pagan year are the Spring and Autumn Equinoxes and the Summer and Winter Solstices. These were originally Norse-German festivals and they took place five or six weeks later than their Celtic counterparts. The sowing ritual, which takes place at the Spring Equinox in many Pagan celebrations, is held at Beltane in Norway. The dates reflect seasonal conditions farther north in Europe.

Some groups wish to remain exclusively Germanic or Celtic and prefer not to celebrate festivals with other origins; but many Pagans have combined the two sets of celebrations to produce a year wheel of eight festivals. This is not followed rigidly all over the world. The eight-festival year works well in relatively temperate climates which have four seasons – spring, summer, autumn and winter. In other parts of the world, the seasonal pattern may be very different and the seasonal rituals are adapted accordingly. In Icelandic Paganism, for instance, there appear to have been only three major festivals, which were called blots or sacrifices. These were Thorriblot at Winter Solstice; Siggiblot in Spring, which was held before the Icelanders went a-viking; and a Harvest festival, when any animals surplus to requirements were sacrificed. There are other differences in other parts of the world, and the exact nature of the festivals varies between traditions, but the following is a pattern which many Pagans would recognize.

The Wheel of the Year

Spring celebrates the coming together of the male and female, Goddess and God. It is a time of seed-sowing and fertility, when day and night, light and dark, are equal and there is a dynamic and creative tension between the polarities of opposites. Pagan Spring Equinox rites often celebrate the emergence of the young God in the world and his mating with the Goddess.

> Isis of Nature awaiteth the coming of Her Lord the Sun.
> She calls Him.
> She draws Him from the place of the dead,
> the Kingdom of Amenti, where all things are forgotten.
> And he comes to Her in his boat called Millions of Years,
> and the Earth grows green with the springing grain. [5]

A Druid Spring rite takes a more cerebral approach.

> Harken to me, all who know sorrow
> and would break from its bondage.
> There is in man a seed which grows
> and, in due season,
> transforms his Earth
> into a Heaven of glorious hues;
> wherein the power of gloom –

born of ignorance –
no longer can prevail.
The seed of love is nurtured in darkness,
when rain clouds burst it germinates
and blossoms into fulfilment of a life that is true –
in light that is health.
Prepare for the day
when that seed in you shall live and grow,
when the influence and the power of the All-Excelling
shall shine forth in your life.
When the time is ripe shall you be led to health –
through a life that is good –
with a faith that is sure –
in the Light-Everlasting. [6]

The fertility symbolism of Spring is found in the Easter eggs which are a custom in many parts of Europe around this time. These were originally the symbols of the German Goddess Ostara, who in Germanic-based languages gave her name to Easter.

Beltane or May Eve celebrates the coming of summer and the marriage of the Goddess and God. This is the point when the male takes on responsibility for the female. Beltane has always traditionally been a celebration of fertility. Nature is abundant. The seeds planted at spring have sprung, the trees are hung with blossom. Until recent centuries, Maypole dancing around a phallic pole was customary in many parts of Europe. May celebrations were suppressed by the Protestant reformers in Europe who were scandalized by the lustiness of some of the country folk's revels which involved the young people of the village going a-Maying before dawn in the woods in order to bring back blossoms to decorate the house – or so they said. Rudyard Kipling captured the spirit of Maying in his Tree Song.

O do not tell the priest of our Art,
for he would call it a sin;
but we shall be down in the woods tonight
a-conjuring Summer in.
And we bring you good news by word of mouth
for woman, cattle and corn;
for the Sun is coming up from the South,
with oak and ash and thorn. [7]

Midsummer is the celebration of the Sun, the Lord of Life. Across Northern Europe, and even in Celtic Ireland, bonfires were lit (and are still lit) on hilltops to celebrate the warmth of the Sun. For those who follow the seasonal cycle of the Horned God, it is at Midsummer that the God is at the height of his power. Born at the Winter Solstice, he comes to full maturity with the Sun's height; but in the cycles and spirals of Paganism, that which reaches its peak is already at the point of decline. From Midsummer, the days begin to grow shorter. All around us, it is still summer and the crops have not yet ripened. The summer has still to reach its fruition, but the signs of hidden decline are there. In some Pagan groups, a battle between Light and Darkness is enacted. This is a battle which the Light wins, but at the same time the Lord of Light receives a wound, which over the coming months will drain away his strength. The wound is symbolic of the inner wound which scars us all – the knowledge of our own mortality, which is the price of consciousness, our glory and our tragedy. Consciousness brings pain because for the first time we see our Earthly lives as they truly are, as mortal and finite. No one finds this an easy path.

> I fear to take this kingship –
> for before me I see
> anguish and pain,
> and blood upon the corn,
> the shadow of my death. [8]

In an Asatru Midsummer celebration, [9] the priest, the Gothi, venerates Balder the beautiful, Son of Odin.

> Hail to Balder, fair as the sea and the Sun
> and the snow upon the mountains;
> Balder, whose soul is pure as water, sky,
> grass and wandering air
> and whose dwelling is in Broad Shining,
> a blessed place in the best of lands,
> where evil runes are not.
> Balder, august, immortal, white and holy,
> we passed days not dark at your side.
> O, that our lives be clad like yours
> in majesty and might. . . .
> For you are Balder,
> whose hair is white with fanning the flames of life.

You are younger than the young
and older than the old.
You are unfolded on the stem of time, like a flower.
Your roots are in the dark Winter.
You are the flower unfolded.
You are new.

The continuity of life is celebrated. Thanks are given to our ancestors and blessings sent to our successors. The Gothi then gives counsel.

Streaming from the stars through everlasting space,
whelming out of Earth herself,
flowing through the green life of the plant,
breaking into the heart of man:
the voice of Balder, the Holy.
A voice as young and ancient as Summer,
like the song of a glad water
flowing down into the night
from a bright morning in the hills,
falling like silver,
as the quiet rain that drops down,
leaf-drenching, from Asgard.
For life is in the seed,
and the ear ripens in the Sun,
and far fairer are the hills of morning.
So let us make bread and eat:
the spark is there wheresoever we strike it.
Kindle the spark and light fire.
Stick, clay and stone are there for building.
Take them, build a dwelling place and live in peace.

At the beginning of August, Lughnasadh or Lammas celebrates the harvest and, in some traditions, the sacrifice of the Corn King, whose reaping is necessary to feed the people. The King accepts the inevitability of the ultimate sacrifice and is cut down by the Goddess, who appears as the Goddess of Death, the wielder of the sickle.

Let us now celebrate the Mystery of Lammas,
the season of the Summer Queen and Sacrificial King.
What most we love we must give back again,
that the Dance of Life may spiral on and on.
From death comes forth new life, and thus rebirth;
from joy to grief and sorrow, and back again to mirth. [10]

The Autumn Equinox is a time of balance, when light equals darkness. It is a time of reflection and of inner change. We stand poised at the changing of a tide. In spring and summer, the impetus of the life force is outwards towards activity and creation. At Autumn Equinox, the tides turn inwards towards contemplation.

Pagan Prayer for Autumn
We stand at the turning point of Summer and Winter.
Summer is the season of action,
Winter the season of rest, repose and contemplation.
It is a time for meditation and for study,
a time to seek the Gods within and not without.
Renew now the power within us, O Great Ones,
so that as the sun wanes,
our unconscious minds may grow more powerful,
and we may descend into our own underworld,
to explore throughout the Winter,
the magic kingdom which we find within.[11]

At Autumn Equinox, the Goddess descends to the Underworld. In some groups, the mysteries of Demeter and Kore are celebrated. The God who was slain at Lammas is now Lord of the Underworld and the Goddess goes to join him. Leaves fall from the trees, birds migrate, the signs of life disappear one by one. Freya Aswynn suggests that in the Northern Tradition, the theme of descent into the unconscious or Underworld can be celebrated by a ritual symbolizing Odin's initiation on the World-Tree.

Samhain or Hallowe'en is the feast of the dead when the worlds of matter and spirit draw close to one another and the dead may pass to and fro through the veils. It is customary to carve Jack o'Lanterns from pumpkins and to place candles in them to guide the souls of the ancestors to the feast. A meal is left out for the ancestors – usually in the garden. In some groups in the Northern tradition, the Festival of the Dead is celebrated on Remembrance Day as Einherjar's or Hero's Day. The emphasis is on the links between past and present and the ties of blood and kin.

In the name of the High Gods. Urd, Norn of the Past,
we offer thanks for the blood ties of our house and family.
Verdandi, Norn of the Present, and Skuld, Norn of the
    Future:

may we not be a failing people and a Springless Autumn.
. . . Now, to our sons' sons and their sons,
we send our words as messengers,
the way we shall not pass along:
Kinsmen! Unseen, unborn, unknown!
Since we can never see your face and never grasp your
    hand,
we send our spirits through time and space,
in Odin's name we greet you.[12]

Yule celebrates the birth of the young Sun God. The Goddess is venerated as the Mother. Evergreen boughs or a tree are brought into the house to mark the continuance of life in the cold winter season. Yule is a time of celebration, gift-giving and great rejoicing; for in the cold, dark days of winter, there is the promise of spring to come. In one ceremony, the God is called upon to bring to his people a sign that light will be restored.

Lord of Darkness, Belovèd of our Lady,
Keeper of the Gates of Life and Death, of Night and Day.
Across the starry heavens, we call unto thee:
the light is failing in our land;
the trees stand bare and skeletal;
the birds have fled;
and plaintive is the song of those who must remain.
The frozen river stands,
unmoving as though dead;
the days grow shorter,
and the crimson setting Sun
falls too soon beneath the tree tops,
bathing the sky in the colour of blood.
Bring us a word, a sign of hope;
speak to thy people, our Lord and our God.

The God then responds:

Behold I answer you:
your hope is reborn.
For in caverns beneath the Earth,
I hear a new born cry;
in the midnight of the year,
my Queen has brought forth our son.
And in the morning at daybreak,
three signs you will see:

a stag upon the hill,
his antlers glistening in the mists of dawn,
the red breast of a cock robin,
singing on the branch of a holly tree,
and all day in the clear blue sky shall hang,
on one side the pale light of the wintery reborn Sun,
and on the other the lingering shadow
of the pale orb of the Moon,
the Goddess' sign,
that her Promised One has come.

I stand for the babe who sleeps in the cradle,
I speak for the King who is to come,
Arthur, Lugh, Balin,
these shall be his names,
and the treasures of the Earth,
to these he shall lay claim.
The Lord of Life is now renewed.
Father of the Child, I come to you,
the light cometh, the Sun returneth,
peace, joy and gentleness descend upon this place,
as we celebrate the Season of the Child.

The Goddess is then brought forth to speak:

In the deep caverns of the Earth I laboured,
and the Sun Child was reborn,
to restore the Earth to fruitfulness,
when winter snows have melted, and he is strong.
Behold the light returneth, the Sun King he is born again!
His father shall furnish him with chariot and horses,
and the Eight Weapons of the Ancients,
I shall give to him as his inheritance.
I shall wrap him in the cloak of the radiance of the Sun,
and arm him with the Shield of Stars,
and the arrows of his enemies shall falter,
and pierce the ground.
The Sword of Truth he shall gird on,
and the Grail of the Wine of Life,
shall inspire his heart and mind.
They will place on his hand the ring of power,
and a crown of gold shall grace his brow.
The Spear of Light shall fly the air for him,

and with the war banner of the Morrigan,
he shall drive back the forces of the dark. [13]

At the beginning of February is Imbolc, the time of the first lactation of ewes, a portent of Spring, when the Goddess renews herself and re-emerges into the world. Imbolc celebrates the transition of the Goddess from Mother to Virgin, i.e. free and independent, once more. Winter is a time of rest, of battening down the hatches and enduring the winter's cold until spring comes again. When the ground softens sufficiently for the first flowers to appear, it is time for reawakening. This is not only a reawakening of Nature, but also a reawakening for human beings, who must now begin to plough the soil to prepare it for the next year's crop. The Goddess walks the land once more, heralded by the appearance of the first flowers. Ceremonies to welcome the Goddess and to welcome the return of the light may be performed here; as too may agricultural ceremonies to bless the new cycle of the year's work, much as the blessing of the plough. With this, the Wheel of the Year returns to Spring. The cycle of becoming begins again.

Celebrating the Seasonal Cycle

I have so far illustrated some of the symbolism of the seasonal rites with poetic invocations and prayers of praise, but this wordy approach is not essential to Pagan celebration. We can revere our Gods in silence, by the lighting of a candle, or the planting of a tree. The essential message is that we are free – to worship how and where we will, and to create and recreate our own forms of celebration which can evolve and change over the years. To mark the seasonal rites, we can create our own forms, or we can work with the rites and forms of one of the Pagan traditions; but we do not use these forms simply because we have been taught them, but because they are meaningful.

The seasonal myths are viewed not as relics of the past, but as expressions of living and eternal truths about humanity and the universe we inhabit. For rituals to be meaningful, they must not become static. They must be a living branch of a tree which is deeply-rooted in the past and stretches upward to reach both present and future. Pagan groups will often examine anew the content of the seasonal celebrations for each festival and tailor them to current needs. Within each festival are many complex levels of interpretation and meaning which can be differently emphasized in different years. As we come again to each festival of the season's round, those things which are most near to us at the time, and those things which have touched us throughout the year, come to the forefront. So, in the symbolism of the seasonal cycle, we see messages that we have not seen before. We examine the rite and we may change it slightly, adding or dropping parts which are more or less relevant to the group. Until recently, the imbalance in outer society meant that many Pagans found it necessary to emphasize the feminine rather than the masculine, Goddess rather than God. Many groups now feel able to orient their rites more towards a balance between Goddess and God and the male mysteries have developed. In explaining this, it sounds as though we consciously decided to invent a new rite, but this is not so. Usually, the need for a new emphasis in the rite comes to us through a dream, through writing a poem, or through an intuitive feeling that something is missing and we must meditate to discover what it is. Thus do the rites evolve and speak to us in the deepest parts of our psyches to express our unity with our Gods and our love for our deities.

1. Marian Green, *The Path Through the Labyrinth*, page 56.
2. Carl Jung, *The Collected Works of C.G. Jung*, Volume 5, *Symbols of Transformation*, page 231.
3. Robert Bly, *Iron John*, pages 107–8.
4. Marian Green, *The Path Through the Labyrinth*, page 40.
5. Dion Fortune, *The Sea Priestess*, page 123.
6. Unpublished Druid material.
7. Rudyard Kipling, 'Weland's Sword', in *Puck of Pook's Hill*, as quoted in Janet and Stewart Farrar, *Eight Sabbats for Witches*, page 91.
8. Vivianne Crowley, *Wicca: The Old Religion in the New Age*, page 195.
9. Stubba, *The Book of Blots: Ceremonies, Rituals and Invocations of the Odinic Rite*, pages 49–54.
10. Vivianne Crowley, unpublished Lammas ritual.
11. Vivianne Crowley, Autumn 1982.
12. Stubba, *The Book of Blots: Ceremonies, Rituals and Invocations of the Odinic Rite*, pages 79–87.
13. Vivianne Crowley, unpublished Yule ritual.

12
Weaving the Web of Wyrd: Shamanism, Divination and Magic

Pagan religion is not only about worshipping the Gods; nor is it merely a system of social ethics. Within the Pagan traditions are means whereby we can contact the Otherworld. There are three major routes to the Otherworld which are available to us this side of manifestation. These are Shamanism, divination and magic. To some extent they overlap.

Many religions have rejected magic, and Christianity fought a hard battle to turn its followers away from the self-help ethos of magic towards the less direct method of prayer. The Pagan view is varied. Some see magic as part of their religious practice; others do not. Many prefer not to interfere in this way in the course of events. Divination is more widely employed. Shamanism is a specialized activity which is pursued by fewer Pagans, not because of ethical scruples, but because it requires abilities which only a minority possess.

The idea of practising Shamanism or performing spells can seem strange, archaic and outlandish to the twentieth-century mind. Even those who accept the possibility of their existence may not believe they themselves have the ability. Paganism's interest in these esoteric sciences is not a regression to the wish-fulfilling world of child, but part of a modern preoccupation which is as much psychological as it is mystical. It is a desire to understand and experience for ourselves other states of being and other states of consciousness.

'Other states of consciousness' is a puzzling phrase to those who have never experienced them. It is difficult to convey these through words, but they are states whereby we can transcend the boundaries of time and space which normally act as barriers in the material world. We can step beyond the here and now to learn of the past, the future, and events happening in other places and in other realms; we can influence and affect those realms; and through those realms, we can also influence and affect the world of everyday reality.

Shamanism

Shamanism is a technique and practice which is of growing importance in modern Paganism. Shamanism originated in Siberia and Central Asia and spread from the Russian steppes westwards into Europe and eastwards into North America. Much of Native American and Inuit religious practice is based on Shamanism. Similar practices are also found in South America, the Pacific region and elsewhere. Shamanism is remarkably widespread. While the similarities between Asian and North American Shamanism may be due to the ideas spreading from Asia to North America via the land bridge which once linked the two continents, this does not explain the appearance of Shamanism in other parts of the world. It seems that many people in many different cultures discovered for themselves the techniques for voyaging in the country of the mind.

Shamanism has been defined as the technique of ecstasy. The role of the Shaman in society is to enter into another state of consciousness, often a state of ecstasis, in order to act as an intermediary between the spirit world and the everyday lives of men and women. Shamanism is a path to knowledge; but this is not achieved through the intellectual questioning and rational analysis of the philosopher and scientist, but through inner experience. In the silence of the forest, cave and sacred space, the Shaman journeys forth to explore the inner world or Otherworld, the country of the mind. The purpose of the journey is not idle curiosity, or even more worthy motives of self-development, it is to serve the Shaman's community. Through their Otherworld explorations, Shamans bring back knowledge of the cause of illnesses and problems in their communities, and why the rains had failed or the crops would not grow. The Shaman can then work acts of healing and magic to solve these community problems. Shamans may also guide others to experience the Otherworld for themselves and so deepen their spiritual lives. The Shaman is also often a 'psychopomp' – a guide through the realm of spirit for the newly-dead.

Much of our contemporary ideas of Shamanism have come from the study of those groups and societies in which Shamanism is still practised. The work of the Shaman was usually dismissed by early Western travellers, researchers and missionaries as ignorance, superstition and misunderstanding of the laws of cause and effect. This attitude displayed not the ignorance of the practitioners themselves, but the ignorance of those who, steeped in their ideas of the superiority of Western science and religion, were unable to see the value of Shamanic practices.

Accessing the Otherworld

In societies where Shamanism is practised, ordinary reality is seen as a narrow band of experience sandwiched between two other realities, those of the Upper and Lower Worlds. This belief is also found in the Celtic and Norse-German world-views. To enter the world of spirit, the Shaman makes an inner journey. This frequently involves descent into the Underworld, but it may also include ascent into heavenly realms – the Upperworld. Together these worlds comprise the Otherworld. The Other-world is just as real as our everyday realm; although what happens would be thought fantastical and impossible in ordinary reality. The Otherworld is populated by powerful beings – often in animal form – who must be propitiated, persuaded and sometimes fought into cooperating with the Shaman's community for its general well-being. The Shaman is entrusted by his or her community with the task of crossing into the Otherworld to deal with these entities. In making the crossing, the Shaman needs protection. This comes in the form of spirit guides or animals who come to the Shaman's aid.

The Otherworld is accessed by changing our state of consciousness and entering into trance. There are a number of ways of achieving this. In some cultures, hallucinogenic drugs are used. Another method is through rhythmic drumming and/or the shaking of a rattle. The shaking of rice in a sieve has also been used. Shamans frequently refer to their drum as their horse or canoe: it is the means by which they make the Otherworld journey. This imagery is found in the Finno-Ugric tradition, where Väinämöinen the First Shaman descends to the Underworld of Tuonola to obtain the three words which he needs to complete his boat.

When drumming is used, this may be carried out by the

Shaman or by an assistant. The beat is monotonous and steady: 205 to 220 beats a minute is the most conducive to facilitate a light trance. Trance does not mean the possession found in voodoo and charismatic Christian sects, where we have no awareness of our physical surroundings, but a change in our brain state whereby we emit brain patterns which are normally associated with sleeping, while we continue to be awake. The Shaman remains at a level of consciousness where he or she retains some awareness of this world. This control is essential as the Otherworld journey may need to be directed and its sights and experiences recollected, mused upon and interpreted. It is common for the Shaman to be able to report back to witnesses on the progress of the journey while still in the process of undertaking it. Sometimes this is accomplished by means of song which forms spontaneously and in synchronicity with the events on the journey.

I go in my canoe
all over
in my vision

over trees
or in water
I'm floating
all around

I float
among whirlpools
all around

I float
among shadows

I go in my canoe
all over
in my vision

over trees
or in water
I'm floating[1]

Entrance to the Upper World is often via a pole which reaches to the sky. This image is found in much Western mythology.

There is the fairy story of *Jack and the Beanstalk*, whereby Jack plants a magic bean which grows up to reach the sky. Jack ascends the beanstalk and encounters a series of adventures. In Norse myth, the pole has evolved into the World Tree whose branches reach to heaven.

Entrance to the Lower World usually takes the form of imagining an opening – a cave, gully or hollow tree, by following tree roots down through the earth, or through diving into a pond or lake. Others take a more direct approach and create an image of diving directly through the surface of the earth. Whatever the point of entry, it is likely that the Shaman will then follow a tunnel. This can be easy or arduous depending on the individual and the circumstances. It can be a gradual descent or a plummeting down. Some describe the experience in naturalistic terms as following underground passages or caves. They are often acutely aware of the roughness of the rock, the smells, temperature changes and the dampness or dryness of the walls as they continue forward. Others see the tunnel in more symbolic terms and describe an enveloping sheath through which they slip or are forced. This image of smooth muscle has obvious associations with the experience of birth. Similarly, a common image is that the tunnel is ribbed and some Inuit Shaman masks incorporate this ribbing in their design. Perhaps it is not so much a case of 'As above, so below', as 'As without, so within'.

The form the tunnel takes – how difficult it is to follow, whether it is almost blocked, and whether by animate or inanimate obstructions – relates closely to the individual for whom the journey is undertaken. It can, of course, be seen as a metaphor for the journey into the unconscious. Most people undertaking Shamanic journeys find that, although their starting-off point is the same on different occasions, the tunnel can appear very different each time. Sometimes it will be more blocked than others. Sometimes it is empty and sometimes it is inhabited with other creatures. These can appear as normal animals – snakes, spiders, etc. – or as mythic creatures and monsters of wild imaginings.

Although variations in technique and practice can be found in different cultures, what is interesting are not the variations but the similarity in the belief systems and Otherworld experiences of different peoples at different times and in the widely-separated counties where Shamanism has been practised. There is no doubt that the techniques used produce profound changes in consciousness and comprise a psychological reality. Many would say that they also represent a supernatural reality; but the distinction is perhaps irrelevant. To those who have explored it, the Otherworld is as real and actual as the ordinary world. People's experiences within it have a commonality which indicate that the Otherworld represents a shared level of consciousness which is present in all humanity. It exists for all who can access it and is more than an individual's private imaginings.

Shamanism in European Paganism

Shamanism involves changing consciousness. A change of consciousness is also essential in magic and divination, which have played an important part in the European Pagan tradition. Magic and divination do not necessarily involve the Otherworld journeying that is the characteristic of Shamanism, but much of European magical and divinatory practice bears the hallmark of earlier Shamanistic culture.

Elements of Shamanism are found throughout European Paganism, but are most obvious in Finno-Ugric religion, where Väinämöinen the First Shaman, son of Ilmater Water-Mother the Creatrix Goddess, helps complete her work of creating the world. Shamanism is also found in the Celtic tradition. Shamans have attributes that are very similar to those ascribed to Druids. Mircea Eliade, in *Shamanism: Archaic Techniques of Ecstasy,* [2] describes the Shaman of the Kazak Kirgiz people of Northern Asia as singer, poet, musician, diviner, priest, doctor, guardian of religious and popular traditions, and preserver of legends. Journeying to the Otherworld to commune with the spirits of the dead in order to gain information or receive teaching was widely practised by the Celts. In the Irish *Flateyjarbok*, there is a story of a man who slept on the burial mound of a dead poet in order to learn the bardic gift. The dead poet appeared to him in a dream and taught him a verse, after which he had the gift of poetry.

Our Norse-German ancestors communicated information from the Otherworld through Sejd, or prophecy. This was an important function of the Volva, whose costume is very reminiscent of that of the Siberian Shaman. The *Eddas* describe the Volva as wearing a dark blue cloak with a hood which was set with stones along the hem. There is an inner hood or head-dress made from animal skin, gloves made of cat skin with the fur innermost, fur boots, a skin bag to contain power objects and a long rune-staff. Archaeological investigations in Scandinavia have found graves with this equipment and with the power objects still intact. These included amber beads, stones, snake bones, squirrel tails, bird claws and sea shells.

Odin the Chief God of the Aesir also has many of the characteristics of a Shaman. The eight-legged horse is a frequent image in Shamanic cultures and one of the ways by which the Shaman can penetrate the Otherworld. Odin travels to Otherworld on such a horse – Sleipnir or Glider – who was fathered by the God Loki on a mare. Sleipnir is therefore part animal and part Divine. We are also told in the *Ynglinga Saga* that Odin made Otherworld journeys where his body lay as though he were asleep or dead. 'He then became a bird or a beast, a fish or a dragon, and went in an instant to far-off lands.'[3] Odin is a God of knowledge, but like that of all Shamans, Odin's knowledge is only achieved at the price of suffering. To obtain wisdom, Odin consults with Mimir's head and drinks each day from Mimir's well, but in order to so, he must sacrifice part of himself – one of his own eyes.

There are many connections between Witchcraft and Shamanism. Rapport with animals was an important mark of both Shaman and Witch; as are power animals and familiar animals and spirits. These are sent out to do the Witch's or Shaman's work. The word 'witch' has a number of derivations, one of the most important of which is to know. Similarly, the Finnish word for Shaman is tietäjä, one-who-knows.

With the advent of Christianity, many Shamanic practices were outlawed, but much was continued by painting a Christian gloss on the original. Spells and charms were 'Christianized' by adding names of appropriate angels and saints. Psychic voyaging using hallucinogenic drugs continued to be used to enter the ecstatic altered state of consciousness which the Inquisition later labelled 'The Witches' Sabbath'. The knowledge of herbal and natural medicine possessed by Shamans became the province of the village wise woman and cunning man.

A typical cunning man is described in Lady Wilde's nineteenth-century collection, *Ancient Legends, Mystic Charms, and Superstitions of Ireland*.

Some persons, even at the present day amongst the
peasants, have strange gifts and a knowledge of the hidden
mysteries, but they can only impart this knowledge when

they know that death is on them, and then it must be . . .
to an unmarried man, or to a childless woman, for these are
the most susceptible to the mysterious power by which
miracles can be worked.

A man now living at Innis-Sark has this strange and
mystic gift. He can heal diseases by word, even at a
distance, and his glance sees into the very heart, and reads
the secret thoughts of men. He never touched beer, spirits,
or meat, in all his life, but has lived entirely on bread, fruit,
and vegetables. A man who know him thus describes him –
'Winter and summer his dress is the same, merely a flannel
shirt and a coat.'[4]

The reference to the cunning man's dress is interesting. One of
the traditional attributes of Shamans, and also of Yogis in the
East, is power over temperature and the elements. Both are
thought to be able to overcome extremes of heat and cold, to sit
naked in the snow without ill effect and to be able to levitate and
fly. Witches were also accredited with these powers; hence
ordeals were devised by the Inquisition to trap the witch into
betraying her supernatural powers to save herself: to float on
water for instance when she should have drowned. This is taken
to its logical (or highly illogical) conclusion in the film of *Monty
Python and the Holy Grail*:

'How can you tell she's a witch?'
'Well, a witch floats and a duck floats, therefore a witch
weighs the same as a duck!'

Shamanism Today

The knowledge of Shamans and Witches was an oral tradition
handed down over the generations and while much was
preserved, much disappeared or its original meaning misunder-
stood. The Shaman's knowledge of natural science and lore often
degenerated into superstition. Oral traditions are very powerful,
but oral teaching can be lost in a generation if it is not passed on.
Sadly, this has happened in recent years in Europe. Traditionally,
like Shamans in other cultures, wise women and cunning men
took on only one apprentice and passed him or her their final
secrets only on their death bed. Many of these were family crafts
and, with the breaking up of traditional family structures, it was
no longer possible to pass on training in this way.

Over the past decade, there has been a tremendous upsurge of interest in Shamanism. This has had some unfortunate results. The spiritual world has always been beset by fads. In the nineteenth and early twentieth centuries, people tried to contact their spirit guides – usually Tibetans, Chinese or Red Indians – who would transmit spiritual wisdom to them. People no longer have spirit guides – they have power animals. Every New Age magazine is advertising born-again medicine men promising to help us to find our animal spirit helpers – for a fee of course.

This growth in *New Age Shamanism* has come about in part because genuine Shamanism is a very difficult path to follow. Despite what advertisements for weekend courses in New Age magazines may imply, it is not easy to become a Shaman. A Shaman is one set apart. He or she was usually identified at an early age as possessing special powers of communication with the Otherworld, the non-material reality around us. Shamans could be apprenticed to learn their trade, but this was uncommon. Usually people became Shamans because they had a spontaneous, severe and traumatic experience – often an illness or spiritual crisis – which forced open for them the doors of the Otherworld. After this, it was no longer possible for them to go back to their previous life. Everything was irrevocably changed. This spontaneous experience happened in a cultural milieu which enabled both the individual and his or her community to interpret it as a Shamanic initiation. Nor was this experience seen as necessarily desirable. The work of the Shaman is considered dangerous and, in many societies, to be chosen as a Shaman is seen as much as a curse as a blessing. Today, those of us who have Shamanic experiences are likely to do so without the support of a mythological and philosophical framework which makes sense of them. Our communities are more likely to interpret our experiences as illness that needs curing rather than spiritual and mystical insight. Recent decades have shown little taste for the mystical.

In the modern world, we are likely to need teaching and guidance if we are to learn the techniques of Shamanism and how to interpret our experiences. This is difficult. It is possible to obtain instruction from those communities which still practise Shamanism, but there are many ethical and practical problems in doing so. The beliefs and practices of these cultures are very far removed from those of most Europeans and many communities were never or are no longer willing to teach them to outsiders. In North and South America, a number of people have exploited the trust of the native peoples who taught them and have turned their knowledge into money-making institutions. There are genuine European Shamans, but these are few and far between. Apart from the traditional wise women and cunning men, who have largely disappeared, there are as yet few people practising the European Shamanic path, although this is rapidly changing.

Divination

Many Pagans use divinatory techniques such as the Tarot, astrology and runes to see into the future. The runes are one of the principle divination methods of Northern Europe. Tacitus,[5] writing in 98 CE, makes one of the earliest references to the throwing of the runes. He describes how the German tribes performed divination by cutting off the branch of a nut-bearing tree, slicing it into strips, marking these with signs and then throwing them onto a white cloth. These would then be interpreted by the community priest or by the head of the family who would select three of the strips.

In Norse-German tradition, the discovery of the runes is accredited to the God Odin. Odin obtains their secrets through undergoing a Shamanic ordeal of being hung from a tree. This aspect of Odin can be equated with the Tarot card of the Hanged Man. The story of Odin's ordeal is found in the *Eddas* in the *Hávamál* or *High One's Words*:

I know I hung on the wind-tossed Tree,
that Tree whom none knoweth whence it sprang,
nine whole nights, pierced with a spear,
given to Odin, myself to myself.

No horn they handed me nor bread;
downwards I looked and with piercing cry,
took up the runes,
and fell to the ground.[6]

The use of runes is also found in the Finno-Ugric tradition. The *Kalevala* describes how Väinämöinen the First Shaman uses slips of alder wood in divination.

Then the aged Väinämöinen,
he, the great primeval Shaman,
hastened alder sticks to cut,
and arranged the sticks in order,
and began the lots to shuffle . . .[7]

Other sources indicate that the strips of wood would have had signs marked upon them. Kati-ma Koppana in *Snake Fat and Knotted Threads* gives us this spell:

I'll cast my slips of alder wood.
Old Mother Kavé, Nature's own,
Golden Kavé, the Beautiful,
come hither to arrange the runes,
arrange the lots with your own hands,
with your own hands the runes to turn . . .[8]

Here the runes are used by one set apart – a Shaman. To use any system of divination, be it Tarot or runes, requires knowledge of the philosophy from which the system springs, its understanding of fate, and the nature of any deities who preside over the divination. Divination should not be engaged in for entertainment or as the superstitious fortune-telling of the fairground booth. To discern the Web of Wyrd is a religious act which must be approached with suitable reverence, sincerity and seriousness. The purpose of divination is to help us look into the pattern of Wyrd, so that we can determine the prevailing trends and then work through them to the end we desire.

The Web of Wyrd

The rationale of Shamanism and magic is interconnectedness – a Oneness of Being. To any Shaman, the concept of Oneness is so obvious that it hardly needs to be stated. There is no separateness in Nature. Everything, both animate or inanimate, is interconnected. Every apparently separate thing, whether a rock or stone, animal, plant, human or event, is linked. All things are part of a greater whole and therefore in communication with one another. The apparent separateness of things is an illusion.

If all things are connected, then by examining any part of the Web of Wyrd, we can gain insights into the whole. The rationale of the Web of Wyrd has been related to a more modern phenomenon, that of the hologram. Holograms are created when two coherent rays of light impinge on an object in their path to produce an interference pattern which can be recorded on film. The film can then be used to create a three-dimensional image of the object. What is interesting is that it is not necessary to have the whole film in order to re-create the object. A tiny fragment will allow the image to be reproduced, although details will be lost as the film area becomes less. From this, it can be argued that each fragment of the universe contains the key to the greater whole. Holograms give us clues to the true nature of reality: that it is a set of interconnected worlds woven around one another, intermeshed and interlinking – the Web of Wyrd.

The magical reality is essentially an holistic one – everything is connected, therefore an action in one part of the physical realm can influence events, people and objects that are separated in time and space. The concept of the Web is important in understanding the concept of time in the Shamanic and magical universes. Past, present and future are seen to coexist. Time is but a measurement of physical change and the realm of Wyrd is beyond the physical. The laws of time do not apply. By achieving a state of consciousness whereby we enter the timeless zone, that deep realm of the unconscious where the personal unconscious merges into the group mind of humankind and that of other aspects of creation, it is possible to discern the future. At the level of the group mind, or collective unconscious, we lose our sense of individual separateness and our minds can merge with those of others. To use an analogy, human beings are a bit like rhizomes – each plant appears separate when we look at the surface of the soil, but if we go deeper, we find they are joined at a common root. To use another analogy, we are like different branches of a tree. When we look outwards we cannot see that we are joined at the trunk. It is only when we turn back and look within that we see that we all emerge from and merge into a central core.

At this deeper level of consciousness, the mind operates outside the time/space parameters which hold good for material reality. We enter a world in which meaningful coincidence or synchronicity occurs. Carl Jung used the term synchronicity to explain those strange coincidences which happen to us on our life's journey and which can often totally alter its direction. We have a dream that if we go to a certain shop we will find a certain book in a certain place. The dream is so powerful that we feel obliged to go and look, even though we feel silly in doing so. We do indeed find the book and reading it changes our view of the world and the course of our lives. This is synchronicity. Marvin Spiegelman writes, in *Hinduism and Jungian Psychology*:

> If we were to translate this into archetypal language, we would say that when one is so deeply connected with the unconscious as to be in touch with the Self, then psychic reality transcends our usual, conscious ideas of time and space, and we are then in the web of existence, in which synchronistic events take place. To be so linked, then, is to 'know' in a different way.[9]

Synchronicity and clairvoyant dreaming are spontaneous transmissions from this deeper level of the psyche. Divination is a way of consciously tuning in to seek information. Certain symbol systems such as the Tarot, astrology and the runes can help us access information from the Web because, by the processes of synchronicity, the pattern of symbols in one place is thought to reflect the patterning of events in another.

Magic

In the Western Pagan tradition, the future is not seen as fixed. If we can discern the pattern of the Web of Wyrd, through spontaneous clairvoyance, divination or a Shamanic journey to the Otherworld, then we can act to change it. This can involve action on the material plane. It can also involve magic.

Magic uses a number of traditional techniques such as candle-burning, talismans, poppets and cord magic. Generally, these are not important in themselves, but are ways of focusing the mind on what is to be accomplished. What is necessary is not the props, but using them to enter a changed state of consciousness, that of trance. This can be precipitated by repetitive movement (dancing or swaying), repetitive sound (chants, mantras, litanies, bells, rattles, drumming); lulling the consciousness through fixing the gaze on an object such as a black mirror or candle flame; and the use of incense. Some means of magic, such as crystals and runes, are more than props. Crystals are thought to act as transmitters of energy; so too are runes. The runes are well-known as a divinatory system, but their use in magic is less familiar. Specific runes have specific purposes.

A spell unknown to queens I know,
or any of humankind:
Help is it named, for help can it give
in sadness and sorrow and sickness.[10]

A fourth I know, if my foes
have fettered me hand and foot,
I chant the spell that chains do break,
flying from hands and feet.[11]

The right chanting and drawing of the runes is a magical act
which activates the forces they represent so that they can be
directed according to the operator's will. In the *Sigdrifumal* is the
following verse which gives instructions on how to deal with a
difficult birth. The *Disir* are female guardian spirits.

Help-runes you should know,
to help bring forth,
the woman of her child:
mark them on your hands,
take hold of her wrists,
and invoke the Disirs' aid.[12]

As I Do Will, So Mote It Be

In magic, 'will' is an important concept. Will is often misunder-
stood in Western society. In the English language, we speak of
wilfulness to mean that someone is wrong-headed and not acting
in accord with the greater good; or willing in the sense of striving.
A better understanding of the nature of will has been provided
by the Italian psychologist Roberto Assagioli, founder of the
psychosynthesis movement. Although raised as a Catholic,
Roberto Assagioli was greatly influenced by Alice Bailey and
other esotericists. The Christian clerics who support psychosynthesis might be greatly surprised if they realized how similar
is much of Assagioli's thought to the work of Aleister Crowley.
Assagioli saw will as having seven qualities: energy; mastery;
concentration; determination; persistence; initiative and
organization. He believed that people should learn to use their
skilful will. This involves not strain or forcefulness but 'a sense
of letting go and yet being fully present. It is cooperating with
the benign forces of the world, which is where love and will are
fully consistent and almost one.'[13] Crowley expressed this as,

'Love is the Law, Love under Will.' The magical will is not about effort. It operates more like the muscles of a trained athlete – at ease and without strain.

The power of the will has also been explored by Dr Serena Roney-Dougal in her book, *Where Science and Magic Meet*.[14] She quotes the Uncertainty Principle of Professor Werner Heisenberg, which argues that truly objective science is impossible: the observer affects the system he or she observes. Serena Roney-Dougal explains that within the human brain, mind exerts power over matter at the synapses, where thinking causes neurones to fire. Tiny electrochemical and other stimuli create changes which result in macroscopic changes to the world outside. She argues that if it is possible to influence other people's minds tele-pathically and for people to produce poltergeist and other paranormal activity through what parapsychologists call psycho-kinesis, then there is no reason why the focused will of a Witch should not cause change through magic.

Magic is on the borders of that territory which has now been claimed by psychology. Bob Stewart, in *Living Magical Arts*, writes:

> The proposition that consciousness may be transformed
> through willed arranged patterns is sometimes found on the
> edges of psychology, but is usually discarded, as no hard
> boundaries can be found for such maps of the psyche. In
> magic the quibbling over maps and boundaries is ignored,
> for after the symbols have been applied and transformations
> of the individual have occurred, the validity or accuracy of
> the maps themselves becomes irrelevant.[15]

How do we achieve the deep connection to the unconscious which enables us to accomplish these transformations? To our ancestors, magicians were those set apart. They were the scientists of the natural world. Reaching behind the veil of matter, they touched the true and deep nature of things. Their work was holy, for in learning the true nature of reality, they penetrated the innermost secrets of creation.

Many modern practitioners of magic see magical ability not as a special gift, but as a skill which many people can develop. Aleister Crowley wrote, in *Magick in Theory and Practice*, that magick was for all – for housemaids, artisans, ladies and lords. While theoretically this may be true, the problem remains that it is difficult for those educated in Western intellectualism to let

go of their rigid thought structures sufficiently to enter trance
states and achieve what Assagioli calls 'letting go yet being fully
present'. Many people gullibly believe what our ancestors
believed – that a four-leaved clover marketed on the pages of a
popular astrology magazine will help them win a fortune.
Others, more sceptical and/or more educated, are put off the idea
of magic by such excesses. Belief of any sort – whether religious
or magical – is not easy for Westerners today. Often people say
how much they envy those who have some firm religious belief,
but that they themselves cannot believe. The Canadian novelist
Robertson Davies has one of his academic characters say to a
Hungarian Gypsy:

> Magic – I hate the word because of what it has come to
> mean, but anyway – magic in the big sense can only
> happen where there is very strong feeling. You can't set it
> going with a sceptical mind – with your fingers crossed, so
> to speak. You must desire, and you must believe. Have you
> any idea how hard that is for a man of my time and a man
> of my training and temperament? At the deepest level of
> your being, you are living in the Middle Ages, and magic
> comes easily – I won't say logically – to you. But for me it is
> a subject of a study, a psychological fact, but not necessarily
> an objective fact. A thing some people have always believed
> but nobody has quite been able to prove. I have never had
> what is necessary – the desire and the belief.[16]

Magic does not require absolute faith; but we need to be open-
minded enough to accept the possibility that it might work. If we
are convinced that nothing will happen, then we will not be able
to let go sufficiently to do magic.

The Ethics of Magic

Traditional practitioners of magic and Shamanism were often
amoral in their outlook. They saw their craft as simply that – a
skill to be used. It could be used for many purposes, both good
and ill, according to what the practitioner and his or her clients
desired. In modern Paganism, magic operates within a spiritual
and ethical framework. This varies with the tradition, but
generally accords with the ethic of 'An it harm none, do what you
will'. This limits the use of magic to those ends which are
beneficial to society. In practical terms, this means that the uses

to which magic is put are much more circumscribed than they were to our ancestors, whose Paganism was often more of the Old Testament 'eye for an eye' variety. Today, Pagans who practise magic will do so if it is really important; but they do not use magical techniques as a prop to avoid dealing with life's problems in practical ways. Magic is not a crutch; nor is it an excuse for exercising the ego and power drives of the inadequate. It is a powerful technique to be used wisely, sparingly and well.

For those Pagans who use magic, to fail to carry out magic in accordance with ethical principles is an act of foolishness; for we are responsible for our actions and must reap their consequences. Christian writer, Michael Perry, observes that Wicca has a high moral code because power brings responsibility.

> The central core of this ethic is expressed in the Wiccan saying 'an [i.e. so long as] ye harm none, do as ye will' – remembering that the 'will' is a key concept in Wicca, and means focused willing, not simply a chance impulse. Wiccans believe that if this teaching is ignored, the harm caused to the other party will rebound threefold on the Witch who was the cause of it, either in this world or in her next incarnation.[17]

A similar perspective is found in the Northern Tradition. Freya Aswynn comments that each sending of a magical spell has a price to be paid.

> In all kinds of magic, energy used has to be compensated, and as each working changes the consciousness of the operator, it follows that each kind of energy invoked will affect your wyrd . . . so do consider very carefully before you embark on any destructive working, as there will be an equal and opposite reaction.[18]

It is important not to be romantic about Shamanism and the magical universe of our ancestors. The idea of interconnectedness means that the concept of accident can be foreign to Shamanic thought. Everything happens for a reason and a purpose. Everything has a cause. In Lynn Andrews' *Medicine Woman*, her teacher tells her that every act has meaning.

> *Accident* is a word born of confusion. It means we didn't understand ourselves enough to know why we did something. If you slip and cut your finger, there is a reason

why you did it. Someone in your moon lodge wanted you to do it. If you knew how to listen to the chiefs inside your moon lodge, you would never do such a foolish thing. The medicine person never makes a mistake. [19]

A world-view which excludes the possibility of accident has both advantages and disadvantages. Positively, it encourages us to take responsibility for ourselves. If something happens to us, it is for a reason and if we don't like it, we can act to change it. Negatively, it can lead to paranoia. It is a world in which illness is the result of curses or transgressions of supernatural laws. To be cured, we must lift the curse or propitiate the spirit we have offended. Usually this means enlisting and paying for the services of an expert to put things right. It is also important to remember that one of the reasons why Witches were persecuted is because people were afraid of what they could do. To some people, the idea that human beings have deep connections with one another is a source of great strength and joy. To others, it is frightening and threatening. As children we often have to fight to assert our individuality and to suddenly find that we are not as separate as we first thought can be alarming and requires us to rethink our notions of reality. This is not always welcome. However, although some people fear it, magic and the state of mind and will which create it are neutral forces. A car driven by a drunk can maim and kill, but this does not mean that the car itself is evil. What is wrong is its misuse.

1. From a free translation by David Cloutier of a Northwest coast Tsimshian Shaman's song. Quoted in Michael Harner, *The Way of the Shaman*, page 74.
2. Mircea Eliade, *Shamanism: Archaic Techniques of Ecstasy*, page 30, quoting J. Castagné, 'Magie et exorcisme chez les Kazak-Kirghizes et autres peuples turcs orientaux', in *Revue des études islamiques*, Paris, page 60.
3. *Ynglinga Saga*, VII, as quoted in Mircea Eliade, *Shamanism: Archaic Techniques of Ecstasy*, page 381.
4. Lady Wilde, *Ancient Legends, Mystic Charms, and Superstitions of Ireland*, pages 100–1.
5. Tacitus, *Germania*, 10, in H. Mattingley (trans.) *The Agricola and the Germania*, page 109.
6. *Hávamál*, verses 138–9.
7. Quoted in Kati-ma Koppana, *Snakefat and Knotted Threads: A Short Introduction to Finnish Magic*, page 76.

8. Kati-ma Koppana, *Snakefat and Knotted Threads: A Short Introduction to Finnish Magic*, page 77.
9. J. Marvin Spiegelman in J.M. Spiegelman and A.U. Vasavada, *Hinduism and Jungian Psychology*, page 52.
10. *Hávamál*, verse 145.
11. *Hávamál*, verse 148.
12. The *Eddas*, *Sigridfumál* or *The Lay of Sigrid*, see Lee M. Hollander, *The Poetic Edda*, page 235.
13. Quoted in Jean Hardy, *A Psychology with a Soul: Psychosynthesis in Evolutionary Context*, page 41.
14. Quoted in Michael Perry, *Gods Within: A Critical Guide to the New Age*, pages 65–6.
15. R.J. Stewart, *Living Magical Arts: Imagination and Magic for the 21st Century*, pages 1–2.
16. Quoted in Robertson Davies, *The Rebel Angels*, page 271.
17. Michael Perry, *Gods Within: A Critical Guide to the New Age*, page 64.
18. Freya Aswynn, *Leaves of Yggdrasil: A Synthesis of Magic, Feminine Mysteries, Folklore*, page 12.
19. Lynn V. Andrews, *Medicine Woman*, page 132.

13
Paganism and Mysticism: The Self and the Grail

The goals of Paganism, and indeed of all religion, are many. There is worship – the honouring of the Gods, the forces which give rise to and maintain our universe. This is expressed in Paganism principally through the observance of the seasonal cycle. There is the teaching of moral ethics and codes. Recent Western religion has often appeared to be dominated by this teaching, which is essentially social rather than spiritual. There is also the inner message of religion, which is found most often in its esoteric traditions and has often been the goal of the few rather than the many. This is the goal of mysticism – achievement of an inner union with the Divine. While many religions promise this after death, mysticism teaches spiritual practices through which this unity may be achieved on Earth.

The seasonal cycle has an underlying message which speaks to us all the more powerfully because it is not overt. This message is that the force of life is eternal, ever-renewing and ever-becoming and, like all things in Nature, we too have our cycles and seasons. We all learn that beneath the fabric of the Goddess' cloak of Nature, there is a spirit which is enduring. It is both changing, but essentially changeless. This paradox is not easy for the Western mind to understand. Our educational system teaches us to think in rational categories where something must be this or that. It cannot simultaneously be both. These truths of the spirit are better understood in the East, where the spiritual seeker is taught to step beyond the traps of the conscious analytical mind. In Zen Buddhism, these truths are taught through koans, paradoxical statements which are designed to confuse our thought processes and teach us their limitations. In Paganism, they are taught through myth and allegory. Myth and allegory lead us beyond the boundaries of the ego and the conscious mind, to travel in the uncharted country of the spirit and to discover our true nature – who and what we really are. The tenets of Paganism are not doctrine, but the importance of personal experience.

Religions which are based on the inner revelations of one prophet and his interpreters must inevitably ossify and crumble. Their teachings are carved, sometimes literally, on tablets of stone and, once their original propounders have passed away, they become over the centuries outer forms and teachings whose original spiritual essence has been lost. We are taught from without, through the conscious and rational mind, what can only be truly realized from within. Spiritual teachings are denigrated into a series of dos and don'ts. If we believe the teachings of one set of ·prophets and follow their prescripts, then we shall be enlightened or saved.

This type of teaching is false. We cannot find salvation or enlightenment from without. We can only find them through experiencing for ourselves unity with the source of all being. If we experience this, then our moral behaviour will be altered dramatically, not because we have been told that this is how a 'good' person behaves, but because we have learned that we are part of a whole which is Divine and are infused with love for our fellow creatures. In loving those with whom we share our planet, then we love the Divine source which is our ultimate home.

Writing in *A History of Yoga*, on the religions of the East, Vivian Worthington comments:

> While more exoteric forms of religion may flourish for a time, along with priesthood, caste, sacrifice, repression, conspicuous wealth, extravagant art, buildings, elaborate theologies or complex ritual, these all eventually expend themselves, and a particular religion either purifies itself or is overtaken by something else. We see this in the rise and decline of the many sects of Hinduism and Buddhism, in China, Japan and Tibet. [1]

A similar process is happening in the West. People have tired of the spiritual poverty of much Western religion and are turning back to the source of religious inspiration – the Voice Within, the messenger of their souls.

My God, enthroned beneath the apple tree,
how I have longed and longed for Thee.
Thy throne of stone, how polished,
vacant sits;
the garden walled is overgrown,
its flowers strangled by neglect.

The church was empty and I found
you'd upped and left – no forwarding address,
a moonlit flit, without a sound.

The priest I saw,
he spoke of garden fetes,
of raffles and of cakes.
His aridness of soul was just like mine,
save that I perceived it,
but that he was blind.

So where are you,
Unfathomable Mystery?
Why do you play,
this game of Hide and Seek with me?

O most elusive deity,
I stand in need of loving thee. [2]

Paganism is a return to mysticism, but it is a mysticism of the West, not that of the East. Most Eastern systems teach austerity and a turning away from the material world. Western Paganism is also non-materialistic, in the sense that wealth and power are not seen as the aims of existence, but to Western Pagans, the created universe is not Maya, illusion; but the work of the Goddess – the Divine made manifest in Nature. In the worship of the Divine both immanent in Nature and transcendent beyond it, we find our true religion.

Pagans do not, in the main, feel the need to create intellectual definitions of their religious understanding. Words such as 'pantheist' and 'polytheist' are not widely used: categorization of our belief systems is not important. We recognize that all such intellectual exercises are ultimately futile. Rational explanations, and the dogmatic theological creeds to which they give rise, were a stage in humanity's evolution, but they are ultimately illusionary. All religious dogma is an attempt to codify that which is beyond the word-based conscious mind. We can only understand it by entering into unity with it.

Isis-Nuit

You sit enthroned within the caverns of my mind,
but Thy throne is empty.
No image will I fashion to grace its seat.
All images are limitation;
and Thou, my belovèd, art infinite beyond all vision.

In realms beyond my imagining,
lies indwelling your eternal spirit,
dreaming to birth the constellations
and nurturing the galaxies.

Hail to Thee, Great Mother,
whose robe is the universe,
whose sequins are the stars!

In the cold places of the night,
I dream of Thy Great Halls:
   three columns of black marble,
   by the pool of the sleeping lotus,
   white petals on dark water.

Where breath turns to mist,
and infinity turns to meaning;
beyond the sound of harp strings,
where the voice no longer echoes,
and silence rings with sound;
where vision can only struggle and fail,
to encapsulate Thy being;
I hear Thee calling and I come –
across the Abyss, below which is Nothingness,
only the empty sighing of the wind;
across the shaking rope-bridge,
which spans the endless chasm.

I walk to Thee in trepidation;
yet seek no other destination;

I do not fear to cross the walk-way,
I do not fear to cross the chasm;
I come with a heart free of longing or desire;
I come to the place of the column
of blue-white-light-fire.

No words now come, or thought, or feeling;
in the reality of Thy presence,
All is as Nothing.
My being fades,
the blue-white consumes,
I-We are One,
are One,
are One. [3]

Mysticism

Contact with and exploration of the worlds of inward reality have ever been the goals of mysticism. It is a goal with a clearly-defined end: that of becoming at-one with Goddess or God, of finding the Divine Self which is present within us all and of uniting our external personality with this Divine centre. The mysticism of all religion seeks to help us integrate the disparate parts of our psyche and to find a point of centredness and peace. In Paganism, we seek the integration of the personality into a coherent and well-functioning whole, which can then find union with the Gods – the divine source of all being. 'Stop knowing and become' is therefore at the heart of much Pagan religious thought; as is the teaching that we are not separate and alone but 'are each part of the interpenetrating, intercommunicating reality that is All.' [4]

The goal of the spiritual quest has been expressed in many different ways throughout the ages; but the mysticism of all religions leads to the same end – unity with the Divine. This fact that mystical Oneness can be achieved through many religious paths and by different means is indicative of the absurdity of religions which teach that there is only one right way. Achieving religious understanding is rather like climbing a series of mountains. We see only what is visible from the top of the particular mountain on which we stand. Each human generation which reaches a peak believes that, 'This is it! We have found the Ultimate Truth.' Then we see that another mountain peak, still higher, beckons and we must begin our journey again. The old truth is only partial. There is ever more to discover; more to be revealed. Then, at the end of our Quest, we discover that that which we sought we carried with us all the time. No outer journey was necessary: we needed only to 'be still and know that I am God'; but therein lies a paradox. If we had not made the journey, we would never have gained the wisdom to know that we already knew what we sought. Such are the strange spirals in the inner journey of the heart.

Although the routes may differ, there are commonalities in the spiritual quest which can be distilled from the wisdom of all faiths. The ultimate experience is often called 'being in touch with the centre' or the Higher Self. Jean Hardy, in her book on psychosynthesis, *A Psychology with a Soul*, argues that this is achieved by being constantly aware of the strength within oneself, and of spirit at work in the world. She distinguishes six attitudes which are important:

being able to see the transcendent and the immanent qualities in other people, in animals, in all creation;
recognizing that a spiritually aware person is on a journey towards becoming aware of what he or she can be;
being able to live and share with other people in a more humble and accepting way;
being able to work well and give to the world from a centred place;
being committed to the causes one sees as important;
and being aware of the creative forces which have occurred throughout human history and upon which we can all draw.[5]

These attitudes may be developed through sincere practice of many different spiritual systems. To poet Robert Bly, this is what is really meant by religion.

Religion here does not mean doctrine, or piety, or purity, or 'faith' or 'belief', or my life given to God. It means a willingness to be a fish in the holy water, to be fished for by Dionysus or one of the other fishermen, to bow the head and take hints from one's own dreams, to live a secret life, praying in a closet, to be lowly, to eat grief as the fish gulps water and lives. It means being both fisherman and fish, not to be the wound but to take hold of the wound. Being a fish is to be active; not with cars or footballs, but with soul.[6]

The realization of unity and centredness in something greater than ourselves is important not just for personal spiritual attainment, but also for society. The achievement of inner unity within individuals is essential if society is to progress. Many religions and political creeds have endeavoured to create a Utopia, a perfect society. However, they tried to do so by changing the structure of society. Society is the creation of those who live in it. If society is deficient, it is because we are deficient. In order to create social harmony, we must first find harmony within ourselves. Otherwise our vision of what constitutes social harmony will be false and distorted by the flaws within our own personalities.

In *The Varieties of Religious Experience*, written at the turn of the century, the psychologist William James explored the difference between healthy and sick ways of living. Much of our society and social structures today are based on sick ways of living because they are created by sick people. In order to transform society, we must transform ourselves. One of his lectures describes the religion of healthy-mindedness which proceeds from an inner unity, 'emanating from a centre that is naturally happy and optimistic and always striving towards growth.'[7]

Much of what has been taught in past religion has taken us far from the religion of healthy-mindedness. Many religions preach love, but in their names people torture and kill others whose views of reality do not accord with their own. True love comes from inner harmony and the learning of wisdom. To achieve wisdom, we must have the humility to see that our views of reality are limited. If we follow our spiritual path with these truths in mind, then our religion can become a force of creativity which will help and benefit the world around us. If we follow our path in order to gain power over others; to impose on others our view of right and wrong; to oppress and maim the spiritual strivings of others, then whatever name we give our religion, it is a religion of tyranny and evil.

The Earth and Her peoples have need of those whose understanding of the needs of humanity is greatest. The spiritual quest can be a selfish pursuit if it is engaged in solely for the benefit of the individual concerned. That is not its purpose. Our minds are far-reaching. They range like spacecraft across the uncharted starry skies of consciousness, seeking to reach the home of the Gods and to know their purposes. Those whose inspiration has helped them to reach heaven's heights and to see the universe as it truly is – theirs is the task of helping humanity evolve on the next step of its journey. The objective of the mystical quest in the Pagan tradition is not to achieve withdrawal, nirvana, shanti, but, as Marian Green writes: 'a desire to serve the rest of Creation by finding and bringing back the Grail of Wisdom by whose waters the whole world will be healed, the Wasteland made green again (for it has been green!).'[8] Those who achieve this unity in the vanguard of humankind and bring back the Grail so that others may drink are its true Shamans, priests, poets and visionaries. They are not greater than their fellows, but are the squirrels on the Tree of Life, running up and down its branches to bring spiritual messages from the crown and the truths of Nature from the base to return to us in Midgard with the nuts of wisdom.

How is this unity achieved? Centredness comes from an inner harmony. In Eastern systems, this is achieved through meditation. This is also important in the Western tradition, but Western systems rely to a much greater extent on more extraverted practice. Whereas the Eastern mind often tends to introversion and abstraction, the Western mind tends to express the mystical process in concrete terms. One way is through participation in ritual with others. By following the seasonal cycle and experiencing and meditating on its symbolism and hidden truths, we come to recognize the enduring nature of the life force and that it is part of us and we of it. This is not just an intellectual understanding. The processes of ritual have a profound effect on the human psyche and bring about deep changes in consciousness, whereby we achieve inner stillness. The ritual processes of the Pagan tradition bring us to this state through exposure to symbols, the enactment of myth, the use of meditation and visualization and, sometimes, Shamanic techniques.

Some modern Pagan rites use ritual as a form of spiritual purification in much the same way as the Pagan Neoplatonists of Greece and Rome used the spiritual exercises of theurgy to achieve oneness with the Divine. Alchemy is a related Western mystical system, which is concerned not so much with the finding of material gold, but with the finding of the true gold of the spirit. The series of purifications and mental disciplines necessary to produce gold bring about a change in the consciousness of the practitioner. The original purpose of the quest becomes irrelevant. It is the journeying which is important. The word 'journeying' appears often in the Western tradition.

The language of mysticism is frequently expressed in terms of a Sacred Quest – a spiritual journey to retrieve a treasure from a giant, a monster or even from death itself. Often there is imagery associated with a descent – a descent into the unconscious. It is portrayed in myth and legend as a heroic journey into the Underworld.

In Wicca, the Goddess descends into the Underworld not to seek a treasure, but to find the answer to a question; to ask the Lord of Death, 'Why dost thou cause all things that I love and take delight in to fade and die?' She discovers the answer to this age-old question which troubles humankind and in return does receive a treasure – the Necklace of Rebirth. Similarly, in the Welsh *Mabinogion*, King Arthur has to enter the Underworld, Annwn, to retrieve the Cauldron of Rebirth. Later stories in the Arthurian cycle describe the quest by King Arthur's knights for the mystical treasure of the Holy Grail. The Grail is a Christian symbol, but it is based on much older Celtic legends of the Cauldron of Rebirth and Plenty which contains all blessedness. The Quest is also often expressed in terms of a journey to the four quarters of the world.

> We came then,
> the last Children of Cerridwen,
> Daughters of Light and Darkness,
> and Sons of Death.
>
> We sought your presence on the wild hills of the North,
> but in the loneliness,
> we found you not.
> We sought your presence in the light of the East,
> but in the mists of dawn,
> we discerned you not.
> We sought your presence beneath the Sun of the South,
> but where shadows shrink,
> we could not see your face.
> We sought your presence where the wind sleeps in the
>   West,
> but in the silence,
> we could not hear your voice . . .[9]

After journeying in all directions we find what we seek at the centre, at the point from which we started. In the Norse-German myth of Freya's descent to the Underworld to win the necklace

Brisingamen, which shines like fire, she must spend a night with each of the four dwarves who forged it. The symbolism of the quest captures the imagination still. J.R.R. Tolkien's *Lord of the Rings* was enormously successful because it spoke to people of a sacred quest in mythological terms. Many modern computer games such as *Dungeons and Dragons* are also based on this theme.

Many people at some point in their lives choose to make a physical journey which is really a voyage to find themselves and who they truly are. As we break away from adolescence into adulthood, or as we make the transition from parenthood to being free adults again when our children leave home to fend for themselves; these can all be good times to make the inner or the outer journey. The treasure which is sought in these quests is rebirth; not rebirth of the body, but rebirth of the personality as the True Self – ourselves as we can be when the fears, weaknesses and imperfections of the outer personality are cast aside. Jung, in *Psychology and Alchemy*, describes the True Self as 'the treasure hard to find [which] lies in the ocean of the unconscious, and only the brave can reach it.[10]

What is this True Self which we so earnestly seek? To describe the Self is difficult. It is an inner experience and as such is beyond words. The language of poetry can sometimes convey it or the language of image. Here is a description from the Hindu texts of the *Upanishads*.

> As an eagle weary after soaring in the sky,
> folds its wings and flies down to rest in its nest,
> so does the shining Self enter the state of dreamless sleep,
> where one is freed from all desires.
> The Self is free from desire,
> free from evil,
> free from fear.
>
> As a man in the arms of his beloved
> is not aware of what is without and what is within,
> so a person in union with the Self
> is not aware of what is without and what is within;
> for in that unitive state,
> all desires find their perfect fulfilment.
> There is no other desire that needs to be fulfilled,
> and one goes beyond sorrow.[11]

The realization of the Self is an experience which is well documented in mystical literature. It is often accompanied by a sense of bliss and dissolution. The boundaries of the personality are found to be false barriers and we discover that within us is a largeness, a greatness, that is beyond our imagining. It is both us and not-us, I and Other. We transcend the boundaries of this world and its consciousness and enter the Garden of the beyond. 'O ecstasy, O ecstasy, I have seen the Kingdom, and it bloomed for me.' [12]

> . . . the self is pure awareness, light and illumination, the fulfilment of one's destiny. It is not the state of unconsciousness of a stone or matter. . . . It is not a metaphysical concept or a hypothesis of science, but a matter of experience, supported by all the mystics and prophets of the world . . . the end and aim of the journey of life. [13]

As well as the language of myth, Pagans use the modern language of humanistic, transpersonal and depth psychology to explain humanity's quest to come to terms with its deeper needs and its spiritual destiny. Many psychologists and those following spiritual paths now recognize that the outer spiritual quest for God is in part an inner spiritual journey. This is not to denigrate the spiritual quest, or by a process of reductionism to turn it into mere psychology, but to recognize that 'if that which thou seekest thou findest not within thee, thou wilt never find it without thee' [14] The Divine is present within us as well as in the world outside and beyond. Jean Hardy, in her book *A Psychology with a Soul: Psychosynthesis in Evolutionary Context* explains:

> In transpersonal psychotherapy terms, the search for spiritual meaning is also the search for the Self, the 'God within', which is linked to the soul of the world. [15]

In entering into contact with universality, paradoxically we do not lose our individuality, but we become more aware of our uniqueness, while at the same time recognizing that we are facets of a greater whole.

Individuation

The discovery, or recovery, of the Self – for it is always there – is what Carl Jung described as the process of individuation. This is the process of becoming who and what we really are. In a sense, it is the aim of all mystical and initiatory processes, in whatever religious symbolism they are dressed. The old outer form is taken from us so that we can find what is beneath. As we go deeper into ourselves through our spiritual training, we come to the core of our personality – the bedrock – where the individual verges on the collective and where we meet with the greater whole – the group mind of humanity. Carl Jung wrote that as we gain in self-knowledge and awareness, and act accordingly, so the layers of the personality are stripped away.

> In this way there arises a consciousness which is no longer imprisoned in the petty, over sensitive, personal world of the ego, but participates freely in the wider world of objective interests. The widened consciousness is no longer that touchy, egotistical bundle of personal wishes, fears, hopes, and ambitions which always has to be compensated or corrected by unconscious counter-tendencies; instead it is a function of relationship to the world of objects bringing the individual into absolute, binding, and indissoluble communion with the world at large.[16]

Individuation is becoming what we were meant to be from the beginning. This process involves letting go of the false images of ourselves which have been built up by our environment and by the projected visions of parents, teachers, friends and lovers. This is often symbolized in initiation rites by the removal or change of clothing. On this symbolic level, the process is simple, but on the inner level it is painful. It involves the destruction and letting go of the ego and all that we thought of as us, but was not. This is difficult. The human mind seeks refuge always in the security of the known. It fears the unknown and change.

There is much emphasis in Paganism on clear-seeing, the original meaning of the word clairvoyance. This is also found in Eastern religion. In the East, it is the task of the guru to help remove the veil of ignorance from the disciple so that he or she may see him- or herself, and also the world, as they really are. It is in seeing-clear and in developing a true understanding of the nature of reality that we can return to the Godhead from which we came. Clear-seeing is hampered by the confines of doctrine, because all religious teachings are only humanity's imperfect attempts to understand the Divine reality. All doctrines will be transcended as we come nearer our goal.

In Eastern spiritual thought, transcendence is achieved by disidentification from attachments to mind and body. Our sensory processes and intellectual processes are seen as traps which attempt to classify the world for us. However, they can only classify the world according to the limits of their mechanisms. In the end they are biologically based and as constrained as any engine or mechanical device. They can only take us so far down the road of understanding. True understanding comes from inner experience which is beyond the classifications invented by the mind and senses.

In order to find the Self, the wiser and deeper part of ourselves, we must make a spiritual journey. This is the process of spiritual initiation. The initiation ceremonies which make us an adult member of society, or which initiate us into a particular religious tradition, are entry points to this process, but they are not the process itself. The process is life long – hence the sight of the Grail often ends in death; for after we have achieved total Oneness with the ultimate reality, then we have reached our spiritual home. No more journeying forth is necessary.

The imagery of initiation is strongly bound up with that of death and rebirth. The old personality dies and a new one is reborn. The initiate is both the same and different. As in reincarnation, something remains from the old, but life begins anew. The close association between the world of dream, individuation and death emerges strongly in Dion Fortune's work.

> There are two deaths by which men die,
> the greater and the lesser.
> The death of the body, and the death of the initiation.
> And of these two,
> the death of the body is the lesser.
> The man who looks upon the face of Isis dies;
> for the Goddess takes him. [17]

> In death men go to Her across the shadowy river,
> for She is the keeper of their souls until the dawn.
> But there is also a death in life,
> and this likewise leadeth on to rebirth. [18]

The ultimate end of the initiatory process is found at the end of many lifetimes. While the East teaches that the journey of lives is an undesirable binding to the material world, Western

Paganism teaches that journeying hopefully is worthwhile and enjoyable in itself. It is also necessary that the more spiritually advanced members of our society do not take it into their heads to dissolve into Nirvana too soon. In the religions of the Piscean Age, the focus was on the salvation of the individual. As we move into the twenty-first century, the lives of the whole human race and of the planet on which we live are at threat. The issue is not our individual needs, but the needs of the world as a whole. We seek the Grail in order to become it – that we may become vessels so that others too may drink from that source.

The Grail
I was a walker of the ways,
and a wanderer of the waste,
I was a mariner upon the deep,
I was a seeker of the most High,
then I came by night to the dark mountainside
and slept and dreamt.

And now I am light in the eyes of the prophet,
I am a sapphire sparkling in the Sun,
I rest upon the breast of the Great Mother,
I am the belovèd of the mountain's heart.

I am a well in the desert,
I contain both light and water,
they may draw from me which they will.
The light of Sun and Moon,
and the rains of heaven replenish me,
I am the Grail.[19]

1. Vivian Worthington, *A History of Yoga*, page 7.
2. From Vivianne Crowley, *Lord I have Furnished a Temple in Your Sight*, Lammas 1978.
3. Vivianne Crowley, *Isis-Nuit*, 1990.
4. Starhawk as quoted in Michael Perry, *Gods Within: A Critical Guide to the New Age*, page 16.
5. Jean Hardy, *A Psychology with a Soul: Psychosynthesis in Evolutionary Context*, pages 60–1.
6. Robert Bly, *Iron John*, page 38.
7. William James, *The Varieties of Religious Experience*, pages 92–136.
8. Marian Green, *The Path Through the Labyrinth*, page 8.
9. From *The Children of Cerridwen*, Vivianne Crowley, Autumn 1984.

10. Quoted in Jean Hardy, *A Psychology with a Soul: Psychosynthesis in Evolutionary Context*, page 61.

11. Eknath Easwaran (trans.), *The Upanishads, Brihadranyaka Upanishad*, Chapter IV, verses 19–21, page 45.

12. From Vivianne Crowley, Imbolc, 1988.

13. Arwind Vasavada in J.M. Spiegelman and A.U. Vasavadas, *Hinduism and Jungian Psychology*, page 157.

14. From the Wiccan *Book of Shadows*, as quoted in Vivianne Crowley, *Wicca: The Old Religion in the New Age*, page 161.

15. Jean Hardy, *A Psychology with a Soul: Psychosynthesis in Evolutionary Context*, page 61.

16. Carl Jung, *Collected Works*, volume 7, page 275.

17. Dion Fortune, *The Sea Priestess*, page 124.

18. Dion Fortune, *The Sea Priestess*, page 125.

19. Vivianne Crowley, April 1988.

14
Becoming a Pagan

As yet, few people are born into Pagan families. For most, the Pagan path is arrived at by conscious decision, rather than through being raised by Pagan parents in their philosophy. If having read and learned about Paganism, we decide that we are or wish to become Pagan, how do we go about it? The route into Paganism is different from that of many spiritual paths. If we want to become Christians, we can attend some local church services and then decide if we want to become more involved. If we want to become Pagans, the path can be a harder and lonelier one. The stages in becoming a Pagan are.

1. Learning about Pagan Gods and mythology.
2. Deciding we are Pagans.
3. Developing contact with Nature.
4. Celebrating the major Pagan festivals.
5. Drawing nearer our Gods through meditation and prayer.
6. Practising Pagan ethics.
7. Deciding whether to join a Pagan group.
8. Deciding to join a particular Pagan tradition.

Learning about Pagan Gods and Mythology

To become Pagans, we must first learn something about Paganism and decide if this is the right path for us. For this, we can turn to those outer sources of knowledge which are most accessible to us. Information about Paganism is obtainable in books which we can borrow from libraries or buy from local bookstores. These may in turn point the way to magazines and more specialist

Pagan books. Some suggestions for reading are contained in the Resources Guide. These sources will give you an idea of whether Paganism is the right path for you.

Deciding we are Pagans

From reading this book and/or from studying further, you may decide that Paganism makes sense and is in accord with your own beliefs. It may be that you have already developed your own spiritual philosophy and have realized for the first time that this can be described as Paganism. To become a Pagan, no formal ceremony of admission is necessary – we become Pagans by deciding that we are; although particular traditions may have their own ceremonies of admission.

Developing Contact With Nature

Contact with the Earth and with Nature is important to all Pagans. The words Pagan and Heathen mean country dweller. Paganism is a religion based on the recognition of the Divine in Nature. Contact with Nature is essential if our Paganism is to be a deeply-rooted and permanent part of our lives. Many Pagans feel a bond with the Earth and with the environment around them which is mystical and very different from the attitude common to 'civilized' human beings today. This attitude was found in earlier times and even in recent history in the native peoples of many lands. It is a bond which is known in farming communities who for generations have tilled the same soil, lived in the same dwellings and have been linked to the same community. These communities were attuned to the land in the most natural of ways – by working it and living its seasonal cycle of growth, fruition, decay, rest and rebirth. In modern times, commitment to the land is important for all of us. Not all Pagans can uproot themselves from their cities and set up organic farms in idyllic countryside; although some do. Those of us who no longer till the soil must create this communion in another way. Creating gardens, taking part in tree-planting campaigns, and visiting sacred sites and natural places full of elemental energy, provide time and space for us to meditate on the forces of Nature and renew our commitment to love, protect and nurture her.

Celebrating the Major Pagan Festivals

We can celebrate the seasonal festivals in many ways. This can involve complex ceremonies or simply communing with Nature at the appropriate times. We can all make some space each seasonal festival to spend time outside. This can be in woods, seashore, moor or mountain, where the forces of Nature are untamed by human hand. However, if this is not possible, it need not debar us from experiencing Nature. We can also observe the growth processes of the seasonal cycle by choosing a tree in the local park and visiting it each festival. Those brought up in an urban environment must relearn the knowledge about and sensitivity to Nature which our ancestors took for granted. If we start out in simple ways to contact the Divine within Nature, we will find that it will begin to reach out to contact us.

If we decide to create celebatory rites we will need to decide on the presiding deities. In this book, I have described a number of different Pagan paths. The traditions I have described do not by any means cover the richness of Europe's cultural heritage. There are also the Gods of the Slavic peoples and the Gods of Greece and of Rome. For some people, these will be the deities to whom they naturally turn.

In some countries, there is one type of Paganism which can be identified as the true Paganism of the land and it is natural for Pagans to turn to these deities and their path. In the English-speaking countries, the situation is much less clear. The British Isles, for instance, have been the destination of immigrant peoples over thousands of years. Its inhabitants are a mixture of Celts, Norse, Germans and Picts, plus in recent years, African, Afro-Caribbean and Asian peoples. In earlier centuries, the pioneering spirit of our Norse ancestors and the wanderlust of the Celts took us to many other lands, whose people and environment were very different from our own. In the New World and Australasia, we created transplanted peoples, who in turn were followed by waves of other Europeans, Africans and Asians. To discover our Gods, we will need to take time to meditate on the different pantheons and deities to find those which seem to speak to us more strongly. It is not just a matter of us choosing them. They must choose us. Some of us may be drawn to the deities whose temples and myths are bound to our own landscape; sometimes we will be drawn to the Gods of our own racial heritage; sometimes other Gods will speak to us.

Many people throughout the world worship the Egyptian deities, whose archetypes are so strong in the collective unconscious that they appear spontaneously to many people in vision and dream.

For some, a synthesis of different Pagan beliefs, drawing on the richness of all our cultural heritages, seems most natural in the modern world. Many followers of the different Pagan movements are keeping their own traditions in private, but in public celebration they are moving ever nearer each other to produce what may be the religion of the future: a new Paganism which is enriched by many streams of thought. The different Pagan paths can be seen as rivers which have as their source one stream. The rivers flow separately and differently through different landscapes and take on different colours according to the soil through which they pass; but in the end all return to the one sea. Philip Carr-Gomm, Head of the Order of Bards, Ovates and Druids, writes of Druidry and Wicca:

> Perhaps we no longer need to polarise our allegiances
> between witch and Druid, allowing ourselves instead to
> enjoy that sense of inclusiveness which enables us to
> explore both traditions in a way that helps us to create the
> path which is unique to ourselves and which explores many
> ways of being which the two branches mediate. Perhaps we
> are approaching the time when once again we can simply
> be followers of the Old Religion, the Old Ways, the Secret
> Faith.[1]

Once we have established a link with our Gods, we need to strengthen our understanding of the ancient deities. We must study their mythologies and decide how we will address ourselves to them. We must not only take the written liturgy of others, but we must also create our own rites and prayers so that our spirituality is a living and ever-growing treasure store within us.

Some ideas for themes for the Pagan festivals are outlined in Chapter 11 on Worshipping the Gods. Further ideas on celebrating the seasonal festivals can be drawn from the books listed in the Resources Guide. The steps involved are:

1. Reading about appropriate seasonal myths.
2. Spending some time outside seeing what is happening in Nature and the agricultural cycle.
3. Setting aside some time to meditate on and/or celebrate the seasonal theme, what it means in our lives – perhaps saying prayers or invocations to appropriate deities.

We can do the latter with or without others; in specially consecrated sacred spaces using the rites of one of the traditions, by sitting down by our living room window or by walking through the forest. The important thing is to set aside some special time when we honour the Gods and the ever-renewing life force, turning our minds away for a time from the mundane necessities which beset much of our lives.

Drawing Nearer our Gods Through Meditation and Prayer

This is not easy. Many of us who start out on the Pagan path are building a spiritual life from scratch, often with nothing but our own intuition and contact with the Gods to guide us. On this lonely road, many of us can feel lost at first; inspired to go forward on the spiritual quest, but unsure how to begin. To go forward, we must have confidence in ourselves and be certain that the way is there if we seek it. Marian Green writes:

> The ancient gates have been restored, and the keys are available to anyone who has the patience, courage and will to find them. The oldest gods have never withdrawn from our world, we have retreated from them behind the false barriers of uninspired religious teaching and solid dogma.[2]

To develop our Paganism, we must reopen the gateways. All spiritual training is based on establishing clear channels of communication with the Otherworld. This can only be achieved by regular communion with it. All of us are bad at regularity and this is doubly hard if we are practising our Paganism alone. We may have families, jobs, educational courses, all competing for our time and attention. How can we fit in another demand?

If our Paganism is to be strong, it must be a part of our everyday life. A remarkable difference between Western and Eastern approaches to religion is the extent to which Hindus, Moslems and Buddhists will take time each day to honour their Gods in totally unselfconscious ways. There is nothing unusual in the East about people stopping in the street to pray. Such behaviour in the West would cause irritation, ridicule and some annoyance to others: the busy lives we lead cannot be interrupted by people prostrate upon the pavement. Overt displays of religiosity are alien in most Western countries and they are not advocated by Pagans; but if we wish to practise our Paganism, it is important that we take a small amount of time each day to be in conscious contact with our Gods. This does not mean that we have to perform elaborate ceremonies, nor does it mean that unconscious links are not present as we go about our everyday lives; but our spiritual life is like a young plant. It must be carefully nurtured, especially at the beginning, if it is to flourish in a hostile climate.

As with other faiths, many Pagan paths advocate daily meditation as a way to draw nearer to the Gods. Pagans talk often of the concept of being centred. This means being tranquil and still within ourselves, listening to the inner voice, the Higher Self – the Divine within us, which is in communion with the Divine without. This centredness is a form of prayer; for prayer to a Pagan is not asking for things from our Gods; it is being with our Gods. We may wish to ask for their help or guidance, but that is not the main object of the exercise. An Odinist writes:

> Odinists in their inveita (praise) call upon the Aesir to approach them in their thoughts as they themselves strive towards the Aesir. Through increased understanding is achieved wholeness, a unity with the Gods that helps us to think out our problems and how they may be overcome. [3]

To take time in the day to centre ourselves and be in communion with the Divine spirit which permeates the universe is like paying a visit to a friend. Often words are unnecessary. Merely to be in the presence of a wise friend refreshes us, makes us clear in our thought and more certain of our purposes.

Practising Pagan Ethics

If we are to call ourselves Pagans, we must live as Pagans. The Pagan ethos has been outlined in this book, but our behaviour may at times deviate far from the ideals of harmony, love and honour which Paganism advocates. To develop our ethical sense, we must be ruthlessly honest with ourselves about our behaviour and motives. We must also have enough self-love to forgive ourselves when we fail to meet our own ideals, and the courage to try again. Some Pagan paths advocate taking time to examine the events of the day and our role in them. A spiritual diary is helpful in this. At the end of the day, in our time of reflection, we consider how we have gone about the day's activities and whether our actions have been centred: that is, proceeding from that centre within us which recognizes what is in accordance with the greater good.

Deciding Whether to Join a Pagan Group

Pagans may worship on their own much of the time; either from necessity or choice. Some Pagans prefer to follow their path alone and attend no religious gatherings. They commune with Nature in her woods and fields and follow the ways of their ancestors. While they may seek an individual teacher, they do not feel the need to meet others or join a group. Others, having decided that they are Pagans, may feel the need to meet and talk with those who share their ideas. Many people find this difficult. They may have tried to talk with friends or family about their beliefs and found rejection, puzzlement or ridicule. At this point, they may write to a Pagan organization asking if they are the only Pagan in the world, they may feel so isolated. Such a feeling is very common in those pioneers who are breaking new spiritual ground. Marilyn Ferguson, in her book *The Aquarian Conspiracy*, comments:

> . . . when a paradigm is shifting, those who espouse the new ideas often imagine that they are isolated individuals swimming against the current. They are amazed when they discover how many people agree with them – sometimes as secretly as themselves.[4]

Pagans conduct religious rituals because they are considered pleasing to the Gods; but worshipping with others also has a social purpose. Group rituals represent a shared enactment of religious myths. Joining together with others to recognize our common spiritual beliefs produces a sense of community between Pagans and a knowledge that we are not alone. This can give us the strength to stand up for our beliefs and to pioneer them in a sometimes hostile society.

If we decide to meet others, this may not be easy. There are open religious gatherings and these are growing, but at present they are restricted to a few localities. Elsewhere, contact with other Pagans is more usual via a national Pagan organization or through a local discussion or social group which may lead to an invitation to attend gatherings. Magazines will often provide lists of events and groups which it may be possible to attend in order to explore the Pagan path more fully. There may not be a group available locally, but there are national organizations which can assist by providing postal tuition, workshops, conferences, etc.

Deciding to Join a Particular Pagan Tradition

If we wish to follow a particular Pagan tradition, we may wish to contact an appropriate group or organization and study for admission. In some traditions, this may not be necessary. Shamanism, for instance, is more usually practised alone; although people may study under a teacher at the beginning and may come together for special ceremonies. Personal contact with others on a particular path can, however, be extremely helpful. Much of Paganism is based on oral teaching and tradition and cannot be conveyed by the printed word. For instance, creating rites and ceremonies when we have never seen any can be difficult unless we are particularly gifted in this direction.

Finding a group may not be easy. The Pagan paths are not missionary religions and do not proselytize. Most Pagans believe that anyone who sincerely seeks contact with their path will be drawn to the right source. Paganism is therefore a path for the persistent. It does not offer easy answers and at present it is not sufficiently resourced to sustain the very dependent. However, groups do exist and someone may be lucky enough to find that there is a suitable group on the doorstep. If this is not the case, we can study through books, and some traditions offer home study courses to assist those who do not have access to a local group. Some suggestions are found in the resources guide.

If you decide to seek admission to a particular Pagan tradition, this may involve a period of training and instruction and passing through a formal induction or initiation ceremony. Whether this is open to you may depend upon your age. Some Pagan paths believe that undertaking a particular religious path is more in the nature of answering a vocation, that is responding to a call from the Gods, and this is not something we are able to do until we reach adulthood.

Having made contact with a group, how do you decide if it is right for you? There are two major criteria – respect and liking. Respect does not mean a one-sided respect for the group and its leaders, if it has them. Respect means mutual respect. Are the people in the group interested in you as an individual and prepared to listen to your views? Do the people in the group seem emotionally stable? Beware of those who claim mystical powers, but whose own personal lives are a mess. Mystical vision alone may be of use to a hermit in a cave, but it is not sufficient to guide a Pagan group whose members must live in the real world. These personality issues may seem far removed from the primary purpose of joining a group, which is to meet with others to celebrate the mysteries of the Gods and possibly, but not necessarily, to obtain knowledge and training from those who are more experienced on the path. However, groups can stand or fall on the personalities, adequacies or inadequacies of their members and leaders.

Joining a group is about finding a group of people with whom we feel compatible. As in all religions, unscrupulous people may masquerade as spiritual teachers in order to exploit others. It is important that we use our common sense when choosing a spiritual group, just as we would when choosing any group of people with whom to work and be friends. This is especially true if we are young and inexperienced in the ways of the world. It is better to be a solo Pagan than to try and join a group where you do not trust or feel in harmony with its members.

Liking is the second criteria for choosing to join a group. It is possible to celebrate the festivals with a group whose members you respect, but who are not people whom you would normally choose as personal friends. Often Pagan groups are very mixed in terms of age, education, occupation and interests. This can be a great source of strength as different members bring different knowledge and life experience to the group. Do not be put off if you find that, when you meet your local Pagans, they are all leather-jacketed, computer whiz kids or New Age grannies and you are not. Find out what lies behind the surface appearance and you may find that what you have in common transcends outer differences. Celebrating together in an atmosphere of mutual trust can lead to a deep friendship and liking between people whose paths would never normally cross.

Do-It-Yourself Paganism

If you are not able to find a Pagan group in your area, you could
set up your own. In forming a group, the advice of others can
be invaluable. This can be obtained from one of the national
organizations representing a particular Pagan path, or from one
of the umbrella organizations which represent Pagans in general.
If you go down the road of creating your own group, there are
a number of practical problems. Premises is one. In the summer
months your group may be able to meet and celebrate outside,
but this may not be much fun on a rainy January night. You may
have to rent a room if no one has a suitable room in his/her home.
Most local authorities have rooms in libraries, etc. Other
organizations such as students' unions and New Age centres may
have rooms they would be willing to rent for seasonal
celebrations.

The next issue is people. At first your group is likely to be small.
You may have a group of friends who share your interests. A
number of you at the local Pagan discussion group may decide
that you would like to create a group to celebrate the major
festivals. You may find that everyone who is interested in the
group has a similar Pagan orientation – be it Shamanism,
Goddess worship, Celtic mysteries or whatever. This simplifies
things. However, you may find that one of you is a budding
Odinist, another is a Goddess-oriented woman not entirely sure
about working with men, and others would really have liked to
join a Wiccan coven, but there isn't one available. Some of you
may want to do ritual in your everyday clothes, others may want
to go back to Nature and throw their clothes to the winds, others
may fancy a nice black hooded robe that your Goddess-oriented
friend thinks looks Satanic. How can you tackle these problems?

Apart from giving up in despair at the first hurdle, the obvious
answer is that there are no easy solutions, but only a difficult
one – compromise. If you are setting up an eclectic Pagan group
and you are yourself a novice, then you cannot impose your own
views and ethos on the group. What has to emerge is a
consensus, which is inevitably a compromise, but which will
enable you to get your group off the ground and working. This
is by no means easy. The psychological literature is full of texts
about the complexities about small group dynamics.

Making compromises is one of the disadvantages of group
working and why many people decide that groups are not for

them. They have a distinct view which they feel is right and do not wish to compromise about the ideals they hold. Such views must be respected. Western human beings, and especially Western Pagan human beings, tend to be individualists. Even those working in the same tradition will not agree entirely on their interpretation of that tradition. On the positive side, one of the beauties of working in a group is learning to interact with others in a meaningful way on deep spiritual issues. We may be the world's greatest Druids, Witches or Shamans, but if we cannot relate to other human beings, then what use are we in the world?

What is necessary in a group is not complete conformity of ideas, but commitment. In order to build a group which works on a spiritual level, it is necessary that people meet together on a regular basis. Some groups may be able to meet weekly. Others may have work and/or family commitments which make that impractical. A pattern of fortnightly meetings often works well and is sufficiently frequent for members to get to know each other and build up a group mind.

Most Pagan groups wish to celebrate the seasonal festivals. Some groups may also wish to celebrate the full Moons. It is good to celebrate these on the exact day, but in practice, unless members live very near to one another, it can be easier to choose a particular day of the week for meetings and to stick to that. People can then plan their other commitments to fit. Most Pagans feel comfortable about celebrating festivals and full Moons on the nearest possible date. It is also important that people pick a pattern of meeting that is practical. Many groups start out enthusiastically meeting every week and then quickly run out of steam. It is better to choose a slightly less ambitious schedule which people can keep.

What can a group do when it meets? Not all meetings need be serious and reverential occasions. Some meetings can be for socializing, reading, discussion, meditation, pathworking or, if the group practises magic, to develop particular magical or divinatory techniques. While there may be no experienced Pagan ritualists in the group everyone will have a little bit of knowledge about something and everyone's areas of knowledge are likely to be slightly different. This is a basis for developing self-teaching and a pooling and sharing of knowledge and expertise.

You may find that no one feels competent to set themselves up as a teacher, but different people can take turns to lead on a particular topic and other people can read up on it and bring their particular piece of research to the discussion. In this way all can contribute and learn from each other. It is possible, for instance, for a group to teach itself about the Celtic tradition by having two members read up on the Irish and Welsh Gods and between them giving a talk on Celtic mythology. Another member could learn the runes and demonstrate a method of divination. Others could devise a rite in honour of some of the Gods and Goddesses of a particular pantheon. The rite might be rather ragged the first time it was worked, but as people became more familiar with the format and revised the rite to run more smoothly, its power and energy would grow.

Developing our Paganism in this way is not so different from studying and practising alone. The big advantage is that it overcomes the laziness and inertia factor. As we all know, studying alone is very hard when we have to parent our children, hold down jobs, study for qualifications and all the myriad other tasks we are trying to perform in the world. The advantage of learning together is that we know we have to do our share when other people are relying on us and so it gives us that extra incentive to persevere.

Group visualization and pathworking exercises are another important activity. To conduct meaningful ritual that is not just a theatrical display by the main participants, it is necessary for everyone to be participating in the ritual on an inner level, not just through external words and actions. Even if people want to work from the perspective of different traditions, it can be a good idea for the group to develop its own way of opening and closing rites which can then be adapted to different pantheons and traditions. Having a familiar opening and closing gives the group a sense of focus and identity. It is a way of saying, 'This is us and this is our space. This is what we are here to do.'

In a newly-formed group, a natural leader or leaders may emerge whom the other group members are happy to allow to take on the organizing role. However, in an eclectic group where no one has the mandate of leadership, this can be a tricky problem. What the group will need if it is to survive is not so much a leader as people who are prepared to take responsibility for some aspect of the group's activities and someone with good enough people skills to persuade the others to volunteer for those responsibilities.

At the outset, it is a good idea to have an administration

meeting and to decide what the group needs to do to organize itself. Does it need a kitty to pay to rent a room, invite occasional speakers, buy candles and incense? Can the group organize itself in another way with people bringing and supplying different items in turns? It is important that some people do not find their generosity taken for granted by the other members or resentments will build up that can destroy what could have been a successful group. If the group always meets in Sarah's flat, are members taking it for granted that she will clean up the ritual space for them, do the washing up afterwards, supply all the candles, incense and maybe even the wine? If so, the group will be short-lived. Groups need to realistically assess the inputs that are needed in terms of time, effort and cash and to make sure that the burden is evenly spread. All these problems can be solved, providing the group makes sure that it gives time and space to admin meetings as well as to its rites, celebrations and learning. A quarterly discussion meeting on how are we doing is useful. Are we satisfied with what we've done so far? What do we want to do next? Is everyone contributing as they should? How do we decide if a new person should join the group? All these domestic issues are mundane in themselves, but the skill with which we learn to deal with them will determine whether we have a creative group which teaches us not only mystical and spiritual knowledge, but also how to relate better with other people – something which will stand us in good stead in the outer world as well as the inner.

Coming Out

Regardless of whether or not we join a group, a decision which every Pagan must make is how public to be about our Paganism. Do you want to 'come out'? Identifying yourself as Pagan will arouse people's interest and they will want to ask you questions about your beliefs. Some people are happy to deal with this; others prefer to keep their beliefs to themselves. However, the more people who are prepared to be open, the more people will come to know and understand Pagans and to see their beliefs as part of the normal spectrum of spiritual belief in our multicultural societies.

Telling people about our religious beliefs when they ask us is very different from preaching to them. Whenever we discover some truth which works for us, it is tempting to try and convince others of its rightness. This can however be very counter-productive. There is nothing worse than the born-again bore and it is insulting and arrogant towards others to ridicule their own beliefs while flaunting the superiority of our own. Marian Green warns:

> Religious nuts are the worst sort, and anyone who goes round preaching some far-fetched cosmic truth will meet with a good deal of opposition. You may indeed acquire privileged information of some kind of direct message from God, but it doesn't give you the automatic right to shout it from the housetops and expect to be believed. [5]

How open you wish to be about your beliefs depends of course on your working environment. If you work in the music business, somewhat exotic interests may be as obligatory as keeping your pet tarantula. If you are a merchant banker, being seen as weird or eccentric may be translated into unreliable and be the death of your career. Much also depends on where we live. In large multi-cultural cities, Pagans arouse no interest at all. In small conservative communities, coming out as a Pagan may lead to ostracization or worse.

There is also the vexed issue of children. In recent years, certain Christian-evangelical inspired campaigns have sought for their own perverse ends to destroy Paganism and to brand Pagans as child molesters and devil worshippers. This is a problem both for Pagan parents and for those who work in the caring professions. Generally, people are more frightened by things they do not know and understand. Parents who are Pagan find that talking to their children's teachers about their beliefs often raises fewer problems than little Rachel going to school one day saying, 'Mummy and Daddy took me dancing round the cauldron with the witches on Saturday.'

Another factor in how public we want to be about our Paganism is the brand we adopt. For Witches, the problems are greater than for Pagans on other paths. The word Witchcraft can be confused with Satanism. Publicity about modern day Witchcraft has done much to dispel misconceptions about it and to educate the public that it is a Pagan religion and not an anti-social cult; but the 'W' word has undoubtedly caused difficulties and some sensationalist, rather than serious, publicity. Many of those who follow the path of Wise-Craft prefer not to use the word Witch, because it creates too much misunderstanding. For some people the words wise woman, cunning man, Shaman, priest or priestess are seen as more accurate descriptions of their religious practice. Others believe, more robustly, that it is time to rehabilitate the word Witchcraft and to educate people about its true meaning.

Our approach to this must again be an individual decision and although Paganism has been denigrated by a Christian fundamentalist backlash in recent years, understanding between Pagans and more thinking Christians is growing. In recent years, conferences have been held for Christians and Pagans which have enabled those from the two faiths to share views and to come to mutual respect. This does not mean that all followers of all religions are going to come to the same view; but it does mean that we can learn from each other and that the insights which we have gained from our respective systems can enrich each others' spiritual lives. Pagans have also participated in interfaith conferences where those on other religious paths have been able to learn that the Pagan viewpoint, while different, shares many of the aims of the spirituality of all faiths. As Paganism has become more widespread, Christian ministers also find themselves meeting Pagans executing their ministry in settings such as hospital visiting and student counselling, and relationships of mutual friendship and respect have been established.

Many Christians now recognize that the crimes and perversions of which Witches are accused bear astonishing resemblance to those from which all persecuted minorities and, indeed, Christians themselves, have suffered from time immemorial. Michael Perry, the Archdeacon of Durham, one of the oldest Christian cathedrals, comments in his book *Gods Within: A Critical Guide to the New Age*:

> The European medieval witch-hunt throve upon the fantasy of 'a baby-killing, cannibalistic, incestuous, orgiastic Devil-worshipping community'. But then, the persecutions of Christians in the early years of our era fed upon similar misinformation, and fear. Their opponents circulated allegations that the Christians had a revolting rite of initiation in which they drowned babies, and that in their meetings, after eating the flesh and drinking the blood of a dead man, they went on to engage in what they called love-feasts where the wine flowed freely amongst the men – and women – who were present (nudge, nudge; wink, wink).[6]

However, while rational Christians may be able to come to an understanding of Pagan religion, there are plenty who still indulge in the knee-jerk response and, whether unwittingly or through maliciousness, perpetuate evil myths about practitioners of Paganism. Michael Perry describes an editorial in an Evangelical magazine – *Prophecy Today* – which suggested that Witches had been working by occult means to undermine family life and marriage, especially among Christians. As Michael Perry says, 'That does not seem to comport very well with "an it harm none do what ye will".' The article then claimed that the discovery of a blackbird hanging from an oak tree a mile or two from a British airport was 'clear evidence of witchcraft activity' and may well have caused the confusion in the mind of the pilot which led to the Kegworth air disaster in January 1989. Michael Perry comments wryly:

> I suppose it is just possible that telepathic activity could
> have confused the pilot's thought processes, though it seems
> an unlikely hypothesis. But to link a dead blackbird with
> witchcraft (when Wicca explicitly renounces any practice of
> sacrifice) shows a complete misunderstanding of that Craft.
> Farm labourers might have put a dead bird on a twig as a
> scarecrow device, or sick-minded characters might treat
> small creatures as flies to wanton boys, but to credit such
> people with wide-ranging psychic powers is unlikely in the
> extreme, and it certainly has nothing to do either with
> witchcraft . . .[7]

Given the range of reactions which Pagans receive, we must decide for ourselves how public we wish to be about our spiritual beliefs, while recognizing that the more that is known about the true nature of Paganism, the easier it will be for those who follow in our footsteps.

The Message of Paganism

Becoming a Pagan is on one hand easy: we can become Pagans without having to seek the recognition or authorization of anyone else. One the other hand, it is difficult. The infrastructure of support is much looser as yet than that for other religions. Paganism is not for the faint-hearted, but for those who are prepared to take responsibility for themselves and for their own spiritual development and learning. This can be daunting and we will make many mistakes and fail often, but this does not matter if we have the courage to go onward in pursuit of our goal. There is only one thing we need and that is commitment. The German mystic, poet and thinker Johann Wolfgang Goethe wrote:

> Until one is committed, there is always a hesitancy,
> the chance to draw back, always ineffectiveness.
>
> Concerning all acts of initiative and creation –
> there is one elementary truth, the ignorance of which
> kills countless ideas and splendid plans;
> that the moment one definitely commits oneself
> then Providence moves too.
> All sorts of things occur to help one
> that would never otherwise have occurred,
> a whole stream of events issue from the decision,
> raising in one's favour all manner of unforeseen incidents
> and meetings plus material assistance,
> which no man could have dreamed would have come his
>   way.
> Whatever you can do, or dream you can, begin it:
> boldness has genius, power and magic in it;
> begin it now.

1. Philip Carr-Gomm, 'Witches and Druids', in *The Cauldron: Pagan Journal of the Old Religion*, No. 68, pages 4–5.
2. Marian Green, *The Path Through the Labyrinth*, pages 62–3.
3. The Odinist Committee, *This is Odinism: Guidelines for Survival*, page 15.
4. Marilyn Ferguson, *The Aquarian Conspiracy*, quoted in Michael Perry, *Gods Within: A Critical Guide to the New Age*, page 13.
5. Marian Green, *The Path Through the Labyrinth*, page 137.
6. Michael Perry, *Gods Within: A Critical Guide to the New Age*, page 69.
7. Michael Perry, *Gods Within: A Critical Guide to the New Age*, page 131.

15

Towards The Future: Paganism in the Twenty-First Century

Towards the Future?

In order for us to worship our Gods, we must have a planet to live on! In Pagan teaching, cycles of creation contain within them the seeds of their own destruction. Since creation is a cyclical and ever-renewing process, in order to make way for new life, all creation must lead inevitably to destruction. All things material are transient. Creation is subject to gradual decay, as well as to periodic cataclysms. Even mineral life, we now know, is subject to the same inevitable process. The Norse-German tradition teaches that Yggdrasil, the Tree of Life which symbolizes the cosmos as we know it, will one day be destroyed. The forces of destruction are ever at work. Four stags (often thought to represent the four winds) nibble at its leaves; two goats chew its bark; the teeth of the serpent Nidhögg, Gnawer-from-Beneath, gnaw at its root undermining it from below. When it has lived its allotted span, the mighty Ash tree will be overthrown. Creation begins, reaches its peak, falls into decline and then disintegrates or is destroyed.

> In the beginning was space and darkness and stillness,
> older than time and forgotten of the Gods.
> The sea of infinite space was the source of all being;
> life arose therein like a tide in the soundless sea.
> All shall return thereto when the night of the Gods draws in. [1]

Creation reaches a point when it can sustain itself no longer, and manifestation is reabsorbed into itself.

In the Norse-German Tradition, the destruction of the world

is known as Ragnarök. It is a fearful time when all boundaries are overthrown, all loyalties discarded, all morality ceases. The forces of chaos are unleashed to do their worst.

Brothers shall battle and slay one another.
Blood ties of sisters' sons shall be sundered.
Harsh is the world. Fornication is rife,
luring to faithlessness spouses of others.

Axe time, sword time, shields shall be cloven;
wind time, wolf time, ere the world wanes.
Din on the fields, trolls in full flight;
no man shall then spare another.

Mimir's sons arise. The dying world flares
at the sound of doom's shrill trumpet.
Loud blows Heimdall, the horn held high.
Odin confers with Mimir's head.

With a roaring in the ancient tree,
the giant is loosened.
The ash-tree, Yggdrasil,
quakes where it stands. [2]

Many would say that we are already entering this destructive phase of society. Here it is described by a modern writer on the Norse-German tradition:

Society reaches a crisis point.
All that was achieved in the past breaks down
and the social structure disintegrates,
leading to the Wolf Age of greed and the Axe Age of war.
Nothing is certain.
Night becomes day.
Day is indistinguishable from night.
Confrontation, terror and chaos rule Midgard.
The fires of Muspellheim ravage the earth,
water engulfs the land.
The old order passes. [3]

Ragnarök brings the return of the Fimbulvetr, Mighty-Winter, a period of bitter cold and lifelessness three winters long. Some see in the description of Ragnarök, a destruction of the type which would occur if a nuclear explosion of great size threw up dust clouds which blotted out the sun. Terrifying though this is, Pagan mythology does not believe that the universe is created on a once-and-for-all basis; nor that it will pass away for ever. In this, the belief which has long been held by Indo-European peoples, both Western and Hindu, differs from the creation mythology of the Near and Middle East. To Pagans, after any phase of destruction, the inexorable process of life will begin again.

Although Paganism teaches that our own planet, the body of Gaia, will, like our own bodies, inevitably grow older, disintegrate and die, this does not mean that human beings should hasten this process. The planet is capable of sustaining us and our heirs for millions of years and we wish to ensure that she does. Human beings as a species are victims of their own success. We have overcome most of our predators – other animals and disease (although disease does fight back) – and have over-bred to such an extent that we are a threat to the world's ecosystem. It is essential for human happiness that we do not rely on Nature to place her own curbs on us, but that we limit ourselves and learn to live in balance with the rest of creation. If we do not, we will destroy our planet.

Does it matter if we destroy the planet? Yes! While the end may be inevitable, we do not want to hasten our demise. Ragnarök might be an interestingly spectacle to observers in other solar systems – the free rock concert of all time on that little planet at the end of the galaxy – but we don't want the show to go on too soon. For those of us who find ourselves in the display, it won't be much fun. Nor would it be for our children, for our children's children, or for the generations beyond. Let's save the final act for as long as possible. The acts before are well worth seeing!

The Living Present

The message of Paganism is to bring love, wisdom and enlightenment into manifestation in the world by returning to those things which we have lost: the wisdom of our Elder Gods. Like the Salmon of Knowledge in Celtic myth, we must return to our ancestral spawning grounds. To make this journey, we must eat of the Tree of Knowledge. In Celtic myth, hazel nuts are the food of the Salmon of Knowledge. The nut is an important symbol because it contains the essence of the tree, which will one day spring forth from it. By eating the nuts of wisdom, our inner spiritual tree is nourished and, rooted in earth, may reach and touch heaven. Paganism has much in common with the mysticism described by Aldous Huxley in his book *The Perennial Philosophy*. It is a spiritual philosophy which:

> . . . places man's final end in the knowledge of the
> immanent and transcendent Ground of all being. [4]

It is the task of Paganism today to give to those who seek its ways the inner knowledge, light, energy and peace with which to live our lives in harmony with one another and with all living creation and to answer the eternal questions of humankind: 'Who am I? What must I do to live well and honourably? What is the meaning of the mystery of life and of the divine?'

Through the dark ages of the past millennia, the truth of Paganism has been hidden from us – buried beneath the rubble of our desolate temples, hidden beneath the churches of another and alien faith. Now the call has rung out from the Rainbow Bridge of Bifrost between the Worlds. Let us rise to answer its summons.

The Fenris-Wolf of Rome devoured the Elder Faith.
Let the Elder Faith be reborn in the hearts of her people;
so that we who worship Goddess and God
made manifest in the beauties of Nature,
within the souls of women and of men,
within the ever-encircling stars,
and beyond all these things –
in the Hidden House of the Spirit;
that we may rise again
and rekindle the eternal flame of truth so long extinguished;
that we may rejoice with chant and song,
with poem and story;
and dance once more the Spiral Dance of Life and Death.
We shall flourish and grow strong;
to take pride in our world, our society and our
    achievements,
and to save ourselves from the descent into madness,
to which the pursuit of materialism and the ignoble doctrine
of man's superiority over all other creatures have brought
    us.
All belief comes from within,
and all truth is sought and found,
in the Cup of the heart,

and the Temple of the spirit;
in the deep places of the forest,
where sunlight patterns the leaf-strewn floor,
and there is only the song of the birds,
to break the silence of the soul.
There shall we find our Gods,
beneath tree and leaf and waving bough,
beneath sky and cloud and in wind and rain,
reborn of the ever-returning Sun
the Phoenix from the Flame.[5]

1. Dion Fortune, *The Sea Priestess*, pages 129–30.
2. *Völuspá*, verses 45–9.
3. Freya Aswynn, *Leaves of Yggdrasil: A Synthesis of Magic, Feminine Mysteries, Folklore*, page 87.
4. Aldous Huxley, *The Perennial Philosophy*, quoted in Michael Perry, *Gods Within: A Critical Guide to the New Age*, page 22.
5. Vivianne Crowley, Beltane, 1992.

Pagan Resources Guide

Where to Find Information, Books, Support and Guidance

Below are listed books, magazines and organizations which can help you find out more about Paganism. The listings are by no means exhaustive. There are many thousands of Pagan resources and it is not possible to cover them all. However, if you buy copies of a few magazines, you will find that they will list other magazines, books and organizations which you can then contact. Most magazines also list groups and events which will enable you to find out what is happening in your own locality.

All Pagan organizations and magazines are run on tight budgets and you should not expect to receive a reply unless you send postage. In your own country, send a stamp addressed envelope and an extra stamp to cover administration costs. To overseas addressess, send two International Reply Coupons. These can be bought in any post office and exchanged for stamps all over the world. Do not send cheques in your own currency to addresses overseas. The cost of cashing them is usually greater than the value of the cheque. Please also write your address on any letter you send, in case letters and covering envelopes are separated.

The magazines and organizations listed are those which have been running for some time and have relatively stable addresses. All have different orientations and can evolve and change with time; therefore listing does not necessarily imply recommendation. The seeker must judge for him- or herself. Costs of magazines and membership fees for organizations have not been given as these will necessarily change, but they themselves will be able to send you up-to-date details. If there is no relevant organization listed for your own country, then write to one of the main bodies in the UK or US. These should be able to help you with international contacts.

You may not find all of the books on the shelves of your local bookstore, but all bookstores can order books for you. The same service is also provided by libraries in most countries. If you find any of the books are no longer in print, then contact esoteric book shops which have a second-hand book service. They will be able to find you what you want. These bookstores will be advertised in magazines.

If you run a Pagan group or organization which is not in touch with the major groups listed here, then you may wish to contact them to foster networking and contacts.

General Paganism

Reading

Margot Adler, *Drawing Down the Moon: Witches, Druids, Goddess-Worshippers and other Pagans in America Today*, Beacon Press, Boston, 1986 ed. An overview of North American Paganism and Wicca with extensive lists of organizations and magazines.

Prudence Jones and Caitlín Matthews (eds.), *Voices from the Circle: The Heritage of Western Paganism*, Aquarian, 1990. Anthology of Pagan writing.

Pagan Federation, *The Pagan Federation Information Pack*, Pagan Federation, London, 2nd ed, 1992. A useful introduction to Paganism.

Groups and Magazines – Europe

Ace of Rods, BCM Akademia, London WC1N 3XX. Pagan contact magazine.

Cauldron, available from Mike Howard, Caemorgan Cottage, Caemorgan Road, Cardigan, Dyfed, SA43 1QU is a Pagan journal of the Old Religion and one of the longest-running Pagan periodicals.

Cercle du Dragon, Moïra, 20 avenue du Général de Gaulle, 24660 Coulountiex-Chamiers, France, is a French Pagan and Wiccan organization which also publishes a quarterly magazine, *Moïra*.

Cheiron, c/o Gramarye, Meadow Close, Bagworth, Leics, is a postal group for Pagans with disabilities and older Pagans.

Gates of Annwn, BM Gates of Annwn, London WC1N 3XX. Pagan contact magazine.

Green Circle, PO Box 42, Bath, BA1 1ZN, organizes discussion groups around the UK for those interested in meeting Pagans and others interested in esoteric subjects. *Green Circular* magazine can be purchased by members.

Hoblink, Box 1, 13 Merrivale Road, Stafford, ST17 9EB, is a network for gay/bi Pagans. Newsletter for members.

Irish Pagan Movement, The Bridge House, Clonegal, County Wexford, Eire, is a Pagan organization and network for Ireland. Also publishes *Pagan Life* magazine.

Norwegian Pagan Federation, PO Box 1814, Nordnes, 524 Bergen, Norway, is an information network which can assist with Pagan and Wiccan contacts in Norway and other Scandinavian countries.

Pagan Federation, BM Box 7097, London WC1N 3XX, is the largest and oldest Pagan and Wiccan body in Europe. It provides an annual conference, local group meetings and contacts across Europe and worldwide. It publishes a very informative quarterly journal, *The Wiccan,* and has a useful Information Pack which gives basic facts about modern European Paganism. There is also a Wicca Information Pack. The PF also sells Pagan books by mail order.

PaganLink, 25 East Hill, Dartford, Kent is a UK Pagan networking organization putting Pagans in touch with one another and with Pagan groups.

Pagan Spirituality Movement, c/o Vivianne Crowley, BM Deosil, London WC1N 3XX, promotes the development of spirituality in a Pagan context. Teachings and workshops.

Pagan Voice, 13 Barnstaple Walk, Knowle, Bristol, BS4 1JQ, is a monthly UK Pagan magazine which lists many events and groups. Useful for contacting local groups.

Quest, BCM-SCL Quest, London WC1N 3XX, is one of the oldest Pagan and Craft magazines. Annual conference also organized. The editor, Marian Green, is a well-known Pagan teacher who runs workshops and correspondence courses.

Groups and Magazines – United States and Canada

Circle, PO Box 219, Mount Horeb, WI 53572, is a major Pagan organization in the US. It organizes Pagan events, fosters contacts and networking, and publishes *Circle Network News*, a very useful and informative journal of Nature Spirituality, which operates a mail order book service. There is a land sanctuary, gatherings, counselling service and many other activities. *Circle* is a legally-recognized Shamanic Wiccan Church.

Church of All Worlds, PO Box 212, Redwood Valley, California 95470, is a Pagan organization which owns land, raises ecological awareness through its subsidiary organization, *Forever Forests*, and publishes the magazine *Green Egg*. Gatherings organized.

Earth Spirit Community, PO Box 365, Medford, Massachusetts 02155, fosters Pagan and Wiccan networking in the mid-Atlantic area and also runs workshops, talks and an annual festival.

Earth Spirit Pagans, PO Box 26476, Colorado Springs, CO 80936, promotes Pagan awareness.

From the Heart, c/o K. Hinds, 2357 Loraine St NE, Atlanta, GA 30319, is a newsletter for Pagan parents.

Gay and Lesbian Pagan Coalition, PO Box 26442, Oklahoma City, OK 773126-0442, publishes personal, group and organization contacts in its magazine *Festive Circles Update*.

Harvest, PO Box 378, Southborough, MA 01772, is an informative Neo-Pagan journal.

MerryMount Messenger, 1016 E El Camino Real, Box 458, Sunnyvale, CA 96087, is the newsletter of the *Thomas Morton Alliance* for Pagan spiritual politics.

Mid-West Pagan Council, PO Box 313, Matteson, Illinois 60442–0313, is an association of Pagan groups in the Mid-West which runs an annual Pagan Festival.

New Moon New York, PO Box 1471, Madison Square Station, New York 10159, is a Pagan networking organization which runs open festivals and publishes *Our Pagan Times*.

Pagans for Peace, PO Box 2205, Clearbrook, BC V2T 3XB.

Pagan Prisoners, PO Box 1510, Ellicott City, MD 21041, runs a free newsletter for Pagan prison inmates.

Pan-American Indian Association, Nocatee, FL 33864–0244, works to revive tribal heritage throughout the world and publishes a newspaper.

Panegyria, PO Box 73, Index, Washington 98256, is a journal of events in the Pacific North-West.

Groups and Magazines – Australia and New Zealand

Church of All Worlds, PO Box 408, Woden, ACT 2606. (See US entry.)

Current Australian Pagan Literature Index, GPO Box G498, Perth 6001, lists magazine articles by Pagan subject index.

Elemental, Box 1028, Strawberry Hills, NSW 2012, is a Pagan newsletter for the Sydney area.

Oracle, c/o The Book and Candle, 86 Victoria St West, Auckland City, is a New Zealand Pagan newsletter.

The Pan-Pacific Pagan Alliance, PO Box A486, Sydney South, NSW 2000, is the contact organization for all branches of Paganism in Australia and New Zealand. Its members' magazine lists groups and contacts and the PPPA can advise on Pagan matters generally. Also has information on the annual Australian Wicca Conference and publishes *Pagan Times*, available from GPO Box G498, Perth, WA 6001.

The Pan-Pacific Pagan Alliance, 516 Huon Road, South Hobart, Tasmania 7000.

The Pan-Pacific Pagan Alliance, 21 Nelson Street, Helensville, New Zealand.

Shadowplay, PO Box 343, Petersham, NSW 2049, is a magazine for Paganism and Wicca.

Goddess and Women's Mysteries

Reading

Zsuzsanna Budapest, *Grandmother Moon*, HarperSanFrancisco, 1992. Seasonal and full Moon rituals from around the world.

Zsuzsanna Budapest, *The Holy Book of Women's Mysteries*, Harper and Row, 1990. Important book on feminist religion.

Marija Gimbutas, *The Language of the Goddess*, Thames and Hudson, 1989. Important book by leading archaeologist.

Esther Harding, *Women's Mysteries Ancient and Modern*, Shambhala, 1990. Insightful book by well-known Jungian therapist.

Janet McCrickard, *Eclipse of the Sun: An Investigation into Sun and Moon Myths*, Gothic Image, Glastonbury, 1991. Important book on solar Goddesses and positive female energy.

Caitlín Matthews, (ed.), *Voices of the Goddess*, Aquarian Press, 1991. Anthology of Goddess writing.

Monica Sjöö and Barbara Mor, *The Great Cosmic Mother*, Harper and Row, 1981. Classic text on the Goddess.

Starhawk, *The Spiral Dance: A Rebirth of the Ancient Religion of the Great Goddess*, Harper and Row, San Francisco, 1979 ed. Influential book on Wiccan-oriented Goddess religion.

Groups and Magazines – Europe

The Fellowship of Isis, Clonegal Castle, Clonegal, Enniscorthy, Eire, offers contacts, teaching and training in Goddess religion worldwide. It also publishes *Isian News* and has an annual conference in London. There are a number of centres offering training in the Goddess priesthood.

From the Flames, 42 Mapperley Road, Nottingham, NG3 5AS, quarterly journal of radical feminist spirituality.

Matriarchy Research and Reclaim Group, Cloverley House, Erwood, Builth Wells, Powys, LD2 3EZ, is a network of Goddess-oriented women who share an interest in women's spirituality. Contacts with groups, annual conference and newsletter.

Sirius, PO Box 428, Denbigh, Clwyd, LL16 4AZ, is a monthly magazine from the *Centre of Vesta*.

Groups and Magazines – United States

Reclaiming, PO Box 14404, San Francisco, California 94114. Center for Feminist Spirituality, a collective of women and men working to unify spirituality and politics. Workshops, summer programmes, public rituals, newsletter. Inspired by work of Starhawk.

SageWoman, PO Box 641, Point Arena, CA 95468, is a quarterly magazine of Women's Spirituality, celebrating the Goddess in every woman.

Woman of Power, PO Box 2785, Orleans, MA 02653, is a magazine of feminism and spirituality.

Groups and Magazines – Australia and New Zealand

Pagan Women's Alliance, Arbour PO Box 109, Bangalow, NSW 2479, is an organization for networking between Pagan women.

God and Men's Mysteries

Reading

William Anderson and Clive Hicks, *The Green Man*, Collins, 1990.

Robert Bly, *Iron John: A Book about Men*, Element Books, Shaftesbury, 1991.

Joseph Campbell, *The Hero with a Thousand Faces*, Bollingen Series XVII, Princeton University Press, 1972.

John Matthews, *Choirs of the God: Revisioning Masculinity*, Mandala, London, 1991.

Robert Moore and Douglas Gillette, *King, Warrior, Magician, Lover*, HarperCollins, 1990.

John Rowan, *The Horned God: Feminism and Men as Wounding and Healing*, Routledge Kegan Paul, 1987.

R.J. Stewart, *Celebrating the Male Mysteries*, Arcania, Bath, 1991.

Groups and Magazines – Europe

Everyman, PO Box 459, Oxford, OX2 2YH, runs workshops for men and also publishes *Passages*, A Journal of Gender, Earth and Soul.

Groups and Magazines – United States

Changing Men, 306 N Brooks St, Madison, WI 53715, is a journal for profeminist men.

Wingspan, Box 1491, Manchester, Maine 01944 is a journal of the Male Spirit.

Wicca and the Craft

Reading

Rae Beth, *Hedgewitch*, Hale, London, 1990, is a useful book for the solitary witch.

Vivianne Crowley, *Wicca: The Old Religion in the New Age*, Aquarian, 1989, insights into Wiccan spirituality.

Janet and Stuart Farrar, *Eight Sabbats for Witches*, Hale, London, 1981, and *The Witches' Way*, Hale, London, 1990. (Also available in a US edition as *The Witches Bible*.) Comprehensive accounts of Wiccan practice.

Janet and Stuart Farrar, *The Life and Times of a Modern Witch*, Piatkus, 1987. Introduction to how Wicca impacts on its practitioners.

Marian Green, *A Witch Alone*, Mandala, 1991, is a useful guide to following the Craft as a solo practitioner.

Julia Phillips and Matthew Sandow, *The Witches of Oz*, Children of Sekhmet Publications, Sydney, 1991.

(See also D.J. Conway in Norse-German section below.)

Groups and Magazines – Europe

(See also Paganism section.)

The Hole in the Sky, Postlagernd 13507, Berlin 27, Germany, can advise on contacts in the German-speaking world.

The House of the Goddess, 33 Oldridge Road, London SW12, is a network of groups worshipping the Goddess and practising witchcraft and Shamanism. Workshops, conferences, rites and training.

The Wicca Study Group, BM Deosil, London WC1N 3XX, provides introductory teaching on Wicca. Introductory evening courses in England and Scotland plus Saturday workshops and correspondence course. The WSG also holds residential workshops and conferences in other parts of Europe.

The Wiccan, BM Box 7097, London WC1N 3XX, is the quarterly journal of the Pagan Federation.

Wiccan Rede, PO Box 473, Zeist, NL 3700 AL, The Netherlands, is an English/Dutch Wiccan magazine which can also assist with contacts in the Netherlands.

Groups and Magazines – United States and Canada

(See also Paganism section.)

Covenant of the Goddess, PO Box 1226, Berkeley, CA 94704, is a federation of Wiccan covens which publishes a newsletter and holds an annual gathering.

Hidden Path, Windwalker, Box 934, Kenosha, WI 53141, gives advice on contacting Gardnerian Wicca.

Red Garters International, PO Box 162046, MH Sacramento, CA 95816, is the official newsletter of the *New Wiccan Church* which is dedicated to the promulgation of English Traditional Wicca. There are braches in other states and the Church will deal with enquiries for admission.

The Wiccan Church of Canada, 1555 Eglinton Avenue, West Toronto, Ontario, N6E 2G9, is a network of Wiccan groups which offers training, information and seasonal celebrations. Also publishes a magazine, *The Chalice and the Blade*, which is available from PO Box 1031, Adelaide St Stn, Toronto.

Witches of Salem, c/o Crow Haven Corner, 125 Essex St, Salem, Massachusetts 01970, runs training and gatherings. Led by the well-known Laurie Cabot.

(See also *Wyrd Network* in Norse-German section below.)

Groups and Magazines – Australia and New Zealand

(See also Paganism section.)

Magic Pentacle, Box 56–065, Dominion Road Post Office, Mount Eden, Auckland, New Zealand, is a magazine of Wicca and magic.

The Web of Wyrd, PO Box A486, Sydney South, NSW 2000, is an informative Wiccan and Pagan magazine.

Shamanism

Reading

Lynn V. Andrews, *Medicine Woman*, Harper San Francisco, 1981. A woman's journey to find the Shaman within her.

Mircea Eliade, *Shamanism: Archaic Techniques of Ecstasy*, Willard R. Trask (trans.), Arkana, London, 1989 ed. Classic text on Shamanism around the world.

Michael Harner, *The Way of the Shaman*, Harper & Row, New York 1980. A modern approach to Shamanistic practice.

John Matthews, *The Celtic Shaman*, Element, Shaftesbury, 1992. Developing Shamanism in a Celtic context.

Kenneth Meadows, *The Medicine Way*, Element, Shaftesbury, 1990. Informative book on modern approaches to Native American Shamanism.

Groups and Magazines – Europe

Dancing Wolf Initiative, 126 Parc-y-Dre, Ruthin, Clwyd, North Wales, LL15 0PH, offers workshops on contemporary Paganism.

Eagle's Wing Centre for Contemporary Shamanism, 58 Westbere Road, London NW2 3RV, workshops, training, gatherings in Shamanistic practice, led by Leo Rutherford.

Moonshine, 498 Bristol Road, Selly Oak, Birmingham, B29 6BD, magazine with Shamanistic approach to Paganism. Also Shamanistic publications.

Pathways, 28 Cowl Street, Evesham, Worcestershire, WR11 4PL, runs courses on contemporary Shamanism and on skills such as drum-making.

People on the Path, 64 Church Road, Richmond, Surrey, TW10 6LN, is a useful quarterly magazine with listings of events.

Groups and Magazines – United States

Center for Shamanic Studies, PO Box 673, Beldon Station, Norwalk, Connecticut 06852, was founded by Michael Harner to offer workshops and training in Shamanic practice. There is also a quaterly newsletter for members.

Shaman's Drum, PO Box 2636, Berkeley, CA 94702, is a journal of experiential Shamanism published by the Cross-Cultural Shamanism Network which contains useful articles and resource listings.

Celtic Tradition and Druidry

Reading

Philip Carr-Gomm, *Elements of The Druid Tradition*, Element, 1991.

Nora Chadwick, *The Celts*, Penguin Books, Harmondsworth, 1970.

Jeffrey Gantz (trans.), *The Mabinogion*, Penguin Books, Harmondsworth, 1976.

Tadhg MacCrossan, *The Sacred Cauldron: Secrets of the Druids*, Llewellyn, 1991.

Caitlín Matthews, *Elements of the Celtic Tradition*, Element, Shaftesbury, 1989.

(See also Hilda R. Ellis Davidson in Norse-German section.)

Groups and Magazines – Europe

Comardiia Druidiacta Armorica, c/o A. le Goff, Bothuan, Commana, 29237 Sizun, France, publishes a review on Druidic studies.

Council of British Druid Orders, 125 Magyar Crescent, Nuneaton, Warks CV17 4SJ, is a federation of Druid Orders which can advise on Druid contacts.

L'Eglise Druidique des Gaules, BP 13, 93301 Aubervilliers, Cedex, France, is a Celtic French-language church which also publishes magazines including *Le Druidisme*.

Irmindade Celtiga, Apartado de Correos 228, 15080 A Corunna, Spain, is a Celtic organization in Spain.

Caitlín and John Matthews, BM Hallowquest, London WC1N 3XX, offer training and workshops in Celtic and Goddess mysteries in the UK and US. Also correspondence course.

Order of Bards, Ovates and Druids, 260 Kew Road, Richmond, Surrey, TW9 3EG offers training in healing, divination, mythology, history and folklore through correspondence course and workshops.

Groups and Magazines – United States

Ar nDraiocht Fein, Box 1022-X4, Nyack, NY 10960, is a Druid Fellowship practising NeoPagan Druidism and offering a journal and training on the Druid path.

Druidiactos, PO Box 472143, Garland, Texas 75047, gives information, advice and guidance on practising Celtic religion today. Also publishes the journal *Parios Andumni*, which is available from the editor, Taranucnos Esugenos, 2922 South Marvin Avenue, Tucson, AZ 85730.

Groups and Magazines – Australia and New Zealand

Caer Witrin, PO Box 6160, Fairfield Gardens, Queensland 4103.

Druidactos Australia, c/o PO Box A486, Sydney South, NSW 2000.

Norse-German Tradition

Reading

Freya Aswynn, *Leaves of Yggdrasil: A Synthesis of Magic, Feminine Mysteries, Folklore*, LLewellyn, 1990. Insightful approach to the Northern mysteries from female practitioner.

D.J. Conway, *Norse Magic*, LLewellyn, 1990, is a useful introduction to celebrating the Norse festivals and working magic in a way harmonious with Wicca and Goddess worship.

Hilda R. Ellis Davidson, *Gods and Myths of Northern Europe*, Pelican, Harmondsworth, 1964. Excellent overview from academic.

Hilda R. Ellis Davidson, *Myths and Symbols in Pagan Europe, Early Scandinavian and Celtic Religions*, Manchester University Press, 1988, is a fascinating academic study which examines the often-neglected similarities in religious practice between these two great European peoples.

Odinist Committee, *This is Odinsim: Guidelines for Survival*, 2nd ed, Raven Banner Editions, London, 1983. Introduction for those seeking the Northern path.

Nigel Pennick, *Practical Magic in the Northern Tradition*, Aquarian, 1989. Very useful for anyone interested in Northern-based Pagan magic.

Snorri Sturloson, *Edda*, Anthony Faulkes (trans.), Everyman Library, J.M. Dent London, 1987. Essential source material.

Elsa-Brita Titchenell, *The Masks of Odin: Wisdom of the Ancient Norse*, Theosophical University Press, Pasadena, California, 1985. Beautiful and inspiring book on the Northern Tradition written from Theosophical and spiritual perspective. Also has translations of principal lays in the *Poetic Edda*.

Groups and Magazines – Europe

Asatruarfelag, c/o S Beinteinsson, Draghalsi, Borgarfirdi, Iceland, represents the Asatru religion in Iceland.

Freya Aswynn, BM Aswynn, London WC1N 3XX, is a rune

mistress and Volva in the old Northern Tradition who conducts seminars on mythology, runes and magical practices.

Odinism Today, BM Edda, London WC1N 3XX, offers guidance for those seeking the Northern path and informative guides on setting up groups and conducting rites.

Odinshof, BCM Tercel, London WC1N 3XX, is a registered religious charity for those worshipping the Norse gods. Contact with groups and correspondence course. Also runs a land guardian scheme.

OR Briefing, BCM Runic, London WC1N 3XX, gives monthly news of Asatru activities.

Groups and Magazines – United States and Canada

Asatru Alliance of Independent Kindreds, PO Box 961, Payson, Arizona 85547, is one of the largest Asatru groups in the US and publishes a magazine, *Vor Tru*.

Asatru Free Assembly, PO Box 1754, Breckenbridge, Texas 76024, works to promote Scandinavian/German Paganism through networking, its magazine *The Runstone* and an annual festival the *Althing*.

Héritage et Tradition, CP 244, Succ. PAT, Montréal, Québec H1B 5K3, is a French-Canadian Asatru newsletter.

Wyrd Network, PO Box 970, Amherst, MA 01004, works to bridge the gap between Wicca and Asatru and to incorporate Norse deities into Wicca.

Yggdrasil, 537 Jones St #165, San Francisco, CA 94102, is published by *Freya's Folk*, and is a quarterly journal of Pagan culture.

Groups and Magazines – Australia and New Zealand

The Runic Guild, GPO Box 2337, Canberra 2601.

Other Traditions

Reading

Marija Gimbutas, *The Balts*, Thames and Hudson, 1963. Useful introduction to the Baltic world.

Marija Gimbutas, *The Slavs*, Thames and Hudson, 1971. Useful introduction to the Slavic world.

Kati-ma Koppana, *The Finnish Gods*, Madragora Dimensions, Helsinki, 1991. Introduction to the Finnish deities.

Kati-ma Koppana, *Snakefat and Knotted Threads: A Short Introduction to Finnish Magic*, Mandragora Dimensions, Helskini, 1990. Fascinating insight into the little-known world of Finnish spirituality and magic.

Elias Löhnrot, *The Kalevala*, K Bosley trans, Oxford University Press, Oxford, 1989 ed. Essential source material.

Groups and Magazines – Europe

For information on Finnish groups and magazines contact Kati-ma Koppana, *Starlight Magazine*, PO Box 452, 00101 Helsinki.

Paganian Europe, 226024 Brivibas Street, 398–104 Riga, is the main Pagan organization in Latvia.

Polish Nature Religion, National Conceptual Study Group, vl Grodeckiego 4 n. 37, 01-843 Warsaw, Poland.

Romuva Vilnius, Elder Algis Jucevicius, Didzioji 11, 2000 Vilnius, organizes summer camps and has information on the practice of Lithuanian religion today.

Groups and Magazines – United States and Canada

Finn Heritage, PO Box 1675, San Luis Obispo, CA 93406, USA, is a contact organization for the Finnish tradition in the USA.

Great Mother's Love Nature Center, PO Box 42, Fairfield, VT 05455. Baltic study and support network.

Romuva Canada, PO Box 232, Station 'D', 4975 Dundas St West, Etobicoke, Ontario, M9A 4X2.

Romuva USA, PO Box 214, Athens, OH 45701, publishes the English language journal of the Lithuanian Ethnic Church Romuva of the USA Inc and can advise on all aspects of Lithuanian Paganism.

Bibliography

Adler, Margot, *Drawing Down the Moon*, Beacon Press, Boston, 1986.

Anderson, William, and Hicks, Clive, *The Green Man*, Collins, 1990.

Andrews, Lynn V., *Medicine Woman*, Harper San Francisco, 1981.

Apuleius, Lucius, *The Golden Ass* (trans. Robert Graves), Penguin, Harmondsworth, 1950, reprinted 1985.

Aswynn, Freya, *Leaves of Yggdrasil: A Synthesis of Magic, Feminine Mysteries, Folklore*, Aswynn, London, 1988, and Llewellyn, 1990.

Auden, W.H., and Taylor, Paul B., *Norse Poems*, Faber and Faber, 1983.

Awolalu, J.O., 'Sin and its Removal in African Traditional Religion', *Journal of the American Academy of Religion*, page 275, 44 (2), 1976.

Awolalu, J. Omosade, and Dopamu, P. Adelumo, *West African Traditional Religion*, Onibondje Press & Book Industries (Nigeria) Ltd, Ibadan, Nigeria, 1979.

Bachofen J.J., *Myth Religion and Mother Right*, Bollingen series LXXXIV, Princeton University Press, Princeton, NJ, 1967, (originally published 1926).

Beth, Rae, *Hedgewitch*, Hale, London, 1990.

Bloom, William (ed.), *The New Age: An Anthology of Essential Writings*, Rider, London, 1991.

Bly, Robert, *Iron John: A Book about Men*, Element Books, Shaftesbury, 1991 (UK Edition).

Bourne, Lois, *A Witch Amongst Us*, Hale, London, 1979.

Bray, Olive, (trans.), *The Elder or Poetic Edda*, Viking Club, 1908.

Budapest, Z., *Grandmother Moon*, HarperSanFrancisco, 1992.

Budapest, Z., *The Holy Book of Women's Mysteries*, Harper and Row, 1990.

Bullfinch, Thomas, *Bullfinch's Mythology*, The Modern Library, New York, no publication date.

Campbell J., *The Hero with a Thousand Faces*, Bollingen Series XVII, Princeton University Press, 1972 (originally published 1949).

Carmichael, Alexander, (trans.), *Carmina Gaedelica*, Edinburgh, Scottish Academic Press, 1972.

Carr-Gomm, Philip, *The Elements of the Druid Tradition*, Element, Shaftesbury, 1991.

Carr-Gomm, Philip, 'Witches and Druids', in *The Cauldron: Pagan Journal of the Old Religion*, pages 4–5, No. 68, Cardigan, 1993.

Castagné, J., 'Magie et exorcisme chez les Kazak-Kirghizes et autres peuples turcs orientaux', in *Revue des études islamiques*, page 60, Paris, 1930.

Chadwick, Nora, *The Celts*, Penguin Books, Harmondsworth, 1970.

Conway, D.J., *Norse Magic*, LLewellyn, 1990.

Cooper, Susan, *The Dark is Rising Sequence*, Penguin, Harmondsworth, 1984.

Crowley, Aleister, *Magick in Theory and Practice*, Castle Books, New York, no publication date.

Crowley, Vivianne, *Wicca: The Old Religion in the New Age*, Aquarian, 1989.

Crowley, Vivianne, 'The Initiation', in Jones, Prudence, and Matthews, Caitlín, (eds.), *Voices from the Circle*, Aquarian Press, 1990.

Crowley, Vivianne, 'Priestess and Witch', in Matthews, Caitlín, (ed.), *Voices of the Goddess*, Aquarian Press, 1991.

Crowley, Vivianne, 'Paganism', in Button J. and Bloom W. (eds.), *The Seeker's Guide: A New Age Resouce Book*, Aquarian, 1992.

Crowley, Vivianne, 'Women and Power in Modern Paganism', in *Women as Teachers and Disciples in Traditional and New Religions*, The Edwin Mellen Press, New York, 1993.

Crowley, Vivianne, *Pagan Spirituality Handbook*, Pagan Spirituality Movement, London, 1994.

Davidson, Hilda R. Ellis, *Myths and Symbols in Pagan Europe, Early Scandinavian and Celtic Religions*, Manchester University Press, 1988.

Davidson, Hilda R. Ellis, *Gods and Myths of Northern Europe*, Pelican, Harmondsworth, 1964.

Davies, Robertson, *The Rebel Angels*, Penguin, Harmondsworth, 1981.

Easwaran, Eknath, (trans.), *The Upanishads*, Arkana, London, 1988.

Eliade, Mircea, *Shamanism: Archaic Techniques of Ecstasy*, trans. by Willard R. Trask, Arkana, London, 1989 ed.

Farrar, Janet and Stuart, *The Life and Times Of A Modern Witch*, Piatikus, 1987.

Farrar, Janet and Stewart, *The Witches' Way*, Robert Hale, London, 1984.

Farrar, Janet and Stewart, *Eight Sabbats for Witches*, Robert Hale, London, 1981.

Ferguson, Marilyn, *The Aquarian Conspiracy: Personal and Social Transformation in the 1980s*, Paladin/Granada, 1982.

Fortune, Dion, *The Sea Priestess*, Star Books, Wyndham Publications, London, 1976.

Fortune, Dion, *Moon Magic*, Samuel Weiser, York Beach, Maine, 1978.

Frazer, Sir James G., *The Golden Bough: A Study in Magic and Religion*, Abridged edition, Macmillan, London 1957 (originally published 1922).

Gantz, Jeffrey, (trans.), *The Mabinogion*, Penguin Books, Harmondsworth, 1976.

Gardner, Gerald B., *High Magick's Aid*, Atlantis Book Shop, 1949.

Gardner, Gerald B., *Witchcraft Today*, Rider & Co, London 1954.

Gardner, Gerald B., *The Meaning of Witchcraft*, Aquarian Press, Wellingborough, 1959.

Gimbutas, Marija, *The Language of the Goddess*, Thames and Hudson, 1989.

Gimbutas, Marija, *The Slavs*, Thames and Hudson, 1971.

Gimbutas, Marija, *The Balts*, Thames and Hudson, 1963.

Graves, Robert (trans.), Lucius Apuleius, *The Golden Ass*, Penguin, Harmondsworth, 1950, reprinted 1985.

Green, Marian, *A Witch Alone*, Mandala, 1991.

Green, Marian, *The Path through the Labyrinth: The Quest for Initiation into the Western Mystery Tradition*, Element, Shaftesbury, 1988.

Harding, Esther, *Women's Mysteries Ancient and Modern*, Shambhala, 1990.

Hardy, Jean, *A Psychology with a Soul: Psychosynthesis in Evolutionary Context*, Arkana, 1989.

Harner, Michael, *The Way of the Shaman*, Harper & Row, New York 1980.

Hillman, James, (ed.), *Puer Papers*, Spring Publications Inc, Dallas, Texas, 1987.

Hollander, Lee M, (trans.), *The Poetic Edda*, University of Texas Press, Austin, Texas, 1962.

Hoyle, Fred, *Of Men and Galaxies*, Heinemann, 1965.

Hutton, Ronald B., *Pagan Religions of the Ancient British Isles*, Basil Blackwell, Oxford, 1991.

James, William, *The Varieties of Religious Experience*, Collins, 1982.

Jones, Prudence, and Matthews, Caitlín, (eds.), *Voices from the Circle*, Aquarian Press, 1990.

Jung, Carl G., *The Collected Works of C.G. Jung*, Vol. 5, *Symbols of Transformation*, Routledge & Kegan Paul, London, 2nd edition, 1967.

Jung, Carl G., *The Collected Works of C.G. Jung*, Vol 7, *Two Essays on Analytical Psychology*.

Jung, Carl G., *The Collected Works of C.G. Jung*, Vol 9, Part 1, *Archetypes of the Collective Unconscious*, Routledge & Kegan Paul, London, 2nd edition 1968.

Jung, Carl G., *Collected Works*, Vol 10, *Civilization in Transition*, Routledge & Kegan Paul, London, 2nd edition, 1968.

Jung, Carl G., *Synchronicity: An Acausal Connecting Principle* in *The Collected Works of C.G. Jung*, Vol 8; Routledge & Kegan Paul, London, 2nd edition 1966.

Jung E., *Animus and Anima: Two Essays*, Spring Publications, Zurich, 1957.

Koppana, Kati-ma, *The Finnish Gods*, Mandragora Dimensions, Helsinki, 1991.

Koppana, Kati-ma, *Snakefat and Knotted Threads: A Short Introduction to Finnish Magic*, Mandragora Dimensions, Helskini, 1990.

Leland, Charles G., *Aradia: The Gospel of the Witches*, C.W. Daniel Company, 1974.

Löhnrot, Elias, *The Kalevala*, trans. by K. Bosley, Oxford University Press, Oxford, 1989.

Lorimer, David, *Whole in One: The Near-Death Experience and the Ethic of Interconnectedness*, Arkana, London, 1990.

Luhrmann, Tanya A., *Persuasians of the Witch's Craft: Ritual Magic and Witchcraft in Present-day England*, Basil Blackwell, Oxford, 1989.

Macalister, R.A.S. (trans.), *Lebor Gabala Erenn*, Dublin, 1938–1956.

MacCrossan, Tadhg, *The Sacred Cauldron: Secrets of the Druids*, Llewellyn, 1991.

Matthews, Caitlín, (ed.), *Voices of the Goddess*, Aquarian, 1991.

Matthews, Caitlín, *Elements of the Celtic Tradition*, Element, Shaftesbury, 1989.

Matthews, John, *The Celtic Shaman*, Element, Shaftesbury, 1992.

Matthews, John (ed.), *Choirs of the God: Revisioning Masculinity*, Mandala, London, 1991.

Mattingly, H. (trans.), *The Agricola and The Germania*, Penguin, Harmondsworth, 1970.

McCrickard, Janet, *Eclipse of the Sun: An Investigation into Sun and Moon Myths*, Gothic Image, Glastonbury, 1991.

McGregor Mathers, S.L., *The Qabalah Unveiled*, 1926, reprinted Arkana 1991.

Meadows, Kenneth, *The Medicine Way*, Element, Shaftesbury, 1990.

Meyer, Kuno, (trans.), *The Instructions of King Cormac mac Airt*, Royal Irish Academy Todd Lecture Series, XV, Hodges, Figgis & Co, 1909.

Michelet, Jules, *La Sorcière*, P. Viallaneix, 1966 (originally published Paris 1862).

Miller, Dusty, *Moonshine* magazine, Birmingham, Spring 1990.

Mone, F.J., *Anzeiger für Kunde der teutschen Vorzeit*, Jahrgang 8, Karlsruhe 1839.

Moore, Robert, and Gillette, Douglas, *King, Warrior, Magician, Lover*, HarperCollins, 1990.

Murray, Margaret, *The God of the Witches*, Oxford University Press, New York and Faber and Faber, London, 1970 (originally published 1931).

Murray, Margaret, *The Witch-Cult in Western Europe: A Study in Anthropology*, Clarendon Press, Oxford 1921.

O'hogain, Daithi, *Fionn Mac Cumhail*, Gill & Macmillan, Dublin, 1988.

Odinist Committee, *This is Odinsim: Guidelines for Survival*, 2nd edition, Raven Banner Editions, London, 1983.

Pagan Federation, *The Pagan Federation Information Pack*, Pagan Federation, London, 2nd edition, 1992.

Pennick, Nigel, *Practical Magic in the Northern Tradition*, Aquarian, 1989.

Perry, Michael, *Gods Within: A Critical Guide to the New Age*, SPCK, London, 1992.

Rees, Alywyn and Rees, Brinley, *Celtic Heritage: Ancient Traditions in Ireland and Wales*, Thames and Hudson, 1961.

Ross, Anne, *Everyday Life of the Pagan Celts*, Carousel Books, Transworld Publishers Limited, London.

Rowan, John *The Horned God: Feminism and Men as Wounding and Healing*, Routledge Kegan Paul, 1987.

Sjöö, Monica, and Mor, Barbara, *The Great Cosmic Mother*, Harper and Row, 1981.

Slater, Herman, *A Book of Pagan Rituals*, Samual Weiser Inc., New York, 1978.

Spiegelman, J.M., and Vasavada, A.U., *Hinduism and Jungian Psychology*, Falcon Press, Los Angeles and Phoenix, 1987.

Starhawk, *The Spiral Dance: A Rebirth of the Ancient Religion of the Great Goddess*, Harper and Row, San Francisco, 1979.

Starhawk, *Truth or Dare: Encounters with Power, Authority and Mystery*, Harper and Row, San Francisco, 1990.

Stewart, R.J., *Living Magical Arts: Imagination and Magic for the 21st Century*, Blandford, London, 1991.

Stewart, R.J., *Celebrating the Male Mysteries*, Arcania, Bath, 1991.

Stubba, *The Book of Blots: Ceremonies, Rituals and Invocations of the Odinic Rite*, The Odinic Rite, London, 1991.

Sturloson, Snorri, *Edda*, trans. by Anthony Faulkes, Everyman Library, J.M. Dent, London, 1987.

Stutley, Margaret, *Hinduism: the Eternal Law*, Crucible, Wellingborough, 1990.

Titchenell, Elsa-Brita, *The Masks of Odin: Wisdom of the Ancient Norse*, Theosophical University Press, Pasadena, California, 1985.

Trikunas, Jonas, *Romuva USA*, No. 8, Sambariai 1992.

Valiente, D., *Natural Magic*, Robert Hale, London, 1975.

Wallis, R.T., *Neoplatonism*, Duckworth, London, 1972.

Wehr, D.S., *Jung and Feminism*, Routledge, London, 1988.

Wilde, Lady, *Ancient Legends, Mystic Charms, and Superstitions of Ireland*, Ward and Downey, London, 1888, reprinted O'Gorman, Galway, Ireland, 1971.

Witt, R.E., *Isis in the Graeco-Roman World*, Thames and Hudson, 1971.

Worthington, Vivian, *A History of Yoga*, Arkana, London, 1982.

Index